MW01045860

Financial Navigation

Powerful Strategies for Investments & Insurance

for

Everyone Who Invests

D. David Campbell

© Copyright 2006 Donald David Campbell.
All rights reserved. No part of this publication may be reproduced, stored in a retrieval
system, or transmitted, in any form or by any means, electronic, mechanical, photocopying,
recording, or otherwise, without the written prior permission of the author.

Every attempt has been made to contact copyright holders for permission to use excerpts
from their printed material. By initial press time we had received most but not all copyright
clearances requested.

The author has attempted to be accurate in every detail. Any errors in this book are my errors
and do not reflect on any company or the publisher. This book gives investment advice. Be
sure to seek individual assistance from a qualified broker. The investment business is fast
paced and changing continually. What made sense in 2005 may not be good advice in later
years. About insurance seek advice from a good company and a qualified insurance agent.

Note for Librarians: A cataloguing record for this book is available from Library and Archives
Canada at www.collectionscanada.ca/amicus/index-e.html
ISBN 1-4120-8205-6

*Printed in Victoria, BC, Canada. Printed on paper with minimum 30% recycled fibre. Trafford's print shop
runs on "green energy" from solar, wind and other environmentally-friendly power sources.*

Offices in Canada, USA, Ireland and UK
This book was published *on-demand* in cooperation with Trafford Publishing. On-demand
publishing is a unique process and service of making a book available for retail sale to the
public taking advantage of on-demand manufacturing and Internet marketing. On-demand
publishing includes promotions, retail sales, manufacturing, order fulfilment, accounting and
collecting royalties on behalf of the author.

Book sales for North America and international:
Trafford Publishing, 6E–2333 Government St.,
Victoria, BC V8T 4P4 CANADA
phone 250 383 6864 (toll-free 1 888 232 4444)
fax 250 383 6804; email to orders@trafford.com
Book sales in Europe:
Trafford Publishing (UK) Limited, 9 Park End Street, 2nd Floor
Oxford, UK OX1 1HH UNITED KINGDOM
phone 44 (0)1865 722 113 (local rate 0845 230 9601)
facsimile 44 (0)1865 722 868; info.uk@trafford.com
Order online at:
trafford.com/05-3171

10 9 8 7 6 5

This book is dedicated to my father who taught me many lessons about life, love and liberty, but not how to manage money. He was one of the reasons I wrote this book.

This book is also dedicated to Gabriela who put up with me writing all weekend and many evenings until well past midnight. She supported my efforts during the many months it took to write and rework, edit and double check.

Thanks to:

CNN/Money
Edward Jones Investments
Franklin Templeton Investments
Institutional Investor
Mackenzie Financial
Raymond James Ltd.
The Globe and Mail
The National Post
The New York Times

These companies gave me the insight though constant reading and education, and taught me to use these powerful strategies combining investments and insurance. Without their help this book could not have been written.

Sharon Crawford helped with the intial edit. I also want to thank my friend and editor Patrick Flynn, who came to the book late in the process and did a very thorough job of editing. He gave me 15 pages of suggestions page by page. Thank you very much Patrick.

Thanks also to Michael Pecar who owns The Dock Shoppe, 162 Queens Quay East, Toronto, Ontario Canada M5A 1B4 (416) 362-3625 or fax (416) 362-8811 for the use of the navigation instruments on the front cover.

Table of Contents

Preface

Why did I write this book?

MAKE NO mistake; I sell investments and life insurance for a living. I wrote this book because it is needed. This is not a feel good book about the lifestyle you can have if only you change your life by getting up earlier, pedaling faster or breathing deeper ... No, this is a book about the hard questions - the ones that keep Canadians and Americans up at night. I'm Canadian and so is this book. That's right, this book contains nothing about 401K's and rolling over your Roth account. This book is primarily for people who invest from the Great White North – Canada. Americans will find some of the chapters on RRSP, RESP and Canadian tax law interesting but not useful. The other chapters contain sound strategies that work well in both Canada and the United States.

Here is the main reason I wrote this book. This information is not taught in school or university. That is a national shame. These strategies you have to learn on your own and sadly many never do. I learned them late but I learned them well.

Most of my clients are well off. That is to say they have a net worth of about $800,000. Some clients are much larger. I find millionaires great clients, often demanding but always fair. This book is written for them but also for the quiet Canadian who has about $400,000 net worth–most of which is in their home's value. People who are not sure if the money they have saved or the pension they have earned will be enough.

It is written to explode a few myths about investing. Are GIC's really the answer? When this was written interest rates were at 40 year lows. Who wants to lock that in? In short, banks want you to invest in GIC's, but that is only thinking about themselves - with your money. Is that right? Is it right for them or more especially YOU?

You can use this book before you see your broker or insurance agent. Definitely read it before you invest or buy insurance at the bank.

I worked for Edward Jones in the West Hill area of Toronto. It is a varied neighborhood with tree-lined streets and well-appointed beautiful homes; not far away are streets of ragged, wretched rental apartments. Solid God-fearing middle class Canadians own the rest of the houses in West Hill. The point is that the people of West Hill are a lot like most Canadians from coast to coast to coast. This book is written for any Canadians concerned about their future, those who are looking for good investment advice and a little Canadian humour.

Most large investors get this kind of advice from high-priced investment counselors and their talent banks. Why shouldn't investors and small business owners get the same kind of expertise? *Financial Navigation* will give you that kind of knowledge. This book is light on the filler material of some investment books and presents hard working strategy after strategy after strategy. If you want, read it with a highlighter.

Now I don't know if you know this, but Edward Jones insists that their people knock on doors the old-fashioned way, the way my father did when he was a young doctor. He made house calls. Those were the kind of calls I made at Edward Jones. For five years I knocked on over 5,000 homes and talked to thousands of people about investments, their future and what they worried about.

I heard the heartbeats of a troubled nation. Old widows who had only "the pension" left to live on. Young people living for today and not thinking about their tomorrows. I saw men weep, after we talked awhile, about the missed chance, the bad advice, the greedy advisor. I can remember only a few people who were really happy with their advisor. Most could not even tell me his or her name.

"Um, Oh I know it, um, she was here last week!"

People are very concerned that they do not have enough saved to retire in dignity.

I wrote this so you can find the answers you are looking for. So you can see that rates of almost 10% are still available with no risk. Did you know that? Or that the perfect investment tip you got at work is best forgotten and never repeated to anyone. What can a widow do? How about a small business owner? Or a suddenly unemployed executive? Or someone who wants to start off in the right financial way?

To all Canadians and all Americans, I am writing so you can find the answers to the hard questions about investments and insurance. I am licensed to sell investments and insurance. I practice what I preach.

Introduction

THERE IS a client of mine. I will not name him or her here. Let's call him Charlie. Well, Charlie had a problem when he came to see me. He hadn't saved enough and he knew it. He had received a small inheritance and invested that in March of 2000. When Charlie told me the date, I winced, because I knew what was coming. Anyone who invested in March of 2000 in stocks or mutual funds hit the height of the bull market right on the nose and from there it was a steep plunge down into a nasty bear market.

Charlie had bought really high and came to me to sell really low. He needed the money for something else. I told him all the reasons he shouldn't sell and told him what he was throwing away. As I recall he sold half and stayed invested in the other half. What he bought with the first half I do not know and he will forget in twenty years. The impact of the decision he made that day will affect his life from that day forward. Charlie was over 60 and he did not have enough time left at work to build up the exchequer.

I remember we got the other half into a few safe investments paying good dividends. Did I do a good job for Charlie? I know I did not. I should have tied him up, stuffed a wad of paper in his mouth, and not let him sign those papers while sternly lecturing him on the time value of money. But then again Charlie would have just thought I was crazy and gone down the street and found another advisor who would probably sell the whole inheritance. Maybe I was just crazy enough to help him by stopping him at 50%.

And that is what I want to do with you. I want to STOP you from making that "sure bet" investment, I want to STOP you settling for a low low GIC rate. I want to STOP you risking it all on tech, on small oil, on last year's winner of the mutual fund contest in the paper. I want you to STOP and think. This is your future we are talking about, your chance to live in Provence or in Tuscany or maybe retire to Elliott Lake. I understand in El- liott Lake you do have a choice. I hear tell that the mosquitoes are so big in the spring that your choice is whether to ride 'em or shoot 'em. Somehow Provence sounds better.

For almost everyone retires one day. Some before they expect to and others even when they are not ready but everyone retires some day. And whether we have enough to sail the oceans of the world or live on "the pension" is up to the decisions we make today.

If you invested in March 2000 or lost it on Bre-X, or Enron or if you sold your small oil just before it became a mid size oil – this book is for you. There is still time to recover for most of us. Doing the prudent things today will help us have a prosperous tomorrow.

A woman I met at her door was like many of us. She felt she knew all there was to know about investing. She was a day trader. Betting all she had on the daily ups and downs of the Canadian Banks. The last time I saw her she ran out to the street to intercept me as I was heading back to my car.

"David stop, I need one good stock idea and I can win it all back!"

She was desperate. Her husband and children had left her. The house was sold out from under her and still she wanted one last stock tip. She was not investing - she was gambling. I advised her to get some help. I remem- ber talking to her wild eyes; her face wore a giddy, flushed manic look. She was in deep trouble. I never found out what happened to her.

But how about you? Will you have enough money saved by retire- ment? Or worse will you live so long that all the money you saved is gone? Will you be able to leave something for the kids? These are the hard ques- tions. These are the questions that keep you and me up at night. These are the questions I will answer in this book.

I know that a book on investing and insurance can be as interesting some- times as reading a phone book, changing a tire in the winter slush or walk- ing in the wind and rain without a raincoat. So seeing as this book is based on my meeting 5,000 people in my door-knocking days with Edward Jones, I have broken up some of the chapters with little stories of what can happen to you when you are out knocking on doors in the mid-day sun. Look for "**Something happened to me on the way to...**" That will be a little funny tale, I hope.

Here is a short story about what can happen if you want advice from the big investment offices. They let you know you are a small fish.

The following is a true story. I got a little taste of what it is like to be a little guy going into a high-end brokerage house. My brother Peter was in Europe. He called and asked me to cash a GIC he had at the Royal Bank. The GIC had not matured and I was told the only way I could do that was take it up with Dominion Securities in downtown Toronto and they could sell the GIC on the open market. The GIC was for $10,000. I walked into the downtown office, and the first thing I noticed was the white marble reception area with the white marble receptionist who was just as cold. "And how much is the GIC for?"

"$10,000."

"Oh, … I see. … Please sit down over there."

She called up a junior trader who came out to the lobby. He was in a real hurry. I felt like I was getting the bum's rush. He took me to a small meeting room and I began to explain Peter's request. Suddenly there was a knock at the door and a trader told my junior that HE had the room and we would have to move to another room. To make a long story shorter we moved to a second and then a third room. Finally I got it sold. Can you imagine if I had asked for investment advice?

That's the problem I will solve for you with this book. Why shouldn't the person who has less than $500,000 get good investment and insurance advice? Doesn't he or she have the same needs? They have families to feed, educate and provide for now, as well as providing for their grandchildren. Perhaps the scale is different but the needs are the same. If the needs are the same; why is the advice different? If you go to a local bank branch you will be told only about GIC's and mutual funds from that bank.

If you have $500,000 to invest you have access to many varied strategies that can work for you even if you do not have $500,000 to invest. The trouble is that the people who help these rich people will not talk to investors with less than that. I heard a story once about Merrill Lynch, a fine old big money firm. They decided that their future was only to be built with investors with over $500,000 in their portfolios. All others had to go to the call centre for advice. An investor from Toronto had a portfolio of $480,000. He called his broker but the switchboard person shunted him over to the call centre. He called in to add an additional $20,000 to top up his account but they told him NO. The powerful strategies that he wanted are throughout this book.

Why am I so passionate about life insurance?

1

LIFE INSURANCE is an odd thing to be passionate about. We can all understand passion for women (or men) and over children or grandkids or with poetry, golf or sailing. Those are the usual passions. So why am I so passionate about life insurance?

What follows is a true story: My father was a doctor in Niagara Falls, Ontario. Dad came there after the war and built up a good practice as an anesthesiologist and a general practitioner. Dad had a good practice, a good wife, six kids and a turbulent temper. He was a good man and always wanted the best for his family. One of the things he always wanted was to own a cottage. We rented for years from a family called the Georges, who had a cottage on Golden Lake, near Eganville. I can recall many summers there. It was grand. But it wasn't our cottage.

Dad knew exactly what the cottage needed. Here is his must-have list: It must face south to catch both the rising and the setting sun; it must have a high rock with lots of water beneath for the older kids to dive off. There had to be a small beach so the younger kids could play in the sand. There had to be a marsh nearby where the boys could catch frogs to scare our sisters. Get the picture? A perfect place but not many cottages had all that. Dad hated lawns; if the cottage had a lawn he didn't even look. "I come to the cottage to rest and read not cut the #*! grass!"

So Dad looked for that cottage over the years. Sometimes on school break he and I would rent an aluminum boat and head down some storm tossed Muskoka Lake to find the cottage for sale, was alas, not perfect. It didn't match Dad's famous list.

One Wednesday, Dad had a meeting with his life insurance agent. Somehow the agent got under Dad's skin and he threw him out and told

17

him to cancel the insurance. He was not going to have that man as his agent anymore. The agent did as Dad told him to do, went back to his office and cancelled Dad's life insurance. That could not happen today but this was 1970.

Dad called up an agent who had been calling him with no success and asked him to come and see him. They set an appointment for the following Monday. So it was all set, Dad would buy new insurance that day. The rest of the week was as usual. Dad did his rounds at the hospital, operating room work in the morning and saw his patients at his office until Friday. On Friday afternoon, Murray McEachearn, a real estate agent in Dorset, called Dad and told him he had found the perfect place on Lake of Bays, on Rabbit Bay. The cottage faced south, it had a diving rock, and there was a small dock, a beach and a nearby marsh. Dad made an appointment to see it the next day.

On Saturday, he and my mother drove to Dorset and went out to see the cottage on Rabbit Bay. There it was. The cottage was run down and looked like it might fall into the bay but could come down quickly and a new place built. It had a diving rock with about 10 feet above the water and lots of good water - if you cleared the granite rock ledge just under the surface. It had a beach and a small marsh just like the agent had said. The price was $13,000. Dad bought it on the spot. Got out his cheque book and made the deal. Finally we had the cottage.

Dad stayed there after Murray left and started to sketch out a new cottage that would sit on the grounds in a few short months. He envisioned the new kitchen, indoor plumbing, and a great family room. A new dock and a ski boat were also planned that day. Dad showed my mother the plans and said this will go here and that will go there. Suddenly he grabbed his chest and said "I need to sit down I'm feeling a little thready". Dad sat on an old chesterfield, went terribly pale and fell over dead. He had suffered a massive heart attack and he was only 56.

It was early July. I was at The University of Western Ontario and got the call when I was holding a Saturday afternoon beer and pizza party with my friends. The phone rang and Dr. Powell, the town coroner for Niagara Falls, and a friend of my father's whose cottage was in the next bay, told me that my father was dead. I remember I only asked one question: "How is my mother?" I asked him.

I said I would be up there as soon as I could. I walked out into the party and told people that I had had bad news and that they should all go home. What a party pooper. They were true friends and not one left me. They all helped me get ready to go up north and get my mother. I remember throwing some things into a bag and walking to the elevator. Andrea Robarts leaned out of my apartment door and yelled, "Do you think you might need this?" It was a dark suit. I guess I was in shock. Doug Caldwell was down in London Ontario to see his girl friend but he volunteered to ride with me to Dorset. He was off to England the following Monday and he still came with me.

Months later, I got a call from my mother. "David, you know that your father died without any insurance."

"Yes, I know that."

"Well I need your help. We are going to lose the house in March if I do not get $15,000 by then."

"Oh."

"Can I leave that problem to you?"

I was the eldest son and the burden was suddenly mine. I was between my second and third years at Western. I had reasonable grades, an excellent summer job working for the Board of Governors of the University and a great girl friend named Kelly but all of that was about to go by the boards - all because Dad had no insurance.

"OK Mum I'll see what I can do and let you know."

How do you earn $15,000 in 1970 with the average annual salary out of school was only $9,000? How could I earn $15,000 in only six months? I had no idea but I did have a good friend in Calgary who might know the answer. I called up Matt Moore Newell. He and I had rowed together at Ridley. I told Matt my dilemma. He told me he would ask his dad. Matt's dad was one of the people who founded the Leduc oilfield north of Calgary. The next day, Matt's dad, a tall Texan, also named Matt Moore Newell, called me to tell me I was heading north to work as a roughneck in the arctic oil patch up near Zama Lake in the North West Territories (as it was called then). I went up there on Boxing Day.

To make a long story shorter I worked that winter for Cantex Drilling. It was so cold. I remember we had an arctic thermometer from Gulf Oil. It had a scale from 120F above to 120F below. One day it was minus 77F and we didn't know about wind chill. I dressed in so many layers, and remember I wrote my girl friend that "I went to work looking like a little outhouse." I managed to stay warm, the food was fabulous and the work hard.

I was green hand when I started and not much better when I finished in March. We punched three dry holes. Then the rig and most of the men went back to Texas.

I say most of the men because our rig started with 16 men and four men died that winter in accidents. I remember pulling one of my mates out of the boiler room. He had gone in there to get out of the cold wind and the carbon monoxide overcame him. I dragged him out by his boots, already stiff from the cold. The rest of us worked harder and longer and sadder.

I remember one night we got bad oil for the five diesels and all five went down at once. We used those engines to heat the trailers, light the area and drive the rig. Dinner was suddenly cancelled. We all worked on the diesels because they were life for us. If we failed to start them soon it was all over since there was only one car on site. I worked like a beaver and every now and again snuck a look at the fabulous northern lights. They hung like a giant green simmering stage curtain and they crackled like giant static on a massive radio. When we lit fires under each diesel they suddenly caught. We had lights and heat again but the incredible northern lights disappeared.

I made a good hourly wage, I made isolation pay, I made 'bottom of the hole bonus' and I got danger pay. In short, I made well over $15,000 that winter. I sent the money home and I returned to London and Western in the spring. All my friends had graduated and moved on. I had to start over again, all that because my father had no insurance. In fact, I didn't get back to university until I was 38. Then I went to California and got an Honours BA with higher distinction. I graduated at 42. Don't let this happen to you. Get covered early and keep your insurance in force. So with that story told let's start talking about how to invest and insure that your family's financial health is well looked after.

Should I buy an RRSP?

2

I COULD just answer YES and end this chapter right here. However, it's not that simple.

One thing I can't do in this book is stand on a high hill and point the finger at all the RRSP non-participants. No, I think my own tale is true for a lot of people. I became aware of RRSP's in my thirties. I heard that it was good in some ways but not for everyone. If you were a student or a commissioned salesperson – you didn't need the tax deferral. If you made lots of money you were better off just investing in an open cash account and getting all the capital gains and deducting the capital losses. There were many theories that sounded right. So I did not open an RRSP until I was in my early forties. Then I was working in Mississauga and it was right before the deadline. I was in the bank just 10 minutes. A teller pointed at three round yellow charts.

"Where do you feel you stand on these?"

"I guess here and here and there."

"That's easy then. Just invest your money in any four of these 16 mutual funds and you are all set."

I was in and out in no time at all. Of the four funds I guessed at three were winners that year and the fourth was a big stinker and dragged the other three down. That year my RRSP went down. So the next year I did the same. After that I stopped guessing with tellers and got a broker. Years later, I became a broker and realized just how hard it is to pick mutual funds, stocks and bonds for anyone else. That is the reason why the bank used the three yellow circles. Did it help Canadians or just make the job easier for the banks?

The RRSP was started by the federal government to help Canadians save some money for their retirement. The rules have changed over the years and some of the restrictions and limitations have been recently removed. The RRSP is still the cornerstone of most Canadian's retirement plans. The "Big But" is that there are Billions of dollars of unused RRSP investment room in millions of Canadian's RRSP's. Why don't we invest all the way in our RRSP and maximize our retirement? I believe it has to do with the record debt levels in North America and Europe. Many people are living pay-cheque to pay-cheque and have no extra cash to put into an RRSP every month.

A trip down the main street of most Canadian towns proves the point. 'Cash Until Payday' shops are everywhere. That says that their customers are living beyond the simple pay-cheque to pay-cheque every month – these people have more month than money. Aren't we all a little like this? You can bet the interest rates at these firms are rapacious. Just hold your breath until next payday. Then plan to do better next month.

The retirement of Canadians is too important to guess at. Luckily now we have good computer programs that can interpret your risk tolerance into a dandy mutual fund program that suits you. If you have never seen this work it is amazing and the results are much better. The computer knows what is best since people well versed in investing programmed it. The program will give you a balanced portfolio. Whether you are a conservative investor, a moderate, an advanced or aggressive investor, there is a balanced portfolio for you. Most large insurance and investment institutions have similar programs.

The RRSP idea works because you can defer taxes owing now and pay them later when you are retired and earning less and at that time inflation has made the dollar worth less too. That's why you should contribute. Now the question is HOW?

How can we get more money into our RRSP's? If you can save $250 a month and start early you can have a rich retirement. To do that you may have to cut out some extras: Make your latte at home using Starbuck's® coffee or if you have to go to Starbuck's, have a simple coffee (if that is possible). That saves a little. Take public transit, if feasible, that saves expensive downtown parking and gas. Take a part- time job. Work nights. These suggestions will not work for everyone. Find one or two things you feel comfortable about cutting out and cut them out every month.

Then find one thing that is tough to give up and give that up too. That way you will always be reminded that your RRSP is more important than even that special thing. To do this I stopped buying beer at the Beer Store. That saves quite a bit every month and keeps me thinner. What can you save?

Why should you bother? Well consider this real possibility:

If you started saving just $250 a month when you turn 23 and did that for 10 years until you are 33. You will have saved $250 X 12 = $3,000 every year. Over 10 years you will have saved $30,000 plus interest. At that point you can stop saving. Leave the money invested for years and years. Resist the temptation to use it for a new car, planned hot tub or sunroom. Keep it from the spender in the family- every family has one. No, it's "HANDS OFF" until you are in your seventies. You will be almost a millionaire.

Albert Einstein was asked, "Doctor Einstein, what is the most powerful force on earth?" I'm sure the reporter expected the answer would be something about nuclear power. But the learned scientist looked him in the eye and said, "Compound Interest!"

Dr. Einstein knew that giving compound interest years to work could make anyone rich.

The example above has several lessons wrapped up in it.

Lesson #1 Start early. By starting in your early twenties you can add years to compound your investment.

Lesson #2 Invest regularly. A consistent month-by-month investment of a small amount can make all the difference if there is enough time (see Lesson #1).

Lesson #3 Hold on to that investment for a long time (see Lesson #1). There is a caveat here. Buy and Hold is not Buy and Ignore for years. Use a good broker and have them review your investments with you once a year. If the account needs to be rebalanced to return to your original investment objectives, do it then. Just don't sell them. Leave it alone and let it grow. You will be richly rewarded.

If you haven't started and time is getting on, that's OK; just start now. Don't put it off another day. Start contributing. If you are older you will have to contribute a lot more than someone younger. Do it anyway. Pour the cash into that registered plan. When you are older you can retire and live a little better because you are drawing down your RRIF or Registered Retirement Income Fund. Your RRIF starts after you wind up your RRSP by the 31st of December in the year you turn 69. After that, you cannot contribute anymore and all the unused RRSP contribution room evaporates. Don't let it all disappear. Start investing in your RRSP today.

In late February we always hear the bank ads cry out, "It's RRSP season!" Nonsense, it's the government RRSP deadline not the RRSP season. The deadline is usually the end of February or the first of March depending on how the weekend falls. You should be investing in your RRSP every month and there is no season to that.

Here's a good idea if you are still earning income in the year you turn 69, you can still contribute to your RRSP. Do it in the December before you wrap up your RRSP forever. Assuming that you have already maximized your RRSP for the last year this will create an over-contribution. The fine will be about $120 and the tax savings many times that. The fine is only for one month since on January 1st your tax problem disappears.

The rules on RRSP's have recently changed. Here are the most current regulations:

The recent 2005 federal budget removed the foreign investment limit of 30%. Now we can invest in foreign investment vehicles without worrying about the limits. Does that mean we should invest in the United States? I come back to that in Chapter 44. Right now I want to outline the basics of RRSP's. You are allowed to invest up to 18% of your last year's earned income into an RRSP up to certain limits. In 2005 the limit was $15,500. It will go up like this:

2006	$18,000
2007	$19,000
2008	$20,000
2009	$21,000
2010	$22,000
2011	Indexed

Earned income includes income from your job, rental income (minus losses), self-employment income (minus losses), and royalties if you are a rock star, author or an inventor.

The best place to find out how much you can contribute is at the bottom of the *Notice of Assessment* that comes to you after you file your taxes. There it will tell you exactly how much room you have to contribute next year. Don't let this number build up. Many people just let it rise until it seems impossible to catch up. Do your best to maximize every year. If you can't maximize, consider taking out an RRSP loan to catch up. Then use your refund to pay down most of the loan. Pay the entire loan off by the end of the year and do another loan the following January. That way you can catch up. Ask your broker about this method of catching up. It's a good idea and above all it makes it possible to catch up. Take advantage of the 40-year low rates and use this time to increase your contributions to your RRSP. By the way, the interest you pay on your RRSP catch up loan is not tax-deductible.

Spousal RRSP

It's about income splitting. Generally that's a good idea since rarely are both spouses earning equally. However, in retirement it is best if you both earn the same amount from a tax point of view. You can use a spousal RRSP to do that. In simple terms, a spousal is an RRSP that you contribute to and only your spouse can withdraw from. You get the deduction and your spouse will pay taxes on withdrawals. The total of your RRSP and the Spousal plan must be within your contribution limits.

Keep in mind that any withdrawals in the first three years of a spousal plan will be taxed back in your hands. For example, if you make a $10,000 contribution to a spousal plan in 2005 and your spouse makes a $4,000 withdrawal in 2007 then you have a $4,000 earnings increase with the accompanying tax bill to pay that year. If you wait until three years have passed the transfer tax is eliminated. However, the spouse still pays withholding taxes on any withdrawal. Withholding taxes are taxes paid directly by the brokerage firm to the government on your behalf.

If you contribute on December 31st you can cut the waiting time down to two years and one day. If you are thinking about making withdrawals in the short term use that strategy.

What can go into an RRSP?

Almost anything. Let's clear up one thing first. Guaranteed Investment Certificates or GIC's are not RRSPs. GIC's can go into an RRSP but they are totally different things. I saw a great deal of confusion on this point, seeing all those people at the door. I blame the banks for this confusion since for a long time banks wanted your RRSPs invested in low–rate GIC's to support their higher margin mortgage business. After a while, in "bank-speak", the terms merged. They are completely different things.

Think of the RRSP as a basket. You can put into that basket (or invest in) cash, GIC's, mutual funds, segregated funds, stocks, bonds, mortgages you hold, some life insurance policies and some annuities, some rights and warrants. If you can't contribute cash one year you can contribute by swapping in stocks, bonds or funds in-kind. Be aware that if the assets you transfer in-kind have gone up in value you will face a tax issue since you bought them and have a taxable capital gain. Meaning that they have gone up in value and that growth is taxable before it goes into your RRSP. Most of these types of transactions need to be set up in a self-directed RRSP at a broker's office as opposed to a managed RRSP at a bank.

Homeowners Plan

If you have not owned a home for four years, you can use this plan. It was started in 1992 and improved in 1998. Now you and your spouse can each withdraw up to $20,000 from your RRSP's tax-free for buying a home. There is a catch and it is a good catch. You have to pay yourself back. You can use this program over and over as long as you have paid off the last loan and sold the house. You also have not owned a house for the last four years. That means that you once owned a house using this plan, rented somewhere for four years and then can use the plan again.

Once you have made a withdrawal from your RRSP you must close the house deal by September 31St of the next year. This date is called the *completion date*. If you can quickly replace the funds by December 31 following the completion date there is no penalty. You must also occupy your home as your principle residence within one year after closing the deal. The home must be on solid ground – that boat you have been dreaming of doesn't qualify. But most homes do: detached, semi-detached, town homes, condominiums, mobile homes, apartment units, a share in a cooperative housing corporation counts too.

Homeowners plan repayments are made to your RRSP over a maximum of 15 years. These payments are not tax deductible. These payments must be made equally over the 15 years but you can pay it off faster. In fact doing that will lower the balance in each of the remaining years. You must start to repay yourself in the second year. If you miss a payment in any year the equal amount for that year will be added to your taxable income in that year. So make those payments on time and enjoy your new home.

Be careful about how you time the Home Buyers plan. Ensure that you leave at least 91 days between depositing funds to your RRSP and then withdrawing funds in your Home Buyers plan. Any withdrawal within less than 91 days and you lose the tax deduction of your deposit.

Should you use this plan? It seems it is right for young people just starting out, but they are the ones who are most hurt by losing the key early growth of that RRSP. Ideally, you should have about 10 years left to build your RRSP before you use it. If you have 35 years or more left to retire the Home Buyers plan doesn't make sense. If you are younger, shop for a low ratio mortgage insured by the CMHC (Canadian Mortgage and Housing Corporation) and keep salting money each month into your RRSP. (See More on Mortgages below).

What should you invest in an RRSP?

The simple answer according to most banks is mutual funds. I think that growth mutual funds and stocks should be in a non-registered account as opposed to your RRSP. If you have stocks and mutual funds in your RRSP, you cannot deduct capital losses each year. You will pay capital gains tax on the non-registered assets but this tax is less than the tax on interest earned on bonds and strip bonds. Interest is taxed at the same rate as salary; whereas, capital gains tax is based on 25% of the capital gains at your average tax rate. Said another way, Capital Gains tax is based on half of the growth on 50% of the capital gain. That number is taxed at your *average rate*. For example, if you buy a stock at $10 and sell it at $16 you have a $6 capital gain. This $6 is reduced to 50% or to $3 and then that number is halved again to $1.50. Say you have 100 shares then you would have a taxable capital gain of $150. Then suppose your *average tax rate* is 30% you would owe 30% of $150 or $45.

Compare that to interest at 6% on a decent bond. If you invested the same amount ($10,000) you would pay taxes on interest at the same *marginal rate* as your salary, which could easily be 40%. You would earn $600 a year and pay tax on that full amount at 40% or $240. The ones that should be in your RRSP are the investments you are paying more tax on - that is interest-earning investments.

The *marginal rate* is the tax rate paid on the last dollar you earned in a given year. It is the highest taxed dollar you earn. The *average tax rate* is just that – the average of all taxes and so less than the *marginal rate*.

So in short, put interest-earning investments in your RRSP, that is, GICs, bonds, income mutual funds and bond funds; and put investments that gain capital gains or lose capital gains, stocks and balanced and growth mutual funds in a non-registered plan. This is advice you will not get at a bank in Canada. They are in the business of selling GICs and only mutual funds.

That being said, I fully realize that not all people can buy bonds since the usual lowest amount sold is $5,000. I also realize that with interest rates at 40-year lows this is not the time to invest in interest-earning investments. Start with the RRSP and when that is maxed open a non-registered account. When interest rates go back up, and they will, then follow my advice.

More on Mortgages

It may seem that I have a bias against banks. Well I do. Here is another example how banks serve themselves and not you. When you buy a home you must have insurance to get a mortgage. Since most people get their mortgages from the bank it seems simple enough to just get the mortgage insurance there. STOP.

Get the mortgage at the bank if you must, but shop around for the mortgage insurance. Often insurance companies have better rates and mortgage brokers can often help, too.

What is wrong with bank mortgage insurance? Let me count the ways. First, as the balance of your mortgage goes down, the monthly payments on the insurance stay the same. Soon you are paying way too much for that insurance. Second, the rates are too high. Compare with a simple 10 or 20-year term insurance contract at an insurance company you will be surprised at the difference. Third, when you buy mortgage insurance from a bank or credit union you are purchasing their group insurance. You are a certificate holder and do not own the policy. The bank can make changes to the coverage without your consent and the coverage is over once the mortgage is paid off or moved to another financial institution. Fourth, if you get new insurance at the new bank you will pay more because you are older and if your health has changed you may be declined.

You own individual life insurance; it is for a fixed amount. If your mortgage is $250,000 and you pay off $100,000 before your death the bank will pay your family $150,000. The insurance company would pay $250,000. You can name a beneficiary and the proceeds are tax-free. The other way the bank gets the money first and then gives the remaining proceeds to you. Individual insurance is fully portable, if you move or change mortgage companies the insurance is still there protecting you all along the way.

Another thing about mortgages, everyone wants to pay the darn thing off. Here is a strategy to get that job completed sooner. Follow this simple rule: The more times you pay the mortgage each month the less you will pay. Pay it once a month and you'll pay the most; twice a month less; and four times a month still less and every week much less. Talk to the firm that holds your mortgage and ask them to change the payments to weekly. Then adjust your savings and pay cheques to make that work.

What you should tell your children about Money and Insurance

3

DID YOU know that investing money the right way is not taught in school? In fact, you can graduate with a PhD. and never hear a single lecture on investing. That is a great national shame. It should be a part of every year's lessons until we start raising investment savvy people generation after generation.

In a way, many parents have taught their children what not to do. They have seen Dad and Mum fighting over money until the wee hours. They have seen their parents invest in tech stocks, Bre-X or Enron and then moan over the loss for years. We teach even when we do not set out to teach. Our example is so loud.

So what should you teach your children? Well, if you have no investment knowledge yourself why not learn together as a family? Start when the eldest is about eight years old. Make the learning fun. Sit down and read a good investment book out loud. Do it once a week as a family group and then do what the book recommends. Have investment nights at home and teach your children. Call your broker and invite him or her over to teach the family one night. Perhaps start a family investment club. Buy stocks together with everyone in on the decision.

At first, invest fictional money. Use the money from the Monopoly game. While you are all learning you can all be saving. When you have saved enough, call your broker over for another evening. Have him or her open a non-registered account in Mom and Dad's names. Since by law you must be 18 to invest money. Then give the broker the money to invest and tell them what you want to invest in. You may find that the broker has another idea or perhaps a very good reason why you should not invest in this fund or company. One note: it is probably best to give your broker a cheque from Mom and Dad's bank account since most investment companies cannot accept cash.

Banks will, of course, accept cash but then bankers do not usually come to your house after supper. Consider opening a special brokerage account with your broker to use for the family's investment club. Open a real account for Mom and Dad at a broker's office and invest for real there. Of course, first get your RRSP maximized every year. Then open a joint open (sometimes called a non-registered) account for further investing.

What should you teach your children? Teach your children about practical wealth building. Show them how investing a small portion of their paper route or baby-sitting money every month is essential.

How much should you save? Here is the best advice I ever heard: PAY YOURSELF FIRST. Pay yourself at least 10% of every pay cheque (see Chapter Thirty One). Teach them this by your good example. Invest 10% of what you make. Here it is up to you if you take 10% of your gross or 10% of your net. Whatever you start continue it every month. Soon you will not even notice it. You will start with 90% every month and live within that. Let compound interest soar. Prove this by doing it.

As your children get older, give them good investment books to read. Get them to talk to you about what they read. Discuss the lessons in every investment book. There is a good list of investment books in the back of this book. Subscribe to investment magazines and some carefully chosen investment newsletters. Read them out loud as a family.

What should you teach your children? As you earn more money give your children money to invest for real. If they are younger than 18 you will have to open an informal trust account or bare trust at your broker's office. This is quite simple and your broker will be happy to do it for you. The statements will come in on a regular basis. Have a look at them together. How are you doing? If you have invested wisely, resist the temptation to sell. This itself is a lesson on holding on. Remember about starting to invest at 23 and investing for the next 10 years at a rate of $250 per month? This is the goal of your teaching. Have them ready to start investing at age 23. You will have started them on a life of investing success.

Pitfalls

Children learn a lot from their parent's attitude to money. If we are fighting over money or moaning over our losses we are teaching a lesson that we may not want to teach. Involve your older children in the family investments. Impress on them that this money is for your old age and their future. It is not for fancy cars or family trips to the Bahamas.

Teach them to be responsible with money. When they are about eight years old, it really depends on the child, start to introduce them to money. Give them an allowance every two weeks and teach them to budget. Tell them they can use it for an extra something they save for or a little candy at the store and when they are older for clothes or whatever. The key to budgeting is that if you spend it all in week one on candies there will be no candy next week. Do not give in and top up the allowance. They will learn budgeting when they learn to plan their savings and save until they can get something they really really want. It will remind them that there is no money tree growing in your backyard.

One pit-fall could be the first car. Young people lust for that first car. My father was quite strict. I got my first car when I was 21 and not a day sooner. Don't let your sons and daughters use their investment money, with a large contribution from you, for their wheels. It again will drive home the lesson about holding those good investments over a very long time. Besides, walking or taking public transit is good for the soul.

Another pit-fall could be a family crisis. They occur in many families. Dad is sacked or Mom is let go. The local plant announces it is closing for good. There are many family crises but what can you do to protect the family against financial disaster in hard times like these?

The Mormons tell their people to have six months of earnings set aside for these difficult times. I am not a Mormon and six months is hard to save when you have a family, are paying the bills and are investing every month. Put aside three months earnings or what you would spend in three months. This will protect you, your home and your investments.

Consider having this money in money market accounts or even safer, invest it in cashable GIC's. When rates improve see which one is paying more and invest the safety money there.

One caution about teaching your children about money. Do not get too caught up in it. After a while teach it once a month and leave it there. Life is about living and money is only a tool that helps us live it to the fullest. What money really does is give us options. Remember money is only a tool.

My father used to tell me "money was like manure. It was no good unless it was spread around and if it sits in a big pile it just stinks." I differ with Dad on his advice. If money sits in a big pile it should be invested and put into your three-month safety money account. He was right though about spreading it around. I think he meant spending it. I now take it to

31

mean diversification. Remember that word, it is a key to investing. Chapter 18 and Chapter 45 are all about diversification.

If you are a concerned parent or an active parent, consider talking to your local school board about investment courses. Call ahead and arrange a meeting. Go with several friends from the neighborhood. Ask that something be started. Even if it starts small, it can grow much bigger as there will be public interest if it is promoted well. Persevere; keep at it until you get some approval. Then find a broker who can teach. That may not be easy. Look for someone who does seminars, as he or she is often comfortable speaking in front of a crowd.

If you are a broker, consider teaching courses on investing at the local high school or community college. Expect it to be an uphill fight. I tried to teach at the University of Toronto's Scarborough branch - something open to the public and students about investing. I planned to offer practical investment advice similar to what you are reading in this book. I got no interest. I may not have spoken to the right person. Maybe I shot too high. I think you will have better luck teaching in a local library, community hall, or a high school. This really should be taught in schools as a regular part of the curriculum.

Should you buy an insurance policy on your children?

Yes! Shocked? Some people are shocked to think that parents would buy a policy on young Johnny and young Jenny. Do they want to profit from their child's (God forbid) death?

The short answer to this question is absolutely not. Lots of parents do that every year. Why do they do it? They do it because they love their children and want to give them a leg-up in the future. Here are some reasons why people buy life insurance on their kids.

It is incredibly inexpensive. Buy a 20-year pay whole life policy on a three year old and it will cost less than $7 a month. But because it's inexpensive is not really the main reason.

If you buy a whole life policy on Jenny, she will have that policy and its' cash value for use later on in life. She can use the cash value to help with the down payment on her first house. Or she can keep the insurance in force and switch the beneficiary to her husband or their first child. Or she can take the policy to the bank and use it as collateral or security for a bank loan.

If her parents have a smart insurance agent he or she will add the Guaranteed Insurability Benefit to the policy. That means that in the future, as long as the policy is kept in force, she can buy more insurance without a medical. Even if she is riddled with cancer at 25 (God forbid that too), she can still buy more insurance.

That option is inexpensive since most children grow up healthy. However, some children don't grow up that way and at this point you can't tell which group Johnny will fit into. This benefit is purchased based on a dollar amount. For example, one client of mine bought a whole life policy on her thirteen-year-old daughter. This was a $30,000 whole life policy with a Guaranteed Insurability Benefit of $100,000. That meant that if her daughter died the policy would pay $30,000. If she wants more insurance later on perhaps when she is expecting her first child then she can exercise the $100,000 option. It costs her $35.00 a month for that policy and it will be all paid up in twenty years. If she had purchased that policy when her daughter was born it would be far less than even that amount.

Two things to note about Guaranteed Insurability Benefits: you still have to pay for the insurance based on your age. It follows then that the sooner you exercise this option the better. Insurance is still inexpensive in your early twenties so that would be a good time to exercise the benefit.

The second point, however, is perhaps you should save that GIB for when you really need it. If you are healthy when you want and need more insurance then price it based on having a medical. The cost of insurance with a medical should be less than the cost without a medical. Check with your insurance agent and price it both ways.

If someone ever tells you that you want to profit from your child's death when you buy insurance on your newborn. You look them right in the eye and tell them that you bought it because you love your child and want the best for him or her in the future. Then suggest that if they love their kids, then they too should give them that important leg-up in the future.

Registered Retirement Income Funds or Annuities?

4

EVERYONE RETIRES one day. Most will retire before they are 69 but there will be many still working. At the end of the year you turn 69 is the deadline for wrapping up your RRSP. That's right, it will be gone and all the opportunity you had to contribute will evaporate too.

You have four choices to make when you wrap up your RRSP. You can:

1) Take it all out in a lump sum.
2) Transfer it all into a RRIF
3) Buy an annuity with it.
4) Some or all of the above together.

If you take option number one – the lump sum. Think long and hard about that since the government will tax you heavily. You will be taxed as if it was salary. You could take it all out and see the world and spend it all on wine, women and song. But that would be a very poor choice especially since you have worked a lifetime to build up this nest egg. However the tax laws do give the option to take it all out and that may be the right option for some in unique circumstances, like a life threatening illness. None of my clients have ever taken that choice. Most have chosen the next option.

Option two - RRIF

Pronounced "Riff", is really the inverse of your RRSP. You make contributions to your RRSP; and you make withdrawals only from your new RRIF. You can stay invested in the same investments that you hold in your RRSP. The government mandates that the money start to come out at a proscribed rate (one set by the government and changeable). The rate is based on your age or the age of your younger spouse.

If you have a younger spouse this can work to your advantage. If she is five years younger than you – use those years to let it grow longer. Arrange so that the first withdrawals are based on when she turns 69 and you can extend the tax deferral a little longer on the RRSP part of your investments.

It is about control. When you retire you can control your Registered Retirement Income Fund (RRIF) to a certain extent. The government still tells you what percent you must deduct at a minimum each year. You do have some control in that you can take the minimum or more if you want. The government sets the withdrawal rate so that the RRIF runs down to almost nothing on your 90th birthday. Happy Birthday Granny. Is that the day you want all your money to be gone? Some happy birthday.

Don't think that you will not live to 90. One of the biggest concerns today for life insurance companies is that people are living longer lives due to medical improvements and innovations. Another reason could be that some of us are smarter about our food choices. Whatever the reason people are living longer. That means you could well live to 90.

A RRIF is a good option for most people except that you could run down your money before age 90, if this is all you have invested.

Here is a chart showing how the RRIF payment diminishes as you get older.

RRIF/LIF

Minimum Annual Payout Schedule

(As a percentage of the January balance)

Age at start of the year	Post 1993 RIFF's	Cash $100,000	Cash per year
60	3.33%	$96,670	$3,330.00
61	3.45%	$93,334.89	$3335.11
62	3.57%	$90,002.84	$3,332.05
63	3.70%	$86,672.73	$3,330.11
64	3.85%	$83,335.83	$3,336.90
65	4.00%	$80,002.40	$3,333.45
66	4.17%	$76,666.30	$3,336.10
67	4.35%	$73,331.32	$3,334.98
68	4.55%	$69,994.75	$3,336.57
69	4.76%	$66,663.00	$3,331.75
70	5.00%	$63,329.85	$3,333.15
71	7.38%	$58,656.11	$4,673.74
72	7.48%	$54,268.64	$4,387.47
73	7.59%	$50.117.93	$4,150.71
74	7.71%	$46,253.84	$3,864.09
75	7.85%	$42,622.91	$3,630.93
76	7.99%	$39,217.34	$3,405.57
77	8.15%	$36,021.13	$3,196.21
78	8.33%	$33,020.57	$3000.56
79	8.53%	$30,203.92	$2,816.65
80	8.75%	$27,561.08	$2,642.84
81	8.99%	$25,083.34	$2,477.74
82	9.58%	$22,680.36	$2,402.98
83	9.58%	$20,507.59	$2,172.77
84	9.93%	$18,471.19	$2,036.40
85	10.33%	$16,563.12	$1,908.07

Age at start of the year	Post 1993 RIFF's	Cash $100,000	Cash **per year**
86	10.79%	$14,775.96	$1,787.16
87	11.33%	$13,101.84	$1,674.12
88	11.96%	$11,534.86	$1,566.98
89	12.71%	$10,068.78	$1,466.08
90	13.62%	$8,697.42	$1,371.36
91	14.73%	$7,416.29	$1,281.13
92	16.12%	$6,220.78	$1,195.51
93	17.92%	$5,106.02	$1,114.76
94	20.00%	$4.084.82	$1,021.20
95	20.00%	$3,267.86	$817.14
96	20.00%	$2,614.29	$653.57
97	20.00%	$2,091.43	$522.86
98	20.00%	$1,673.14	$418.29
99	20.00%	$1,338.51	$334.63
100	20.00%	$1,070.81	$267.70

As you can see from the chart your money runs down when you are older. Happy Birthday Granny! Also, all of us need a lot more than $100,000 invested by age 69. You can't live well on that much plus government pensions.

Another way to give your investments in your RRIF more time to grow and to defer taxes as long as possible is to transfer from an RRSP to a RRIF in December in the year you turn 69. But do not take any money out until December the next year.

Remember in Chapter Two, I urged you to also have investments outside your RRSP? This next option is when they can really help.

Option three – Annuities

This is the exact opposite of a RRIF. You have no control but you do have a guarantee (if it is set up right) that you will have a steady income for the rest of your life. With a life annuity you can never outlive your money. Isn't that reassuring?

There are many different flavours of annuities. Basically the choices can be broadly grouped into *term certain annuities* and *life annuities*.

Term certain annuities are what they say they are. They will pay you a certain sum every month or semi-annually for a certain term. Most are 10, 15 or 20-year annuities. The big drawback to term certain annuities is that you can outlive your money. If you live longer than the term it can all be gone.

On the flip side these pay more compared to life annuities so your paydays are better.

Don't expect to leave any money for the kids with term certain annuities. For example, if you buy a straight term certain annuity for a term of 10 years and die in the fifth year, the money goes back to the company you bought it from not to the kids. If you buy them with a guarantee period that is a little better. For example you could buy a 20-year term certain annuity with a 20-year guarantee if you are less than 70. That way if you live 15 more years and die in the fifteenth year of the contract the other five years are commuted to your estate or your beneficiaries. Commuted means the remaining money owed is totaled up and your heirs get a lump sum in most cases. If this concerns you, it can be set up so that the heirs get monthly payments for the rest of the term instead of the lump sum. As I said earlier annuities can be customized the way you want them. Of course every bit of customization reduces the amount paid out. Most payouts are semi annual but monthly payments are also quite popular.

I think the best annuity is a life annuity. They offer the best income protection. That is an annuity that is guaranteed to continue to pay you for the rest of your days even if you live to be 110. Now the payout is lower on these but the payments until you die makes it worthwhile. You can never outlive these.

Every investment book or newspaper article I have read that mentions annuities says don't buy them if interest rates are low. That is true if you are 65 or less but it is not true if you are older. Most people who buy life annuities are older so this popular advice is just plain wrong.

Life annuities are based on two factors not just one. True they are based on interest rates; but they are also based on mortality tables. These mortality tables can increase the rate you get on the annuity to great rates even today as long as you are over 65.

Ten Percent?

Remember in the preface where I wrote that you could still get rates of 10% safely? Here is one way to get a return of almost 10%.

I have a client who is 78. Let's call him Sam Dominion; he has $100,000 to invest in a life annuity. Based on a payout I ran this week,

Sam would get his own money back at a rate of 9.34%. He would be paid $778.12 every month for as long as he lives. This is a guaranteed annuity that is guaranteed for 12 years (until Sam is 90 -that is the maximum age). To be clearer, the annuity will be paid for at least 12 years, in this case to age 90. Remember, if he lives longer than 90, the payments continue until he dies. If he dies before 90, the balance to 90 is computed and a cheque mailed out.

How do I calculate that 9.34%? I simply take the monthly payout and multiply it by 12 to make it an annual payment. Or I could take a semi annual payment and double it to get an annual payment. Then I simply take that annual payment as a percentage of the total invested and I get a rate. In this case 9.34%. Now these rates are from insurance companies and being conservative they will never say that you get 9.34%. Because they cannot tell you the day you will die so they cannot accurately say what rate you will ultimately get. And of course the balance goes down as you are paid. But the fact remains. I can say it this way and it is true. Sam will get monthly payments of $778.12 for the rest of his life and right now works out to an annual payment of 9.34%. Keep in mind that you are really getting your own money back with a guarantee that it can never run out.

The way I sell life annuities is in Option four. See if it makes sense for you too.

Option four- Combine a RRIF with a life annuity

The RRIF gives you regular payments and runs your money to ground at age 90. The life annuity pays you semi annually as well but it never runs out until you do. A combination of these options gives you the best of both. The life annuity cannot be guaranteed past 90, it is guaranteed to leave money to your heirs if you die before 90.

For example, say you are 72 and you have some money in a non-registered account that has built up over time. You had this account outside your RRSP so the money did not go into the RRIF. This is your real retirement money. The RIFF is nice but for most of us it is not going to mean too much. When you die not much will likely be left for your sons and daughters and it runs down at 90. Happy birthday.

One point to note: If you have a RRIF and want to turn it into a life annuity that can be done too. That becomes an LRIF. See Alphabet Soup Appendix I.

Back to our example, you are 72 and decide that you had better ensure that you never run out of money. You simply buy a life annuity with a guarantee of 18 years. The law says that we cannot extend a guarantee period beyond age 90. That is the guarantee that any balance after death will be commuted to your heirs cannot be set past 90. If you live past 90 the life annuity will continue to pay like clockwork. However, when you die after 90, that's it. Then there is no annuity money left for your heirs.

But if you live until you are 85 there will still be five years left in the guarantee period. (Remember we bought that guarantee to age 90) So the last five years monthly totals are added up and the lump sum is commuted to your beneficiaries or your estate.

It depends on the individual which of the four options is right for you. Fact is you have to pick one or two. The two I like are a combination of a RRIF and a life annuity guaranteed to age 90.

I just read an article in *The New York Times* entitled "Who is Preying on your Grandparents?" The article tells people the dangers of annuities. I get so angry at publications that publish as if it was gospel – a grand lie about all annuities. That article fails to say it is speaking of one specific kind of annuities that most companies in Canada don't even offer and they apply it to the entire world of annuities like it is God's Truth. In fact, the article just makes it harder for good people to sell good high quality annuities to people who really will benefit from them.

Let me be more specific: Remember I told you that annuities come in all shapes and sizes? Well one shape they come in is called deferred annuities. These are investment vehicles that let the interest grow for 10 or 15 years before they start paying out. This type of product is fine if you are in your 40's but really wrong to sell to people who might not live to see their money start to flow from the annuity. Manulife sells these in Canada and they have a good sales force. I doubt whether the same kind of problems would occur here in Canada. The article is about some elderly people that bought deferred annuities and then found that the widows could not get at their money after their husband died without great withdrawal penalties. These people should not have been sold deferred annuities.

They would be quite happy with a guaranteed life annuity. Let's take the article's lead example. If the couple had purchased a guaranteed life annuity on the husband, when he died they would have gotten all the money back that remained on the contract. Suppose he was 78 when they bought the guaranteed life annuity. Suppose the guarantee was to age 90 that would be a 12-year guarantee. But he died in his 82nd year. What would happen? Would his widow have a hard time getting the rest of the money? NO, not at all. She would get a call from her agent and he or she would bring around a cheque for the total of all remaining payments. At $250 a month that would be eight years or 96 months equals $24,000. If their American agent had done it that way *The New York Times* would have had to find another story.

Something happened to me on the way to. ...Here is a little story that even most people in West Hill would not dream existed in that prim and proper enclave by the lake. I went up to a house on one of the central streets of West Hill; I knocked briskly on the door and stepped back the required eight feet. The door opened a very little bit, "Are you the one o'clock"? She asked.

"No I'm David Campbell with Edward Jones." The door opened wider and there was a women dressed in a little bit of a dress that hid too little and lots and lots of beads.

"You're not the one o'clock? I was expecting a man who looks a bit like you. Are you sure you're not the one o'clock?"

I remember I tried to look her right in the eye and tell her that I wished her well but I was not the one o'clock. I gave her a card (habit I guess) and I never expected her to call me. But she did months later; she made an appointment to come to my office to invest some of her ill-gotten gains. She never showed up. I guess her one o'clock arrived and she was busy.

Two years later I was back on that street and the house of ill repute was gone. There was a middle-aged lady tending the garden. She and her husband had just bought the house and she was fixing up the yard. I didn't have the heart to tell what her new home was before. But if the walls could talk ...

Insurance - Permanent or Term?

5

THERE ARE lots of myths in Canada about this issue:

1) "Buy protection only, that's straight term."
2) "Whole life is forced savings, I can save on my own."
3) "Whole life is a rip off"
4) "Whole life is too expensive."

The list of misconceptions goes on and on. There is a simple way to look at this issue.

When we are young we have short-term insurance needs. We start to have a family, we need to make sure that if something happened to Dad or Mom then the money to payoff the mortgage, run the household, pay the bills and look after the educational needs of the children would be there. The thing all these needs have in common is that they are relatively short-term. Most of them would be taken care of in 20 years.

For example, if Dad dies at age 30 then Mom has to continue on her own. It's not easy to think about this possibility but we must. Since bad things do happen to some. As the French say, "Merde fait". Or as the German "Scheisse passiert". We all know what the English version of this is. Bad things do happen.

Short-term needs should be taken care of by term insurance. If you are in your twenties or thirties, you will find term insurance very inexpensive. It is useful to cover a mortgage in a cost-effective way.

Term insurance has many other uses. It is an inexpensive way to buy insurance for a small child. It can be the backbone of a business continuance plan. If one of the partners dies in the short-term it can be used to buy out his or her share of the firm. Term insurance gets quite expensive as we get older. It ends completely at age 80 or 85. So that cannot be all you need.

No, since you also have long-term needs too. You have the need to pay for funeral expenses, and other debts like the final bills. The monthly bills will keep on coming even though the prime wage earner is gone. When you are young you will not need a lot of permanent insurance, although if you buy it now it will be much less expensive. However, let's assume that the reality is you have kids and dental bills, a house to run, the odd night out and so on. We know that more money for a large permanent insurance policy is not usually affordable. So if you are in your twenties or thirties buy a small permanent policy. Something like $50,000. That will take care of the final expenses and other payments you may have at the end of your life some 60 or 70 years from now.

Let's take another example; our fictitious couple is Bill and Sue and their three children Nat, Pat and Tat. Nat is 16, and Pat and Tat are twins and 12 years old. Now things are fine. Bill and Sue have purchased enough 20-year term to cover the mortgage, the higher education of Nat, Pat and Tat as well as enough money to pay the bills until the kids are through university. How much term is that?

If the mortgage is $300,000 and the cost of university will be $6,000 per year in 10 years. Then the cost of university education for Nat is $24,000, for Pat is $24,000 and for Tat $26,000. Let's say that Tat works for a few years and then decides to go to university. We can assume that by the time Tat goes to university the costs are $6,500 per year due to inflation. All together that is $74,000. Then if we want Sue to have the freedom not to have to work after Bill dies we add in 10 year or 15 years of household expenses. We will assume that 10 years is enough to see Pat and Tat though university.

The mortgage is paid off with the term insurance bought at purchase, so there are no more payments there. There are other monthly expenses. (These numbers are an example only).

1) City taxes $2300 per year so $192 per month
2) Groceries $800 (at $200 per week)
3) The bills (water, hydro, phone, fire insurance, cable, internet etc.) $700 per month
4) The car (monthly payment, gas and insurance and maintenance) $500 per month

5) Hockey, dance lessons, Kumon® and other child expenses = $300 per month
6) Dental set aside $150 per month
7) House maintenance $100 per month

I may have left out some of your expenses, this is not meant to be an exhaustive list. Our example has household expenses of $2,742 per month. The annual expense then is $32,904 and 10 years of those expenses are $329,040. Let's use $330,000.

How much term for Bill and Sue to cover the short-term needs if Bill or Sue dies prematurely?

Mortgage paid off at first death $300,000 (usually a separate policy)

University Education for three children $74,000

Ten years of spousal and family support $330,000

Total $704,000

That would be roughly $800,000 minus $300,000 already in place equals $500,000 of 20-year term (a little more in case we forgot something and to account for inflation). If Bill is 28 and Sue 26 that would cost in 2005 in 20-year term about $ 103.50 per month.

Their permanent life insurance last to die of $50,000 would cost about $61.65 per month.

So for less than $170.00 per month a couple the ages of Bill and Sue can take care of their insurance quite inexpensively.

But wait 20 years to do it and the cost will shock you. For the same amount of insurance $500,000 of 20-year term and $50,000 of permanent last to die insurance, the $50,000 of 20 year last to die whole life insurance is now $152.73 per month and the $500,000 of 20-year term costs $393.30 for a total of $545.60. If they wait another 10 years it would cost $1,066.70 per month for the same coverage.

One very good thing to remember about permanent or whole life insurance is that you are owners of the company in a sense. You get a vote at the annual meeting. You can attend and you will get annual statements just like a stockholder.

Tax experts and financial columnists agree insurance has a place in every investment plan. Here is a short list of the kind of things life insurance can do for you.

You may need life insurance for these reasons: sons and daughters, spouses, retirement lifestyle, education, pay capital gains tax at death, leave a good inheritance, business succession, funding shareholder agreements, for an investment that grows tax free, keeping key employees, transferring wealth from one generation to the next, burial expenses, collateral, critical illness, disability, and health plans. There are many more ways to use life insurance – the strategies in this book will go over each one in detail.

Here is the key to many of the strategies: If the policy is a tax-exempt policy (the accrued income not subject to tax), the tax-free accumulation can be considerable over the long-term.

Let me repeat that:

The death proceeds of life insurance are NOT taxable.

Our government seems to want to tax anything that moves but if they ever started taxing the insurance payouts for widows and orphans they would be soundly defeated at the next election. Some things are too important to tax.

Do you think that the insurance for Bill and Sue is too expensive? Term insurance has come down a long way in the last few years as more women are covered. If you bought term insurance in the 80's or early 90's have a look at your policy. You may save money by replacing that policy with a current one. Check this carefully before you replace your policy.

This key fact that life insurance payouts are not taxed leads to some innovative ways of using permanent and term life insurance. I'll explore these ideas in future chapters. Right now let's see how this lack of taxes (hallelujah!) can work for you.

If Robert dies at 79 and if he owns life insurance when he dies. Then the life insurance company gets the certificate of death from the funeral home or the local coroner they issue the cheque. This cheque is the sum of all the dividends the policy has built up and the cash value. The life insurance company will add it all up and issue the cheque.

Please note that this cheque is not subject to probate even if the rest of the estate is subject to probate. Life insurance avoids probate and goes straight to the beneficiary. This usually happens in about six or seven business days sometimes even sooner. As a life agent I have had the pleasure (can I really call it that?) perhaps not really pleasure but it does feel good to present a large cheque to the grieving widow or widower. It does not replace Mary or Charlie but it sure helps. I usually get a hug from the widows and a good strong handshake from the widowers. Sometimes it is the other way around but they almost always show me that they are grateful.

Think about it, everyone else is clamoring for money: Funeral Parlor, Coroner, ambulance transfer, florists, delivery companies. All of them phoning the survivor or dropping in to collect. He or she keeps putting them off until their insurance agent arrives with the cheque to take care of all the clamorers and give them some peace of mind. Like I said it feels good. As I write this, I know that a cheque for a grieving client will be coming in this Monday. It is now Saturday afternoon. I will deliver that cheque as soon as I get it.

What are the advantages of Term and Permanent insurance?

The chief advantage of term insurance is that it is less expensive when you are young. It is true that term insurance is pure protection. It is useful for short-term consideration e.g. covering the mortgage. For example, I hold a $460,000 term insurance policy on my life. It is only for ten more years. I am almost 56 and by 66 I believe that term life insurance will be too expensive. I also have $200,000 of joint permanent life insurance. This is intended to pay off my last expenses and keep my wife in good stead the rest of her days. In case she dies ahead of me, she holds another $200,000 of term and the $200,000 of joint permanent to keep me in whiskey and waffles until I'm too old to enjoy them. I do practice what I preach.

How do I know that my life insurance company will pay off years later? That should not be a worry. The only modern day Canadian insurance company failure was the fall of Confederation Life. They invested too much in real estate and the bubble burst at the wrong time. (See diversification Chapter 18 and 45). However, most people do not know the rest of the story. Every shareholder and policyholder in Confederation Life got his or her money back. In the long run nobody lost money although that happy conclusion did take a while.

Look for a large company that has been around a long time. For example London Life was established in 1847. Great West is a little younger and owns London Life. Both are very good. Manulife, Standard Life, Sun Life and Canada Life are good too. It is my opinion that life insurance companies that are really network marketing companies should be avoided. Their focus seems to be on recruiting more salespeople rather than looking after your real insurance needs.

Some companies are better than others for permanent insurance. The one that holds the great majority of permanent life insurance in Canada is London Life. In fact London and Great West together account for 25% of all life insurance sold in Canada. Speaking of London Life, they have a participating fund backing up their permanent accounts of $13.6 billion and growing.

It is invested very well. 95% of it is invested in extra safe fixed income investments. For example, bonds from the federal and some provincial governments are most of the holdings. There is quality real estate and also corporate bonds and municipal bonds from big cities. There is also cash. That makes up 95% and the other 5% is invested in equities. The equity investments are safe as well; investments like Canadian banks and large insurance companies and some large safe firms. The mandate is that equities cannot exceed 5% of the total portfolio.

How does it do? What does a typical company's investment return look like?

		Return on par account assets After investment expenses	S&P/TSX	5 year GIC
30 years	1974 – 2003	8.7%	10.2%	8.6%
20 years	1984 – 2003	8.8%	8.8%	7.4%
15 years	1989 – 2003	8.2%	8.6%	6.3%
10 years	1994 – 2003	7.6%	8.6%	5.0%
5 years	1999 – 2003	7.2%	6.5%	4.2%
1 year	2003	7.5%	26.3%	3.1%

Permanent insurance is based on receiving dividends on an annual basis. How are these dividends calculated? In most major insurance companies it works this way. The company looks at three areas to figure out the annual policyholder dividend. One is the expenses of the corporation, another is how the par account has performed and last the mortality rate among the policyholders. They tumble these numbers and announce the annual dividend. In the past two years it has been set at 4%. That means that all the participating or "par" accounts will be credited 4% of the assets held in each policy. Over time that can really build up since the growth is tax-free. If you own an old whole life policy have a good look at it soon. It may well have grown over the years. I had an old one that my father bought for me when I was a little boy. It was from Imperial Life, which has long since been absorbed into another firm. I kept it for years and finally cashed it in. If I had been wiser at the time I would have had very inexpensive coverage for life. Like I said I cannot stand on a high hill and say do as I did. But if I knew then what I know now, ... the central idea is if you have an old whole life policy, it is probably paying for itself by now. Let it run. It will pay some of your final expenses at least.

How do whole life policies pay for themselves? It is simple. After a long while the dividends have grown larger than the premiums. If that is the case with any of your older policies, call your insurance company and ask for the forms to go on "Premium Vacation". Fill them out and send them in and that is that. If the dividends have a couple of bad years, then the insurance company may call you to add more money to the policy. It is likely going to pay for itself until you die. However, if you keep paying the premiums the death benefit will be higher since you will build up the cash value. The choice is yours if you need the money go on premium vacation. If you can keep up the payments do that. Your kids will want to thank you but they will not be able to. When you buy permanent insurance you can ask about the offset date. That is the date that the company expects, but of course cannot guarantee, that the policy will be large enough to pay for itself.

I just heard a horror story at work. A broker I work with was talking to his neighbour over the back fence. The neighbour told him this story: He bought insurance 40 years before and thought it would build up enough that he could use it to partially pay his retirement at 65. Now he is 63 and he finally got the policy out and showed it to my friend. It has no cash value. It was a term policy sold as a permanent policy. The man didn't check for years and nobody came from the insurance company to tell him. He bought term to 65 and thought it was Whole Life to 65.

What is the lesson here? Put this book down and go and read your policies. Make sure that you know what you have. I mean it – go and check right now.

The Raw Power of Insurance

6

I HAVE just come from a meeting with a past client of mine. She has been investing in houses, which she bought in the early 80's. Now she is selling them. The problem is they have gone up about 400% in these 25 years. Now how is that a problem? The taxman licks his lips in anticipation. There are plenty of taxes to pay.

In 1991 you could crystallize the growth of non-registered investments. So how much did the house go up since 1991? The answer is 350%! That was an excellent investment because houses values were growing quickly in the 80's and 90's but are they still great today? If you plan on living in them for the next 25 years they will treat you well but if you are buying them for an investment in the short term beware. There could be a bubble that crushes the prices. It has happened before. Luckily in Canada we have many immigrants who fill the demand for houses annually.

What can my client do about the impending burden to her estate? That is the capital gains tax on the housing investment. Keep in mind that this does not apply on your home that you live in. That is called the matrimonial home and it cannot be taxed. However, all other houses, cottages, ranches, farms etc. will be taxed at the second death.

Here is where people who have money can use insurance creatively. Remember I wrote that the tax act says that the proceeds of insurance are not taxed at death and that they are allowed to grow tax-free.

This idea works well if you have money you will not be using in your lifetime. She can use insurance to make sure that the housing investments and the stocks and bonds go to her children intact. If she invests $50,000 each year for the next ten years she will have invested $500,000 and will leave almost $2,000,000 to pay for the taxes on her estate. That investment has to be a last to die policy.

If her husband dies first then she will inherit his RIFF directly as well as any non-registered investments. His pension will also go to her at about 60% of the previous level.

The tax hit comes at the second death. In this case, when she dies. That is when she is "deemed" to have sold all her investments the day she died and has to pay taxes on the capital growth of these investments.

That law always creates a funny picture in my head. Imagine if you will a person on his deathbed who gets up and calls his broker and says, "Sell! Sell it all." Then he goes back to his bed and dies. That is nuts. But that is how the taxman sees us. We are "deemed" (like it really happened) to have sold all our investments the day we die.

In the meeting I showed my client how investing $50,000 a year for 10 years would take advantage of the income tax act and save all the investments for the kids. I'll find out if I sold it soon. Whether I sold it or not it is still a very good idea to shelter investments with permanent life insurance.

There is a big objection: "It only pays when I am dead. It does not help me." OK, lets look at that. Did you know that you could use a life insurance policy as collateral? A life insurance policy can benefit you and benefit your family. You can take a life insurance policy to the bank. They will give you a loan based on the built up cash value of the policy. However, not all insurance policies are created equally. You will get about 90% back on a whole life policy, about 50% on universal life and nothing on a term policy since there is no built up cash value. You never have to repay this loan. The bank holds the policy and the annual dividends pay the interest. When you die they take out their loan plus any interest owing and send your beneficiaries the balance. The key is that during the term of the loan the interest should be paid by the building dividends. See Chapter Fourteen for the important details.

The funny thing about investing is that when you invest you have *already decided* to pay taxes on your investments. That goes for RRSP's, Non Registered accounts too. Have you ever thought about it that way? When you and your spouse die your estate will have to pay the taxes. Would you wish that burden on your kids?

Use life insurance to cover that burden and your kids will thank you.

The rich can use insurance in other ways too. They can fund Buy/Sell shotgun business agreements this way. They can use insurance to freeze and protect their estates for their kids or use it now to guarantee a loan. I'll get to all these methods in future chapters. See Estate Planning 301 - Chapter 9.

Here is how many rich people are investing these days. With the stock market unsure and bonds in the basement there appears to be little to invest in for growth that is safe. Some clever wealthy people have noticed that whole life insurance can be their next big investment. Here is how it would work if you can invest $466,000 per year for 9 years and are 56. I have a prospect/client looking at this investment as I write. He was knocked out by the growth of the dividends and death benefit in only twenty years. Here are the numbers: Keep in mind that this is not an illustration of any policy; a true illustration must have a cover page and a 25% less example. That being said it is a true example of how an insurance policy would pay out for someone 56 and in good health.

Age	Cash Value	Death Benefit	Out of pocket
56		$10,000,000	$466,000
57	$108,200	10,227,182	466,000
58	237,288	10,484,073	466,000
59	388,306	10,770,036	466,000
60	562,057	11,083,985	466,000
61	760,513	11,427,175	466,000
62	986,363	11,802,037	466,000
63	1,512,824	12,211,745	466,000
64	2,343,153	12,659,369	466,000
		total	4,194,000
65	3,280,060	12,358,416	0 retires
66	4,188,774	12,084,955	0
67	4,368,492	11,842,225	0
68	4,552,492	11,633,223	0
69	4,764,968	11,462,088	0
70	4,987,081	11,328,070	0
71	5,229,925	11,230,468	0
72	5,490,626	11,162,956	0
73	5,766,336	11,119,773	0
74	6,044,714	11,096,365	0
75	6,326,654	11,092,908	0
76	6,623,326	11,109,968	0
77	6,895,797	11,147,883	0

Age	Cash Value	Death Benefit	Out of pocket
78	7,164,463	11,206,157	0
79	7,448,711	11,283,010	0
80	7,748,383	11,377,480	0

My prospective client will have invested $466,000 for nine years = $4,194,000 and have a cash value of $6,623,326 after 20 years (**That's Plus $2,429,326**). When he is 80 the cash value will have risen to $7,748,383. And if he dies at 80 his family will get over $11,000,000. Great West Life's Whole Life department invests very conservatively so these returns are sure but not guaranteed. The reduced example would drop the numbers by 25%. I believe the returns will be better than this but only time will tell. Looking only at the cash value his investment of $466,000 will have risen magnificently whenever he dies. If you have that kind of money give your lucky agent a call.

However, if $466,000 is too rich for you, OK let's show you what you can do if you can put into insurance only $833.33 a month. Here is what happens to $10,000 a year.

As you look over the following numbers I want you to remember that pants have two front pockets. Remember that analogy because if you look carefully at these numbers you will soon see that when you put in $10,000 in one pocket the cash value goes up MORE than that after a few years. **This is the most powerful strategy in this book. Learn this information well.** You are only taking from one pocket and putting **more** into the other pocket. Here is where you can see that insurance is an investment not an expense. You are paying yourself with this strategy. First carefully check the following numbers and remember this key fact - **this growth is <u>tax-free</u>. Not <u>tax deferred</u> like RRSP, which you will pay taxes on one day. There is no better safer investment – watch it grow.**

Sam Dominion who, in this case, is 35 buys a 20 Pay Life Participating policy with a death benefit in the first year of **$330,796**. He pays $10,000 each year for 20 years. So when he is 55 his insurance is paid up for life. Watch these numbers and learn a big secret about whole life insurance:

Yr	Age	Out of Pocket	Yearly increase in Cash Value	Total Cash Value	Death Benefit
0					$330,796
1	36	$10,000	$4,932	$4,932	$348,484
2	37	$10,000	$7,857	$12,789	$367,497
3	38	$10,000	$9,945	$22,734	$388,094
4	39	$10,000	$10,674!!!	$33,408	$409,016
5	40	$10,000	$10,245	$43,653	$430,272
6	41	$10,000	$11,128	$54,781	$451,995
7	42	$10,000	$12,051	$66,832	$473,719
8	43	$10,000	$12,873	$79,705	$495,169
9	44	$10,000	$13,701	$93,406	$516,310
10	45	$10,000	$14,582	$107,988	$537,170
11	46	$10,000	$15,386	$123,374	$557,776
12	47	$10,000	$16,276	$139,650	$578,154
13	48	$10,000	$17,180	$156,830	$598,546
14	49	$10,000	$18,287	$175,117	$619,617
15	50	$10,000	$19,517	$194,634	$641,565
16	51	$10,000	$20,907!!!	$215,541	$664,635
17	52	$10,000	$20,676	$236,217	$680,037
18	53	$10,000	$20,673	$256,890	$715,478
19	54	$10,000	$26,690	$283,580	$747,973
20	55	$10,000	$28,191	$311,771	$781,740
21	56	$0	$19,365	$331,136	$808,303
22	57	$0	$20,297	$351,433	$834,792
23	58	$0	$21,211	$372,644	$861,239
24	59	$0	$22,232	$394,876	$887,843
25	60	$0	$23,388	$418,264	$914,976

Yr	Age	Out of Pocket	Yearly increase in Cash Value	Total Cash Value	Death Benefit
26	61	$0	$24,617	$442,881	$942,651
27	62	$0	$25,886	$468,767	$970,896
28	63	$0	$27,158	$495,925	$999,678
29	64	$0	$28,466	$524,391	$1,029,014!
30	65	$0	$30,097	$554,488	$1,059,466
31	66	$0	$31,913	$586,401	$1,091,216
32	67	$0	$33,799	$620,200	$1,124,266
33	68	$0	$35,260	$655,460	$1,157,875
34	69	$0	$36,757	$692,217	$1,192,110
35	70	$0	$38,223	$730,440	$1,227,031
36	71	$0	$39,569	$770,009	$1,262,445
37	72	$0	$40,883	$810,892	$1,298,399
38	73	$0	$42,186	$853,078	$1,335,042
39	74	$0	$43,514	$896,592	$1,372,399
40	75	$0	$44,860	$941,452	$1,410,566

By year four it is paying you more than you put in. By year 16 your annual investment is more than doubled. After 20 years it is growing by itself with no investment from you. That is amazing. Whole life is an excellent investment. Older clients tell me that and young people don't believe it.

Now that Sam is 75 he can take out a collateral loan from a bank that he never has to pay back. With whole life he can borrow up to 90 percent. The bank interest payments are met by the yearly increase in cash value. At 75 Sam has $941,452 in total cash value to borrow against. Let's suppose he needs 90% to augment his retirement funds. That would be $847,306 that he could borrow. And all he invested was $10,000 for 20 years or $200,000. The growth was tax-free and he has lots of money for the rest of his life. If Sam dies at 75 he leaves almost $1.5 million. All because he did the right thing when he was 35.

If Sam lives to 80 plus here is what his insurance looks like then.

Yr	Age	Out of Pocket	Yearly increase in Cash Value	Total Cash Value	Death Benefit
45	80	$0	$50,971	$1,184,404	$1,613,493
50	85	$0	$56,757	$1,456,500	$1,837,306
55	90	$0	$61,281	$1,757,037	$2,085,056

Sam dies at 90 having lived a good, full life. His collateral loan comes off his final death benefit and he leaves $2,085,056 minus the loan of $847,306 minus the interest. See the account keeps going up despite the loan against it since the bank only holds the insurance policy as collateral. The interest payments can come off at death. Suppose the loan rate was 7% and the length of the loan was fifteen years. Sam would pay $45,445 in interest and leave an estate of **$1,192,305.** To repeat all this happened because he did the right thing at 35.

There is no safer investment. Look at the annual growth without any of the ups and downs of the stock market. This policy grows risk free, tax free and steadily. This is the big secret of life insurance. Buy whole life and prosper.

A goal of most well off individuals is to be able to self-insure their family fortune. At least that was what I was taught as a lad. Now it seems that life insurance can be used to protect an estate, fund intergenerational wealth and protect the family. Life insurance can be the family's best investment.

Universal Life Insurance

7

ANOTHER WAY the rich use insurance is with Universal Life. This is the fastest growing area of life insurance in Canada. The major difference between this and whole life insurance is that this is not participating insurance. Unlike whole life insurance you do not get automatic dividends or get a vote or an invitation to the annual meeting. Most people don't go anyway so that is probably not a large concern. People buy universal because they can get a large amount of insurance at a cheaper cost than whole life. You do get some growth unlike term. Universal life insurance is really a hybrid between whole life and term insurance. Universal life invests in several mutual funds of your choice. The one big caveat is that you are expected to manage the investments yourself. You pick the mutual funds that the insurance is invested in. You take the risk. But the total amount of insurance at the outset is guaranteed no matter what happens to the investments.

There was a 44-year-old man, let's call him Tony, who bought $400,000 of universal life from Manulife and invested it all in high tech companies in 2000. As we all know his investments plummeted that year. He was driving on the 401 and may have fallen asleep at the wheel or something similar - no one will ever really know. He was killed when he left the road at high speed and hit a tree. His family was shocked of course and when they checked his policy the value was down to $240,000 from $400,000. Manulife paid off the entire $400,000. They took his investments and sold them and added $160,000 to cover the guaranteed amount. That is what you get with good companies – no quibbles. "Dad is dead; please pay up" – and they do.

Universal has a guaranteed value that is established at the beginning. The growth comes from investing the money in whatever kind of mutual fund or segregated fund you want. There are equity funds, international funds, growth funds, growth and income funds, income funds, emerging markets and disappearing markets (I'm joking). The point is that there are over 45 different funds we can be invested in with universal life.

Universal life insurance is not for everyone. One of my clients was almost sold universal life by one of his other agents. The turning point came when I recommended whole life instead hung on one point. "When you are dead your wife will handle the investments, right?" She was in the room, but to be fair she had never taken an interest in the investments; that was his job and she trusted him completely. The idea that she would be handling the investments with her husband gone and me retired, at best, was not a pleasing prospect. He discussed it with her and quickly opted for the whole life and we wrote the policy that day.

With universal life insurance the investments are your responsibility and you must manage this type of life insurance. Most universal life policies have a minimum monthly investment and a maximum investment. You can only pay the minimum or some amount in between or you can pay the maximum. Paying over the maximum gets you into tax trouble. Most universal life policies are sold with the client only told about the minimum they must pay. So most universal life policies are sold minimum funded.

This is a shame and should not be. If a client is only going to minimum fund his universal life, he can get the same coverage cheaper with term to 100 insurance. That is simply term insurance that lasts until you are 100. Your family will get the same insurance payout without the worry and angst of investing correctly when you are in your 80s and 90s. However, with term to 100, you have to pay your entire life. You can't offset term to 100 nor can you offset (premium vacation) universal life - you pay for both all your life. You cannot go on premium vacation with term to 100 nor universal life since they are both non – par (non participating) policies and non-par products do not build up large cash values to fund the premium vacation.

Universal life was originally brought out in response to a desire of Canadians for more transparency in insurance. "Show us the inner workings of insurance."

Whole life, it seems, was a mystery. The money is simply invested in fixed income investments like government bonds, some high quality corporate bonds, commercial mortgages and the like with only up to 5% of the fund in equity investments, in other words, stocks. But all that happens at the head office of the insurance firm. From the point of view of the agent and the policyholder, it just happens.

Universal life is quite different; when you buy it, the whole internal workings of insurance are on view. You see the actual cost of insurance broken out, the effect of a bonus spelled out. An estimate of the value is there, too. The cost of buying the mutual or segregated fund is outlined for you. Some people want this level of detail; others do not.

Universal life is generally less money in premium than whole life, but the buyer should be able to manage his or her investments very well. Ideally you will have an agent that understands investing, too. Handle it just like a stocks and bonds portfolio and meet with your agent at least once a year to see if the funds need to be moved around or rebalanced. Some companies have computer programs that do the rebalancing daily for you. That may work well for you, but if you want someone or something else to handle the investments you should be buying whole life and not universal life.

Most universal insurance comes with either a bonus clause or without a bonus clause. Ask your agent to calculate it both ways. Most of the time the most insurance for the least money is without the bonus. Be sure to check how it was calculated.

Something happened to me on the way ... One day I knocked at the door of a solid middle class brick home in the West Hill area. A man about 55 answered the door. I introduced myself and asked him a few questions about himself and about his investments. He laughed and told me he had no investments. "I live off the people of Canada."

What do you mean? I asked thinking he was a nation-wide con man or worse.

"I retired from the Federal civil service and I have the best pension in Canada! I never have to work or save again. Your taxes keep my account growing. I live off the people!"

I left quickly. Don't you really hate people like that?

Critical Illness Insurance

8

DO YOU remember the Doctor who did the first heart transplant? His name was Dr. Christian Barnard from South Africa. His brother Marius, was also a doctor, who noted that people who got very sick these days generally recovered as opposed to likely dying, as in the past. He added that becoming seriously sick is very difficult on your finances.

Using the slogan, Critical Illness insurance – "Not because you're going to die, but because you're going to survive," he founded the first CI company and this concept has spread around the world. In Canada it is sold by only 23% of advisors and is starting to grow. For some reason we are slower than the rest of the world, to pick up this grand idea. The likely cause is our high taxes, which the governement cannot bring themselves to cut no matter how high the federal budget surplus grows.

But I digress. If you get a dread disease such as cancer, heart attack or a stroke you are out of action for quite a while. You can't work and probably have to take it easy for weeks, if not months. What a hit to your finances! How would you handle that?

I know it could never happen to you. I'm healthy, too, but I know the numbers and here they are:

During their lifetime:

- 1 in 2 men (50%) of men suffer heart disease; one in three women will do the same.
- 1 in 2.3 men and 1 in 2.6 women in Canada will develop cancer
- 1 in 9 women will develop breast cancer
- 1 in 12 Canadians will develop lung cancer
- 145,500 new cancer cases occurred in 2004

- About 50,000 Canadians have Multiple Sclerosis the ratio is 2:1 women to men.

Source: Heart and Stroke Foundation & Canadian Cancer Society

These numbers can scare you. It could happen to you and me.

I had been busy and had neglected to call my buddy, Ben, for about two years. We just did not call. He was busy and so was I. We had gone through this before and just picked up where we left off. He had a book published about the RESP and I wanted to ask him how he went about contacting a publisher. I called him once and left a message, he did not call back. I called again about two weeks later and left another message. A few weeks later I was on the golf course, at the third tee and my cell phone rang. It was Ben's wife Silvia, "David, I was so touched by your phone calls I guess you didn't know, Ben died a year ago." I was stunned. Ben was in his early 50's and he was gone. He died of cancer. Did he have insurance? I don't know. If he had CI and lived 90 days from his diagnosis, he could have left Silvia more money. Ironically, his last book was called "Now You're a Widow."

There is some good news for those who suffer a heart attack or stroke - 80% survive the initial event. That should be good news for the 4 out of 5 people but now comes the cost of the cure. Here are the costs in Canadian dollars:

Cost of cures:
Heart transplant (stay in hospital two to four weeks) **$240,500 to $390,000***
Coronary artery bypass (1 to 4 vessels, in hospital 5-7 days **$87,750 to $122,200***
Radiation Treatment re cancer for six weeks **$58,500 to $78,000****
*Transplant Financial Services – Mayo Clinic Rochester Minnesota
**National Cancer Institute of Canada: Canadian Cancer Statistics 2004

These treatments may not be covered by OHIP. It depends if your doctor recommends the operation and, of course, if you can wait for months or not. If not, you may have to go to the United States.

Where do the funds come from to pay for this calamity? You probably do not have that much cash just sitting in a savings account. If you do, call me and we'll conservatively invest it. But seriously, where do the funds come from for the average Canadian?

Possible Sources

You could cash in your RRSP but that is bad idea for several reasons. You will pay withholding tax to the federal government that is quite high. 10% on the first $4,999; 15% on the first $9,999 and 20% on anything higher. That is quite high taxation, you are supposed to save with an RRSP and the growth is tax-free, so if you withdraw it the government slaps your wrists. The biggest problem is that if you take the money out of your RRSP it loses its chance to grow over time. If you have $80,000 in your RRSP, which is the Canadian average, and you planned to let it grow 20 years at 5%, you could have $212,263.82 when you retire. But if you use it too early you have nothing. Think of the difference that will make in your retirement. "On the pension" or in Monte Carlo every four years.

You could ask your parents, if they are still around. They are likely retired and have a little stashed away, why not ask them? You'd probably get some of the money and ruin your parent's plans for a comfortable retirement. Suppose we leave them out of it. Ok, how about cousin Fred? NO. It is a lot of money and you likely can't pay it back.

How about a bank? Remember that old saw about a banker? They give you a new umbrella when it is sunny outside and ask for it back when it is raining. Well, if you get cancer or have a stroke or suffer a heart attack, brothers and sisters, it is raining. The bank will politely turn you down. If you die you cannot repay them, so no deal. Can you turn over your life insurance to the bank and get a loan? Sure you could, but that is not why you bought it and if you do die your family will need it badly.

A business owner has other options: he can sell equipment, he can liquidate shares, and he can take the cash out of retained earnings. Each one of these ideas takes away from the business just when that business may go through a hard time because the owner got very sick.

There is not a good way to fund your cure - except insurance.

Critical Illness is one of the few types of insurance that pays off when you are alive. Here is how it works: If you survive 30 days after a heart attack or a stroke or 90 days after the diagnosis of cancer you get paid. You can then use that money to make changes to the house to accommodate a wheelchair if necessary, or you could go to Rochester Minn. for a cure at the Mayo Clinic. Or if you need a change and some rest you can take a long vacation if you choose. The money is yours and you can do what you want with it.

I am 56 and I got this insurance recently. First I checked what this insurance would cost me. It is only $158.26 a month for $100,000. That is for coverage from the big three: heart attack, stroke or cancer. 83% of claims are for these diseases. You can buy it with level payouts, which is what I bought. That simply means that the payments are the same each year the policy is in force. The alternative is to buy it with declining payouts. That means that the policy would pay $100,000 in the first year but if the problem happened in later years the coverage would drop $10,000 each year. If one had a heart attack or stroke or contracted cancer in the fifth year, the policy would only pay $50,000. Declining CI is cheaper, it would have only cost me $91.00 a month. I got the more expensive and better level insurance. It will pay me $100,000 if I have a problem as above, at anytime in the next ten years.

What if you get a different disease? For a little more, mine cost me $37 more –total $195 per month, you can get covered for these other nasty illnesses; A large insurance company calls this option the Enhanced Critical Illness Rider. It covers:

- Alzheimer's,
- Aortic Surgery
- Benign Brain Tumour
- Blindness,
- Coma
- Coronary Artery Bypass
- Deafness
- Heart Valve Replacement
- Kidney Failure
- Loss of Independent Existence
- Loss of Limbs
- Loss of Speech
- Major Organ Transplant
- Motor Neuron Disease
- Multiple Sclerosis
- Occupational HIV Infection
- Paralysis
- Parkinson's Disease
- Severe Burns

All these diseases have specific markers, or standards that must be met, with most large firms. Other firms have more general markers. I prefer the specific markers because they are not onerous - they are the hospital standards. Also, I like to know that there is an objective standard not a subjective one. An insurance sales trainer used this analogy that I like: Suppose you and I are entered in the Major League Home Run Derby. Now because we are amateurs we have a subjective judge. If he feels we hit the pitch a long way then he may or may not call it a home run. That approach worries me. Suppose we have to hit it over the fence and that is a home run. There is no debate then. Is it over the fence or isn't it? Check if your insurance company uses clear definitions of the disease. If it could be an area of debate or conflict it likely will be trouble. Go to an agent who uses clear sharp definitions. Is it over the fence or isn't it? If it hits the top of the fence did it fall back inside the park or did it trickle into the stands? Is it over the fence or not?

There is an option that is wonderful, too. It is called the Return of Premium Option. If you live to 75 and have made no claims you get all your premiums back. You do not get any interest on this money – what you put in you get back. Still if you get a large sum when you are 75, it could be just what you need when you get it. This option increases the cost quite a bit so look at it both ways, that is, with and without this option. Banks offer this insurance but do not offer anything beyond the basic three of cancer, heart attack and stroke. The other 19 are not covered. Also compare the costs of bank insurance with the same coverage at a large insurance company. You will be surprised or perhaps you will not be surprised: there is a pattern to overcharging for bank services, isn't there? Compare costs and coverage before you buy from a bank.

I believe this type of insurance is a must for businesses large and small. I have seen the effect of a heart attack suffered by the president of a large international client I worked with years ago. Despite being sick he would not leave his post even for a holiday. It was very messy. He lasted over 30 days. If Critical Illness insurance had been around, the transition would have been much smoother.

Do you need any another reason to buy this insurance? A director at my office told me today about another reason to buy critical illness insurance. His father in law is a doctor and was discussing the drugs available to breast cancer patients recently. These drugs are wildly expensive. A year's worth could cost $100,000! The federal and provincial governments have reluctantly said they will cover these costs. The good doctor thinks they cannot do it for long. The bills are going to simply be too high. Provincial Health Plans will have to let the private hospitals take this over. Private hospitals will have the drugs but the patient will have to pay. This is true not just for breast cancer victims but also for many other diseases. Exotic drugs will be developed to control or cure these diseases and may not be covered by any government-funding program. The patients will have to pay for it themselves. You know where I am going – Critical Illness can help you finance these new exotic drugs.

Critical Illness Insurance is affordable and can make all the difference in your business life and your family's life

Estate Planning

9

WHAT EXACTLY is estate planning? The answer depends on our income and the size of the estate in question. For most people it's as simple as getting an updated will and keeping it where your family can find it. One man I heard of kept his will in a safety deposit box. He left the bank for some reason and soon after that he died. The family did not find the will until after he had been declared intestate which means that he had died with no will. When that happens, the government divides your estate as they see fit, not as you saw fit.

It depends on the province that you live in, but in Ontario basically the spouse gets the first $200,000 and then the spouse and children share the excess over $200,000 equally. If there is no spouse, the children share equally, and if no children, the parents, and if no parents, the brothers and sisters, and so on. This is a mess just waiting to happen. You can avoid the whole thing by having an up-to-date will.

There are several other ways to get the estate from your hands to the people you wish to receive it without the taxman getting too big a bite. The government has closed many of the former loopholes. The Kiddie Tax stopped a very good way to transfer wealth to the children. One way that still works is a trust. There are many different types of trusts. Something is held "in trust" for someone else.

What exactly is a trust? A trust is not defined in any law of Canada. The idea has a long history of use under English law. Simply, it is the fiduciary relationship between two or more persons. One is the Trustee, and he or she holds legal ownership and control of a property for the benefit of someone else called the beneficiary. This separation of the legal ownership and the right to beneficial use of some property or asset is a basic and key part of a trust. A trust is not a legal entity like a corporation. Rather, it is a formalized relationship between the trustee and the beneficiary. The person who sets up the trust, called the settlor, is not part of the trust. He sets it up but is separate from the relationship between the trustee and the beneficiary.

Who can be a trustee? An individual, a corporation, an officer of the court, or a government official can be a trustee.

Broadly speaking, there are trusts that are implied and trusts that are express. An express trust is written and is clear from its wording. An implied trust is clear from the nature of the transaction. For example you give money to a courier. He has to and will deliver it to the intended beneficiary or he or she will not be a courier in the morning.

One thing to keep in mind about trusts is that they expire every 21 years. If you are 55 and want to leave an asset or property to your only son, the trust could expire when you are 76. So as an estate tool it has some limitations.

The wording of a trust should be certain. It is best to get these written up by a good lawyer. The term is the "three certainties" and this refers to "words" (the settlor's words), "subject matter" (what we are writing this trust about i.e. land or stock portfolios) and lastly the "objects" or the persons intended to have benefit of the trust.

A trustee must be loyal to the beneficiary. That duty is Job One for a trustee. That means no conflict of interest and no personal profit from the trust. The trustee must be governed by the central idea that it is all for the benefit of the beneficiaries and no one else. Also the trustee must treat all beneficiaries equally. For example, he or she cannot favour one son or another. Even if the trustee is acting in good faith and is not being paid, a trustee who improperly delegates his or her authority may be held personally liable for any resulting losses. There is precedent setting case law: Wagner vs. van Cleef (1991) Ont. Div. Court.

A trust can be revocable or irrevocable. Generally a revocable trust is not desirable as it may create a tax problem for the settlor. Specially, the will may result in an income and capital gains for the settlor if revoked. Remember he or she is not part of the trust. Attribution rules may come in to play to eliminate the tax benefit of a transfer. (Attribution Rules are part of Canadian tax law. These rules say that, when you attempt to transfer income to your spouse, children, in-laws, nieces or nephews by transferring income-producing assets or property to them, *you* will be taxed on the income, not the person you intended to pay the tax.)

Generally irrevocable trusts are more commonly used. A good example of an irrevocable trust would be that the trust property cannot revert to the settlor, and the settlor is prohibited from amending or terminating the trust after its creation. A settlor can have some control by wisely choosing the trustee. In some cases the settlor can be the trustee. Check with your lawyer on that one.

All trusts can be classified another way: For example, Inter Vivos and Testamentary Trusts, these two trusts are quite different and opposite. The Inter Vivos Trust is created during your lifetime and the Testamentary Trust is created at your death. Any trust during your lifetime is Inter Vivos and any trust after your death is Testamentary.

In the case of cash or property transfer into a testamentary trust on the death of a taxpayer the taxpayer is deemed to have sold all his property at fair market value. As the assets have likely increased in value, the trust would immediately owe capital gains tax. This can also occur at the second death. Most of the time the man dies first and his estate passes to his wife. When she dies that is what is called the second death. At the second death, the trust can be activated.

There are also discretionary trusts. These are used, for example, when a trust is created for a disabled beneficiary. The trustee can distribute income or principal as they see fit. This brings us to a brief discussion of "Henson Trusts."

Henson Trusts are the use of a trust for a disabled person who holds a beneficiary interest in a trust that is being distributed as a Discretionary Trust. In Ontario the provincial government gives certain benefits to disabled people. However, if they earn or receive too much money, those government benefits can be withdrawn. In the past, if a disabled person received money from the discretionary trust, the government benefits would be clawed back. This was unfair so the courts in 1989 created an exception. The courts have held that if a disabled person is a beneficiary of a discretionary trust, holding that discretionary interest in that trust will not, by itself, cause the individual to lose any government services.

It is the responsibility of the trustee to distribute the money in such a manner that the money will not be enough to overturn government services. If the individual has large expenses during the year, these can also be paid for by the trust.

I had an instance of this happening when I worked at Edward Jones. A lawyer called me to ask if I had any safe investments for a young client of his. Turned out that a young boy had been badly hurt in a car accident. The insurance payment to the lad was about $400,000; the lawyer wanted a safe investment that paid over 5%. The judge had told him to see if he could do better than a GIC at the bank. I found a province of Alberta bond paying 5.7%. It paid in March and September and would give the family enough cash to keep up with the boy's annual on-going expenses for 15 years. At the end of that time the bond would mature and the $400,000 would be repaid to the family. The judge was pleased that we had found a grand solution. I met the lawyer two years later, and he recalls setting up a trust to help the family until the boy was old enough to manage on his own.

There are many different types of trusts. There are Inter Vivos trusts for minors, multiple testamentary trusts, spousal trusts, creditor protection trusts, non-resident trusts, constructive trusts and insurance trusts. See a good lawyer if you think any trust would help your family or your corporation.

Estate Freezes

An estate freeze is a common estate-planning tool. In general terms, an estate freeze is an estate planning tool to freeze or fix the growth of capital property held by you during your life. Any future growth of the capital property after the freeze, is transferred to your heirs. As an example, if you own a business, and if your business is incorporated, then the shares you own should increase in value. On death, the income tax act says that you must pay taxes on that growth. It often means the business must be sold to pay the taxes. That could be a problem since it might not be a good time to sell the business, for instance, in a down market. Note: insurance can eliminate this tax headache.

The way it is generally is done is by changing your common shares for an equal value of preferred shares. The heirs get the common shares, which will grow in value, and you get the preferred shares. Preferred shares do not participate in the growth of a company but they do pay tax-preferred income.

The creation of an estate freeze is complex and should be left to tax pros. Here are the benefits:

1) You pass the future growth in the asset's value to the next generation, you will defer taxes on that growth for many years. The taxes will be paid when your heirs die or sell the asset.
2) That will also give the asset more time to grow before it is taxed.
3) By freezing the value of the asset you will be able to estimate your tax obligation at your death fairly accurately. Preferred shares have a set value. This allows you to plan for payment of these taxes.
4) There is no need to give up control of the frozen asset during your lifetime.

There is no more doubt about the death benefit. It will not apply to all estate freezes but you may be able to take advantage of enhanced capital gains exemption if you own shares of a "qualified small business" or "qualified farm property." This can shelter up to $500,000 of capital gains. The shares must be QSBC shares. What are they? It is complex but you must have owned shares in a qualified small business or farm property for two years and that company must be using 90% of its assets in Canada to carry on an active business in Canada. There is more on this in Chapter Thirteen. It is in subsection 110.6 (1) of the Income tax Act. If you think this applies to you see your professional accountant.

How do we freeze assets?

It is too complex for this book. You would be bored beyond belief. It is enough to say that there are two common methods for freezing estate assets. One is a corporation and the other is a trust.

First the corporation: one way is to transfer your growing assets to a company of your creation and take back in return preferred shares in that company that are frozen in value. The common shares, which can grow, are transferred to your heirs.

The second method is a trust. It is an inter vivos trust (done when you are alive). You transfer some of your assets to the trust for the benefit of your children or anyone else. For either method, you will need the services of a tax pro like your professional accountant. Transferring any asset can trigger taxes, but an accountant can show you a way to avoid this with a corporation.

Setting up a Testamentary Trust

This is another way to income split. You can set this up in your will. All or a portion of your assets would be transferred to the trust when you die. Your heirs are the beneficiaries of the trust. Let's suppose you want to leave an annual amount to your heir. The trust is considered an individual for tax purposes. This concept is useful if the surviving spouse has an income of her own. If she inherited the money paid directly to her every year, she would have to add this money to her own and pay taxes on the total at a higher tax level. By splitting the income with the trust we lighten the tax burden. Both the trust and the heir pay taxes but at a lower rate.

Insured Asset Transfer

This is for money you will not need during your lifetime. You could invest this money in GIC's and leave them to your children. Or you could invest the money in stocks and bonds and leave that to your children. Both of those ways the growth will be taxed with capital gains tax. If, however, you utilize an insured asset transfer to your heirs your investment grows tax-free. You do that by buying permanent life insurance policy either a whole life policy or a universal life policy. That money will grow within the policy tax-free and the amount left to your heirs will be much larger. Manulife calls this an Estate Bond. It is the same thing.

Giving to Charity

There is a whole section on this in Chapter 12.

Business Succession

There is a whole section on this in Chapter 13.

There are entire books written on Estate Planning. This one chapter just hits the main ideas. If you need more, see the list of books in Appendix II for some ideas. There are many other strategies which apply to estate planning in other chapters.

Who gets the cottage when Mum dies?

10

MOST PEOPLE leave the cottage to their children in their will. My mother left the cottage on Lake of Bays to all six of her children equally. What she really left us was a very messy situation. Who could use the cottage on what weekends and so on; it became quite a nightmare.

You should talk with your children before deciding who gets the cottage in your will. It could be that some of your children don't want the problem of handling the bills, taxes and upkeep. They may not go up there often and would rather sell the old place. Some others will be horrified at selling the cottage. That is especially true if the cottage has been in the family since the days of granddad or even great granddad.

The law is that when the cottage passes from the second death of the parents to the children, a capital gains tax is due. This could be quite a tax since many cottage properties have gone up in value many times since granddad built it.

The rules are that one half of the growth since 1971 must be included in income for the year when the property is disposed. Proper estate planning can solve this problem.

Your principal residence is not subject to capital gains. So if you claim the cottage as your principal residence you must pay capital gains on your home. Figure out which has increased the least and use that one for the capital gains tax.

Ideally, leave insurance to cover the capital gains tax. and set up a fund to take care of the upkeep on the cottage as well.

What other options do you have? Well you could set up a corporation or a trust. Both of these concepts have their limitations. If you set up a corporation you must file taxes annually and the creation of the corporation could trigger a tax problem right away. As mentioned in the last chapter the downside of trusts is that they have a "deemed distribution" every 21 years. That means they wind up.

There is a simple way to do this if you have enough of an estate. Leave the cottage to one child and leave assets of equal value to the other children. That is the rich person's solution.

If you are not rich, then try another method of distribution. Leave the cottage to all the children to use and enjoy equally but insist that the children execute a buy sell agreement between them or amongst them all that contains a "shotgun" clause. This clause says that any child can name a price for the cottage and the others can sell to him or her at that price or buy him out for the same price. That ensures that the property is sold to one of the children at a fair price.

The best way is to have enough insurance to cover the capital gains tax.

How did my family handle it? It worked out but it was a little messy. We all used the cottage for a while. My sister and her husband did the most work on the cottage and stayed up there almost all summer. My sister died of ALS and my widowed brother-in- law used it all summer with his three daughters Eventually one of us ran up debts (not me) and to bail that person out we sold the cottage to my brother-in-law with the reservation that any of us can use the place when we want if we call him first. That seems fair. Some of us got our own cottages and one other got a sailboat and eventually it all settled down. That was not the best idea but it worked.

My ex-wife's parents did it better. In fact, they did it the right way. First, before they died, they fixed up the cottage so the maintenance would be minimized. Then they bought insurance to cover the capital gains tax on the cottage at the second death. They then added another large insurance policy to pay for the continual upkeep and taxes on the old place. Now my ex-wife shares it with her brother and it is manageable. The boathouse needed a new roof and a new dock. Those needs were taken care of by the interest on the insurance proceeds. If you can do it, that way is the way to go.

What is the best insurance when you are starting out?

11

I REMEMBER when I was young. No one could tell me anything. I knew it all. I rented and played hard and then I woke up at 26 and asked, "What was I thinking"? I quickly took good advice, settled down, got married and kept a steady job. In that little history, I know, I was like a lot of my friends. We were early Baby Boomers and we worked hard and played hard. Until we got serious. Until we got commitments. Until we got a mortgage.

After that an insurance agent friend called me up and we made an appointment to sit down and discuss the situation. Of course, I thought I could not afford insurance. After all I was paying a mortgage, but time passed and I called him back. "Warren, can you come over and have a talk?" I was almost 30 and suddenly knew I could die someday. Warren came over with his flip chart book and showed us how insurance is an investment, not an expense. I remember we bought something quite new called universal life. I kept paying that off every month until one month years later I missed a payment. That was when we moved to California to go back to university and left the universal life behind.

Years later we returned and Warren found us again. We all attended the same church. He came over and told us that we had put so much money into that policy that even with the four years that had gone by we still had a choice. We could restart the insurance or take the cash value that was now $10,000. We were starting over so we took the money and ran.

Was that the right thing to do? As I have said before if I knew then what I know now... What's that old line? Too soon old, too late smart. Learn from me and let me stop you from doing it the way I did.

When you are young universal life is usually too expensive. When we bought it we could afford it, but later it was too much. So I advise you not to buy universal life in your 20s and early 30s if you do not hold a solid steady job or plan to move to the U.S.A. If you can afford it – it's great do it. But there is another way.

Let's look at it from the point of view of need. What would happen if Mike died? We would have to bury him and that would cost about $12,000 to $15,000 today. Then Bonnie, if she were not working, would have to start working. But what if she was home because she and Mike have three young kids? She can't work – she is busy enough. With the added burden of her husband's death, she has a lot on her plate.

That means we need to cover the living expenses for Bonnie. Is the mortgage paid off? Probably not. How about the education of the three youngsters? These are all expenses that are hard to pay for on a single mom's income.

OK, first thing we do is divide the expenses into **permanent** expenses and **temporary** expenses. The permanent expenses are: Bury Mike = $12,000. A small permanent insurance policy will solve this long-term problem. A whole life policy for $12,000 will take care of the final expenses for Mike or Bonnie today. Let's think about $20,000 because the costs will be higher in the future.

The other permanent expense would be a small policy on each of the children. A permanent life insurance policy provides a financial asset that will help the child in the future. The low cost of this insurance is wonderful and if you want to do the job right add a rider that guarantees that the child can purchase insurance regardless of his or her health.

A client of mine recently bought a 20-year permanent Whole Life policy on her 11- year- old daughter. I recall we purchased $50,000 of whole life and $100,000 of guaranteed insurability. That means that the daughter will be able to purchase $100,000 of insurance in the future even if she is terminally ill. It costs about $31.50 a month. The rest of the expenses are all temporary.

Let's look at it with no insurance. If Mike dies prematurely and there is no insurance, Bonnie will eventually get a job. The house will be sold and they will be forced to rent. The three kids probably won't go to university. The temporary issues will be solved but not the way anyone wants them solved.

There is a better way. The permanent insurance would cost this much in 2005. I have included guaranteed insurability and disability waiver. If Mike is 28 and Bonnie is 26 and their kids are Billy who is ten, Cathy who is eight and Fred who is five. $20,000 of Whole life would cost the parents

$17.69 per month. For the kids, their whole life insurance would cost this much each month: Billy $23.94, Cathy $20.28 and Fred $21.75. So insuring the whole family with whole life would cost $83.60.

Lets look at the temporary problems again.

Living expenses for Bonnie: Remember that the three kids are 10, eight and five. Let's ideally provide enough living expenses for Bonnie for 10 years. That would be enough to pay the house taxes (we will keep the house, too), pay for monthly food and entertainment. How about new clothes and an annual trip? You love her don't you? Add that all up and it becomes:

Living Expenses for Bonnie

	Month	Month	10 Years
House taxes		2500	25,000
Food	700	8400	84,000
Annual trip		3000	30,000
Entertainment	100	1200	12,000
Clothes	200	2400	24,000
TOTAL			175,000

Let's round that number up to $200,000 in case we left something important out. Then we simply have to buy the much cheaper term insurance for $200,000 coverage.

If the mortgage is not paid off, add that to it now. Remember the advice about bank mortgage insurance - don't get it. It is too expensive and the payments do not go down as you pay down the mortgage. In essence, the price of it keeps rising! Buy term insurance to cover that too. If you have another $200,000 left on the mortgage, then add it to the other $200,000 and get $400,000 worth of term coverage.

I recommend you buy 20-year term insurance to cover off all these temporary expenses. You could buy 10-year term but when you get to the end of the first 10 years and want to renew, you will be in for a big surprise. You insurance rate will likely be a lot higher. After all you are ten years older. Twenty-year is a little more, but the rate is the same for 20 years. After a while the payment will seem easy.

To buy $400,000, of Twenty-year-term policy on the parents, Mike and Bonnie, would cost in 2005, $90.00 a month. Total insurance both permanent and term, each month for our fictitious but normal family, is $173.66.

Let's summarize. What do we really need? Whole life enough to bury Mike or Bonnie would require a joint first-to-die whole life or universal life policy on both Mike and Bonnie. Both are forms of investments. Whole life grows with dividends; universal life is based on Mutual Funds. You must maintain a personal watch on the investments. I recommend Whole life. Just have the small payment come out of your bank account automatically and you will never miss the money. If Mike and Bonnie are 28 and 26, whole life for $20,000 is $17.69 a month. The total monthly cost for all the kids' whole life costs $65.97.

The $400,000 term 20 insurance would carry for $90 a month. That all totals to $173.60. That would mean that for less than $175 per month the whole family could be prepared if the worst happened. And the children have guaranteed insurance for life. That is a good place to be. It will give you peace of mind and you will sleep better because of that. A combination of a little permanent insurance and a lot of inexpensive term insurance is the way to go when you are starting out life together.

Changing Needs and Various types of Insurance

12

AS YOU grow and change, let your insurance change with you. When you are young you need different types and amounts of insurance than when you are older. Let me explain. You might be thinking of starting your own business or taking a sabbatical or even early retirement. Insurance and a good agent can guide you through these life stage changes.

I hope you are beginning to see that insurance is based on need. If you are rich, you can be what is called "self-insured." That means you have enough money to cover off any disaster or change in circumstances. Most of us are not in that happy boat. We both work outside the home. The kids may or may not go to university. If they do go, they may be saddled with huge student loans.

Let's have a look at some of the strategies that help when needs are changing:

Starting a new business. You can borrow against the cash value of a permanent or whole life policy. The bank may advance you up to 90% of the cash value. That can give you the leg-up you may need.

Taking a Sabbatical You may be paid part of your salary when you are away in Africa or exploring the Andes, but you will have to fund some of the adventure yourself. The cash value of a whole life policy dedicated for this use is a fine way to ensure you have a wonderful year off.

Early Retirement This largely depends on your pension and whether you have been wise enough to stick it out in one firm or government office for

30 years. But if you can do it – hats off to you! You can supplement your retirement with a life annuity that is guaranteed to pay you for the rest of your life.

Paying off the mortgage This is usually the cause for a good party. To have that party earlier, you should consider ways to pay it off faster. One of the best ways is to pay your mortgage more often. In fact, the more often you pay your mortgage, the less you will pay. So every other week is better than monthly, but weekly is better than every two weeks. It depends how you are paid and how you can budget. In general, the more often you pay the mortgage, the sooner you have it paid off.

If the mortgage is closed, open a special savings account to put money aside to pay the mortgage down when the term ends. Before you take another mortgage, pay the total down. Set a goal to save $10,000 or $25,000, or $100,000, and time it so you can apply it to the mortgage before you renew.

Be careful about the amortization period, if you can handle the payments, a shorter amortization period can save you tens of thousands of dollars over the life of the mortgage.

Protect your Spouse's lifestyle This is another job for insurance. Use inexpensive term insurance. If either wage earner should die prematurely then the insurance will pay off and the one left can carry on. (See the discussion of this in the last chapter).

Paying off a large loan Perhaps you have a hobby that requires a large investment. Perhaps a racing sailboat or a powerboat or you may enjoy racing cars or perhaps you own a horse ranch. All of these take fairly large sums of capital to keep current. What happens when you die and you still owe money on your plane or speedboat? Term insurance to cover off all your obligations is a fine idea. Use 10-year term here or if you think you may not have it all paid off in 10 years, consider 20-year term. This is one area where the need is temporary and the insurance should be temporary too.

Providing Long term care or home care You can use permanent insurance here too but another solution is Long Term Care Insurance. If you cannot look after yourself, and there are some tests to determine if you can look after yourself, you can qualify for this insurance. There are usually four questions: 1) can you feed yourself? 2) can you dress yourself? 3) can you go to the bathroom by yourself? and 4) can you walk without assistance? In general, can you look after yourself? Each insurance company is a little different but these questions are the ones that are usually asked. Long Term Care Insurance will pay the costs of a nursing home. The whole trick of insurance is summed up here. **You have to buy it when you do not need it.** See your insurance agent if you think this might be what you need.

Providing retirement income You need income in retirement. Term insurance does not build up cash values, so it is not appropriate for your old age. Whole life and universal insurance both develop cash values that you can access tax-free. Besides spending the cash values you can use the cash value as collateral for a consumer loan at a third party institution. What that means is if you have your insurance with Manulife you cannot get a loan against that insurance from Manulife. Get the loan from a bank. They will lend you up to 90% on a whole life, about 50% on universal. Term insurance usually will not be accepted, as it has no cash value (see Chapter Fourteen). The bank keeps the policy and if you die, they send in the forms and get the money. They take what they are owed and send the balance to your family.

Consider combining a single-life annuity and a permanent life insurance policy that can maximize your pension pay out while providing funds for your beneficiaries. (See information on this in Chapter 4).

Planning for the upkeep of the cottage Suppose you own an old beautiful family cottage in Muskoka or in Manitoba or a ski lodge in B.C. You can leave it to your kids but can they pay the taxes and upkeep on the property? You can leave a whole life policy to pay for the maintenance of the buildings and property. Consider a whole life policy for $100,000 - $400,000 to handle this job and spell your wishes out in your will. The interest on the payout should take care of a leaky roof.

Providing for your grandchildren's future Consider that you could leave your grandchildren some of the insurance in your will. Another way to provide for their future is to buy some life insurance on their life. Add the rider that guarantees future insurability. Your grandkids will remember you fondly. They will anyway, but if you give them this kind of gift it will go a long way to protecting your children's children.

Ensuring that the final taxes are paid This is a good use of permanent insurance. Capital gains tax is owed on all assets except the family home. That means the cottage, the hobby farm or ranch (if it is not your matrimonial home). Buy enough insurance to pay the capital gains tax at death. That way your kids can keep an asset and not have to sell it to pay the darn taxes.

Leaving a Legacy Not the way one federal leader wanted to leave a legacy; but suppose you wanted to benefit your Alma Mater. Perhaps the local Boys club or the Girl's Club needs a new roof or a new wing or a new pool table. Whatever you think is important you can leave behind. All it takes is a little planning now.

I remember a fellow at Camp Ahmek when I was only about 13. His name was Peter Benning and why would I remember Peter? Because Peter Benning got a dime and put it in a thick paper sleeve and thumb tacked that sleeve to the only pay phone at camp. He called it the *Peter Benning Memorial Dime*. We all used his dime to start our calls home and when it came out of the pay phone at the end of the call we put the *Peter Benning Memorial Dime* back for the next person. You can do the same with a more grown up idea and you can benefit society just as much as Peter did in 1962. You, too, can be remembered.

Although I saw something sad the other day in this regard. I drove past a school building that was being torn down in a school expansion. I passed just when the name of an original donor on a brass plaque hit the torn up earth. There is no saying your gift will be there in 100 years. In fact, it likely won't.

A carefully arranged planned gift can be tax effective too. You can leave it outside of your estate to your favourite charity. Using permanent insurance which will pay off when you die is a good way to do this. Insurance avoids probate and goes right to the beneficiary, in this case a charity. Term is not appropriate, most term policies end at age 80 or 85. You could live longer than that.

Using permanent insurance can leave a meaningful gift. You can buy policies for millions of dollars. Of course they are not inexpensive and you better be in perfect health. Generally insurance companies do not attempt to create wealth in heirs. Most people who want a large policy have proven resources to pay the premiums. There is more on gifting in Chapter Twenty Three.

You can also leave a cultural property. The government has allowed a generous tax treatment of cultural gifts to retain "national treasures" in Canada. The only catch is that the Canadian Cultural Property Export Review Board must approve the cultural gifts. If your gift is approved, you will not pay any capital gains tax on it. That will give you a tax credit somewhere else in your final return.

You can also use insurance to replace the capital value of your gift. The donation usually has to happen within three years of the death of the donor.

What Insurance does a Business Need?

13

THERE ARE many needs for insurance in any business. In this chapter we cover insurance for small to medium sized businesses. The insurance uses in any company can vary from protecting a key employee, partner buyouts, to business succession. There are several uses other than these three that we will discuss in this chapter. If someone asked, "what is the best type of insurance for a business?" I would have to answer, "It depends." That is not the best answer or the one you want to hear, but that is the real answer as there are many types of businesses.

However, we can make some good assumptions. Because you are the owner or manager of your own business, a vast majority of your wealth is tied up in your enterprise. You may have a large requirement to protect what you have built against the unforeseen problems like death, disability, and to ensure liquidity for reasons like partner buy out and eventual business succession.

If you have just started, you will need to protect your ability to repay your start-up loans in the event of your death or disability. If your business is well established and growing you will want to protect those employees you really depend on and are so glad you hired. Later on when you are thinking of retirement, you will need to ensure the continued well-being of your family and the selling of your enterprise. Or you may want to give to a hospital or your favourite charity. Insurance can help you do all these things.

Let's look at the **Key Employee** first:

Term insurance does not work here simply because this strategy depends on the insurance building up cash values and term does not do that. In addition, the key individual insured may outlive their term insurance, which, I repeat, ends at age 80 or in some cases 85. Policies that build cash values on a tax-advantaged basis can be used over and over within the lifetime of the business. One use would be to insure the life of the key employee.

Who is a key employee? It could be the owner manager themselves, or a key scientist, or the best manager. This type of insurance can be used to attract and retain new employees as well. You can also use insurance to pay for the retirement of a long-term key employee as well. Simply use the cash value built up over time. Take that money and invest it in a money market fund or a collateral loan or perhaps a partial surrender of the policy. All these strategies will be discussed in more detail in Chapter Fourteen.

You can use the built up cash value to fund the purchase of your business by the key employee or third-party buyer when you retire or die. You can use the money to lend to the new buyer and take back a mortgage on your business. Talk to your lawyer about this and get ironclad contracts (more on this later in the Chapter – see Business Succession).

The main idea here is to have those cash value dollars built up in the policy over time. You have to start now to have these abilities in the future. Also the cash value that may be available depends on how the policy is funded and on whatever tax laws are in force when the money is withdrawn from the policy. Understand also that using the cash value will reduce the death benefit of the policy.

Business Partner Buy Out

Another need could be to have the funds to buy out a business partner's interest in the firm after their death. The danger you run without this protection is that you may be business partners with someone you did not anticipate - his wife or her husband.

Convertible term insurance can work in this case in the short run. It is inexpensive and can be converted to whole life later on. Be aware that the cost of converting the policy to whole life may cost more than a brand new whole life policy. Why? The guaranteed conversion may not require underwriting so the insurance company will charge more to cover the risk of the individual being quite sick at the time of converting the policy. On the other hand, if you are healthy, consider a new whole life policy when the firm can afford it.

Critical Illness Insurance

Another form of insurance that business owners should consider is critical illness insurance. This is insurance that pays the owner a lump sum of money if he or she becomes ill and survives 30 days or 90 days in the case of cancer. Most policies cover the big three: heart attack, stroke or cancer. Some cover up to 19 different illnesses. If you skipped the chapter on Critical Illness (Chapter Eight) go back to it for more information.

For most people this wonderful insurance may seem expensive. However, for a corporation to ensure a key executive, a partnership or for a small business owner, this insurance can make all the difference. You can use the lump sum proceeds in any way you want. It can be used by the company to replace or buy out the sick employee or partner. You can travel to the Mayo Clinic for a cure or jet to Miami for a vacation; you can buy that yacht or motor home. Whatever you want. If it is affordable, buy the option that lets you get all the premiums back if you stay healthy until 75. That is a great way to supplement your retirement when you may need it.

Business Succession

Should a business have a succession plan? When you are busy with the day-to-day running of your business you probably do not think too much about passing it on to your child or exactly how you will sell it. The main task is to make money so that the business survives long enough for this to be an issue. One day the thought arrives that says "we've made it over the hump. We're pretty safe now, we are well established." You and I both know that any business can fail, but the thought will start to grow in your head that you really should do something about planning the eventual transfer of your business. The sooner you have this thought the better the succession plan will be. Remember insurance takes time to build up cash values and insurance is a main plank of these plans.

Exactly what is a business succession plan? This is really an extension of your own estate planning. A business succession plan determines how your business will be transferred to your child or a third party. It outlines the steps necessary to prepare the changeover. The plan affects you, your family, your employees, your clients, your suppliers, creditors and others. A good succession plan will exactly outline your wishes for the business should you suffer a serious disability, or a disease that makes you unable to run your business from day-to-day. It can help you ease into retirement and provide retirement income. Remember, after you die and the business passes to your spouse, when she dies capital gains tax will be owing.

There are a series of six steps that are required in each business succession plan. There are business and personal issues to include, which all have to be considered together. Therefore, bring in your lawyer, your accountant, your stockbroker, your insurance advisor and your tax professionals to hammer out a great unique plan for you. Here are the six steps:

1) Look at your business as it actually is.
2) Discuss your goals for your business and your family.
3) Identify and prioritize action plans and responsibilities.
4) Select the best action plan.
5) Document your decisions.
6) Implement your action plan

Start by looking at your business as if something will happen to you tomorrow. Here are some questions you may want to think about: If you died while running your business, how do you want to divide the estate so it is fair to all family members and anyone else you may want to leave money to? What other assets do you have and who will receive them? How much control do you want to have over the business after you retire? Where will the money come from to fund the purchase of your business and fund your retirement? How will your family retain their lifestyle in the event of your death or disability? How will you ensure your business runs smoothly after you are gone?

Changes in life circumstances can impact your business succession plan. For example, a divorce or a new marriage can force a change in your plans. Death, of course, will put the plan into action.

There is no way to guarantee your good health. However, you can start an action plan with a properly funded buy-sell agreement.

My grandfather on my mother's side owned a men's clothing store. He was a haberdasher. He sold men's suits and shirts starting when he came back from the First World War. He called it "Chapman's Men's Wear." He had the main store at Bloor and Yonge in Toronto, right across the street from Frank Stollery's. Frank is at number one Bloor, and granddad was his competitor and friend. Granddad often told me stories of selling during the depression in the thirties. He and Frank would meet in the middle of Bloor (imagine that today) and Granddad would say, "How's business Frank?"

He'd say, "Abe, I sold one handkerchief"

Granddad would reply, "I sold the other one, Frank" and they would wander back to their stores.

I was in his store when I was just a lad. He had two piles of handkerchiefs at the cash register. One was priced at $1.00 and the other at a nickel. I asked him why he had two piles of handkerchiefs. He got a little twinkle in his eye and answered, "When people see two piles of handkerchief, they know that nobody wants a 5-cent handkerchief."

"Granddad, if everyone buys the dollar handkerchiefs, what do you do when that pile is empty?"

"I just take some from the 5-cent pile and put them on the dollar pile."

He was a good merchandiser but he did not have a good succession plan. Frank Stollery's store is still there today. What happened to my grandfather's business? He did not have a clear succession plan. He left it to his son who expanded to three stores and lost the business when the neighbourhoods he expanded into changed their demographics totally.

Buy-Sell Agreement

A buy-sell agreement is a plan that provides for a proper and orderly transfer of ownership under established guidelines, for example, when a business owner dies or become seriously disabled. A good buy-sell agreement establishes a fair value for the business, both now and in the future. A good buy-sell agreement sets out the way the ownership shares of the deceased will be sold. It also states what you want to happen when you retire. Also, the family members of the dead owner must receive proper value for the owner's share of the firm. How this is funded is very important, as likely the firm cannot afford to simply pay for this out of cash flow. A properly funded buy-sell agreement can do more that just look after the family members. It can assure creditors that the funds will be available to pay their bills. Some lenders require a properly funded buy-sell agreement before giving you a loan. It can assure existing employees of continual employment. It will make a market for the shareholder's interest in the business. It sets the terms under which you and your shareholders agree to buy and sell their interests in the business. It will provide the heirs with a predetermined price for their shares. It can protect other shareholders from unwanted shareholders, such as family members of the dead partner. It can allocate the shares to all shareholders in a fair and equitable manner. It can also be a method to establish the value of the business.

How to determine the value of your business: That is really the task of your accountant, but I will outline some proven ways to value your business since it is important to understand the likely valuation procedures your accountant will utilize.

1) **The Fixed Value Method**. This plan simply sets a value for the business and this is updated annually. The advantages are that it is clean, simple and easy to explain. The shareholders can easily figure out the value of their shares. The disadvantage is that the value must be recalculated annually.

2) **The Formula Method**. The purchase price is valued on a formula based on some clear measure of the firm. For example, it could be the book value of the firm or the adjusted book value. Another formula could be a multiple of earnings or a multiple of sales. The advantage of the formula method is that it does not need to be reviewed annually. Also an analysis can be determined quickly and inexpensively.

The disadvantages of the formula method are that the terms book value and adjusted book value have no set definitions and could lead to disagreements. These disagreements can occur even if the definitions of the terms are set out in the agreement. Once set these terms may be out of favour with accountants in 25 or 30 years. It is also difficult to evaluate the value of property and goodwill with this method.

3) **The Fair Market Value Method**. The advantages of the fair market value method are that the shareholders and family will get the price the market says the firm's shares are worth. Usually that will be an even-handed solution for all.

Often the valuation can be accomplished by negotiation using terms specifically set out in the agreement. Note well that the insurance proceeds must not be included in this calculation. They will be used to fund whatever is agreed upon.

The advantages of the fair market value method are the shareholders and family will receive an equitable value for their shares. It should be a n evenhanded solution for all involved.

The disadvantages are that these valuations can be expensive and may not establish a value fast enough in a fast changing dynamic business. Also as the market changes these values can vary widely from year to year.

Perhaps the best solution to these issues is the famous Shotgun clause.

The Shotgun Clause Method. This clause applies when there is a disagreement among shareholders or one shareholder has a desire to sell or buy all the shares. Here is how it works: A shareholder who wants to buy offers to purchase the shares from the other shareholders at a certain price. The other shareholders then have the right to sell their shares to the first shareholder at the price he mentioned or to buy back the shares of the first shareholder at his price. He must offer enough to buy and not so little that he is bought out. These negotiations can be dramatic.

On the other hand if a shareholder who wants to sell asks too high a price for his shares, the other shareholders would refuse to buy his shares at that price. However, they would happily turn the tables and sell out to the first shareholder at the excessive price. He can't ask too much for his shares or he may own all the shares at his high asking price.

If the selling shareholder asks too low a price he or she would be leaving money on the table. A shotgun clause is a balancing act and should result in a fair price for the purchase and sale.

A good buy-sell agreement provides peace of mind and security to the business owner. He or she can know that solid plans are in place should death or disability strike suddenly. These agreements are often complex and unique and require a full-court press by all your advisors. I recommend you call in your accountant, broker, lawyer, tax-expert and your insurance advisor. Working together they can help you establish the right plan for you, your business and your family.

If you own a small business, when you die your business may transfer to your spouse. If you don't plan now it could all be gone to taxes when he or she dies. On the second death capital gains taxes will come due. This is usually the business breaker. (Thanks, oh wise government.) Protect yourself by buying permanent life insurance to cover that predictable expense when you are in your early years – thirties or forties. It will be less expensive then. This is key.

Corporate Asset Transfer – is an excellent idea for getting the assets out of a company you have built up from the beginning. If you want to 1) retain excess cash flow within your successful company, 2) want to maintain that surplus and use it to grow the value of your estates, 3) want to use that excess cash in your personal account, and 4) want to minimize additional tax at your personal marginal tax rate.

If this sounds interesting to you, see your insurance advisor. The concept is based on using a corporately funded tax-exempt permanent insurance policy. Often, it can also provide greater benefits in both personal and estate values when compared to traditional taxable investments.

A corporately funded, tax-exempt permanent life insurance policy allows corporations to accumulate growth inside the policy without having to pay tax on that growth. This growth will not be subject to taxes or the

"Refundable Dividend Tax on Hand" (RDTOH). (An attempt by the government to equal the taxing field between corporations and individuals.) See your accountant on this one. Insurance trumps it. See your agent.

The death benefit amount from the corporately funded life insurance policy is received tax-free by the beneficiary private corporation and will be credited to the Capital Dividend Account (CDA). Capital dividends may be paid to the CDA as a tax-free capital dividend to surviving shareholders or the estate and may also provide funds for business succession or other tax issues.

Small business is often considered the backbone of the national economy. More people work for small companies than for large multinational firms. Yet 60% of small businesses will change hands due to retirement within the next five years. Despite being so important to the national economy, well over 60% do not have a succession plan. Only 10% of small businesses survive to the third generation, due to a poor choice of successor or a profound lack of planning. I know you are busy - but are you too busy to ignore this?

If you ignore this advice and even if you live long, hale and hearty and still run your business into your 80s, when you die there will be massive tax headaches for your family. Call those advisors together and get them working.

If you own shares for at least two years in a "qualifying small business corporation," when you want to sell them you may be eligible to use the $500,000 Capital Gains Exemption. The formula is a bit restrictive in that only privately owned Canadian companies can qualify. The corporation must be using 90% or more of its assets to carry on an active business primarily in Canada, the same must be true for 50% or more of its assets throughout the two-year period that you have owned the stock. Every Canadian can use this $500,000 capital gains exemption but only on "qualified small businesses" and "qualified farm property." Please note that if you sell shares in a "qualified small business" and you sell a "qualified farm property" that the total of the deduction allowed is $500,000, not $500,000 for the QSBC and a second $500,000 for the farmland.

I have simplified this complex tax relief by hitting only the highlights of it. Check with a small business accountant to be sure your corporation qualifies for this excellent tax exemption.

Individual Pension Plan

One underused strategy is the **Individual Pension Plan (IPP)**, but this requires a knowledgeable actuary and the creation of a corporate trust or an individual trusteeship to manage the pension. If you need creditor protection please consider this strategy.

Pensions are creditor proof unlike RRSPs. The big advantage is that the Individual Pension Plan allows the owner to lower the taxes paid by the business while funding the owner's retirement. Any income earned above $300,000 is taxed at the highest corporate rates, but contributions to an IPP will reduce the income earned on the bottom line. In other words, with this strategy you will pay for your own retirement while lowering the corporate taxes.

Small business owners can name their spouses and themselves as members of the pension and draw on it after retirement. But on the second death the pension's assets are considered part of the estate and are subject to capital gains taxes and probate.

But there is a way to help your business last into the third and fourth generation and in doing so generate real wealth for your grandchildren. You simply defer indefinitely the taxation of the pension assets. How do you do that? You add your children to the pension. When you and your spouse die the pension carries on to the children. They can do the same thing and name their children as owners of the pension plan and so on and so on. The children have to work for the business for this to be neat and tidy. This, of course, can erode the RRSP room for your sons and daughters. To avoid that problem, make the pension a 1% employer-paid, defined contribution plan.

To be clear, there are broadly two types of pension plans in Canada. There are defined benefit plans, where an employee knows exactly what his pension will be when he retires. The other type is called defined contribution plans. There the payer only knows what he or she puts into the pension every paycheque.

There are other opportunities available with the IPP. For example, the company can continue to contribute to your IPP even after you retire. The company can contribute to top up the IPP as long as the assets do not earn over 7.5%. If the IPP is invested safely in bonds and the average return on your bond portfolio is 5.5%, then the company you helped build from the ground up can chip in the other 2%. That is good for the company as it lowers the taxable earnings at the bottom line and it is good for you. If the assets perform above 7.5%, the company cannot add to your IPP. I have just hit the high points of this Individual Pension Plan. If you want to start one, see a good accountant.

When it comes time to sell your business it makes good sense to maximize the value of your business. Here is a tip to legally pump up the value. Every business owner has at some point told the tax people in Ottawa about some business losses. Since 1998 the government tax people have been faithfully keeping track of this for all of us. Usually, this total does not affect us in any way. The problem is that this total can erode a small business owner's Capital Gains Exemption. Look at it this way: If a small business owner wants to claim a Capital Gains Exemption of $150,000 and has a capital loss total, (called the CNIL balance), of $50,000 then he or she can only claim $100,000 in capital exemptions.

The solution to this question, as almost all businesses built up capital losses in the early years, is to increase the dividend payments small business owner pay to themselves. Ottawa considers these dividend payments investment gains, and they will offset the CNIL balance. It is a good idea to reduce the salary a small business owner pays to himself or herself at the same time. This will avoid raising your personal exposure to tax and also avoid excessive drainage of the company's assets.

In our example, the small business owner would only need to pay himself or herself $40,000 in dividends as the payment would be grossed up by 25%, to $50,000, which would eliminate the CNIL balance of $50,000 and enable the small business owner to claim the full capital gains exemption (See Chapter Nineteen).

Short Term Disability

Many small business owners trust the Canadian government for disability benefits when their employees suffer a disability at work. If the employee cannot do the job due to injury they are sent home and the employer expects Employment Insurance (EI) to cover the costs. When the employee is better, he comes off EI and gets back to work. Have you ever really done that? Here is what really happens in most cases.

EI does not pay enough any more. The payments are based on 55% of the employee's gross income and are maxed out at $413.00, per week. That is never enough and the employer gets a call from the employee and usually has to help out financially. The business owner is not covered. The benefits, such as they are, are fully taxable, and there is a waiting period of at least two weeks. There is a much better way.

As a business owner, did you know that the regulations for EI are worth looking into? When you do you will discover that EI says if you can get private coverage that meets or exceeds the EI coverage for less, then you can opt out of paying the EI payments. Did you hear that? You can opt out of the EI payments. Check this out at 1-800 561-7923 that is the EI hotline for Premium Reduction. All you need is a better cheaper plan.

Here it is:

For starters, with short-term disability coverage, business owners are covered so if you get hurt on the job you can claim - unlike UI. The benefits are based on 67% of the employee's gross income and are capped at $1,384 per week. That is 3.5 times as much as EI and is likely enough to pay the bills. Depending on the option chosen, you can have a zero day waiting period. If the employee pays for the short-term disability insurance the proceeds are not taxed.

In addition, the employer saves $0.30 for each $100.00, of payroll. That works out to a savings of $1,800 per year. Isn't that a much better plan? However, the freedom the government gives, it also takes away. They tell you what to do with the employer portion of the savings. The employer portion of the $1,800 must be passed on to the employees. The entire amount can be used to pay for group life insurance payments, group RRSPs, a raise in pay, a staff party or any other way you can think of as long as it benefits the employees and not you the owner.

Raises for employees

In the old days if an employee did a good job he or she was rewarded with a small raise and everyone was happy. That idyllic world has come to a complete stop. Government tinkering and cutbacks, increasing drug, hospital and paramedical costs have risen sharply. The old system of a 3% raise just does not cut it any more. Here are two charts, one comparing the cost to the employer and another showing the benefit to the employee of a 3% raise on a salary of $35,000 vs. a same size increase in Group Benefits.

Cost. for the Employer

	Raise	Group Benefits
Pay increase	$1,050	$1,050
EI	$30.87	N/A
CPP	$51.98	N/A
WSIB*	$22.99	N/A
Sales Tax**	N/A	$84.00
Payroll Tax	$10.29	N/A
Total	**$1,166.13**	**$1,134.00**

*Workplace Safety and Insurance Board. Using industry average for 2003

**8% Ontario retail tax

Net of this chart shows that it costs the employer $30 more to give a raise in pay as opposed to group benefits. The real difference is in the relative benefits to the employee.

Benefits for the Employee

	Raise	Group Benefits
Pay increase	$1,050	$1,050
EI	($22.05)	N/A
CPP	($51.98)	N/A
WSIB*	($51.98)	N/A
Sales Tax**	N/A	($84.00)
Income tax	($362.40)*	N/A
Total	**$613.57**	**$966**

*This is the total additional tax deducted over 12 pay periods.

Which would you rather get? It seems obvious that due to increases in EI and CPP premiums, plus high income taxes, this example shows that it more attractive to receive group benefits than a 3% raise in pay. In the future, depending on plan usage, a group benefits plan has the potential to pay out far more to the employee than $1,050 premium investment – it can grow sharply over the years.

It is clear that both the employer and the employee have more to gain with a sound group benefit plan as opposed to a raise in pay. Please note that results will be a little different for each province. I have used an Ontario example.

How to profit from your life insurance – during your lifetime

14

MANY OF you have insurance policies that you have owned for years or may be considering buying one soon. You know somewhere deep inside that you have done an altruistic thing, but did you know that you may be able to benefit from that insurance during your lifetime? We buy insurance so that the people we love – our spouses and our children, will be protected in the event we die. We all know that but this chapter will show you how to profit from your life insurance before you die. There are four ways. Each one of these options has tax consequences and I will discuss these in detail. Keep in mind that governments change and tax law changes with government budgets. Check with your insurance agent if you ever want to do one of these strategies in the future.

Let's deal with the worst one first and get it out of the way. If you are terminally ill you can get part of the insurance payment before you die. The percent varies with insurance companies, but if you or an insured loved one is terminally ill and needs some money your insurance company can advance it before the death. Of course, it comes out of the total death benefit. If you need it, check with your agent.

The three remaining strategies require the types of insurance that have cash values. There is one exception to this and I will point it out when we get there. By cash values I mean either whole life or universal life. It should be permanent insurance.

Insurance policies are tax exempt and woe to a government that would tamper with that. Some may try in the future and if they ever dared they would get a huge backlash from most thinking people. You buy life insurance with after tax dollars – the tax has already been paid. These strategies work as long as the taxman keeps his grasping fingers out of this area.

After you have owned the insurance for years, it has built up a cash value and you can access this cash value in the future. The key idea here is that you are able to access it if you need it in the future for financial emergencies or to add to your income or for any reason you may have.

Here are the three most common ways to access the cash value of your permanent insurance policy:

1) **A policy loan** is just what it sounds like. The insurance company will lend you some of the cash value. This method keeps the cash inside the insurance policy. However, it does come out of the death benefit if not repaid.

2) **Partial surrender** of the cash value directly from your policy. The cash payout option allows you to access the dividend and the dividend growth that has accumulated in your policy. This also removes part of the death benefit, but if the insurance policy is large this may well be a fine option.

3) **Collateral assignment** of an insurance policy as security for a loan or line of credit. In Quebec, the policy is accepted as security for a loan by way of a moveable hypothec (that is what collateral assignment is called in Quebec, it's the same thing).

The first two methods will likely attract some taxation. The dividend cash value of the policy has been steadily growing tax-free for all those years. When you withdraw some of that growth, it will likely be taxed. The third method does not attract tax at this time to the policy owner.

These are methods or strategies that you will likely not employ at this time but may apply them in the future. This is not why you bought your policy but this is how it can be used. You will likely not make a decision about which method to use until you are much closer to actually needing the money. Of course, if you have owned a policy for years you can employ these strategies tomorrow.

As I have explained many times one of the great benefits of permanent insurance is that the growth of the dividends is tax-exempt. Keep in mind that its tax status changes when you withdraw it from the policy in any other way than as a death benefit. So partial withdrawal is taxed at the same rate as though the entire policy was surrendered.

For policies issued after December 1, 1982 the amount that is taxable is the approximate difference between:

- The cash taken at the time of withdrawal and
- The Adjusted Cost Basis. (ACB) is a new term in this book and it is used extensively in the discussion of the taxation of insurance. It is defined as: the total premiums (excluding those for additional benefits) you have paid, less the cumulative cost of pure insurance over the years, less any dividends that were not used to purchase additional insurance or pay premiums for the policy, less any policy loans taken out in the past. This number is called the Adjusted Cost Basis or ACB.

The end result of that calculation assuming that payments have been paid in full is that:

- Very little is taxable if the policy is cashed in the very early years.
- About half (50%) is taxable if the policy is surrendered after 15 or 20 years.
- All or almost all is taxable if the policy is cashed after 25 or 30 years.

While the larger percentage of the cash value is taxed in later years, the policy owner has benefited from years of tax-exempt growth. The exact amount taxable will vary depending on the type of insurance, the age of the insured and how much premium has been paid.

Now lets look at the last three methods in more detail:

Policy loan

This method does not actually take money out of the policy. The insurer advances you some of the cash value in the form of a loan. You pay interest for the use of this money but your policy continues to grow as if the money was not withdrawn from the policy. This is the same as borrowing from a bank instead of using the money in your bank account.

On the first loan the insurer will draw money against the tax-free adjusted cost basis of the policy. Once the ACB is gone, every dollar taken from the cash value will be taxable. Using the same policy as we used in the partial surrender example let's say you wanted two loans over a period of two months. The first loan is for $40,000 and the second is for $20,000.

For the first loan:

Loan amount	$40,000
Adjusted Cost Basis (ACB)	$40,000 (but the ACB is now zero)
Taxable amount	$0

For the second loan:

Loan amount	$20,000
ACB	0
Taxable amount	$20,000

This example shows that the adjusted cost basis equaled the first loan so no taxes will be paid. If I have used a different amount there would have been some ACB remaining and on the second loan that ACB would be used up first and the balance would be fully taxable.

Here are some other important points you should know about policy loans:

- The interest payable may be added to the loan balance (the term is capitalized). That means you would not repay the interest out of your pocket. However, if the total loan exceeds the maximum value available you may be asked to pay interest out of pocket. Keep in mind that the dividends should pay the interest.
- The total amount you can borrow including capitalized interest is limited to a percentage of the cash value. This varies by insurance company; see your agent for exact details.
- If the loan and the capitalized interest after a while exceed this percentage of the cash value, you will be forced to surrender the entire policy if you cannot make a loan payment to get back under the specific percentage. If you surrender the policy, you lose all the protection it provides.
- If you desire, you can repay the amount of the loan. This will restore the value of your policy cash value. If you do not choose to repay the loan, the total amount of the loan plus any interest not paid will be deducted from the death benefit.
- If you repay the loan, you can claim a tax deduction equal to the taxable income you declared when you took the loan out. The amount repaid not including any loan interest paid is added back into your ACB. If you repaid $30,000 of the total of $60,000 in the

above example, $20,000 could be claimed as a tax deduction and the ACB would be increased by $30,000.

- If you pay interest it increases your ACB.

Partial Surrender of cash value

This strategy uses the withdrawal of some of the built up cash value of the policy. Using the cash value before the death benefit will affect the future growth of the policy, as the growth will now be on reduced capital. Also it will, of course, reduce the cash value of the policy.

Partial surrenders can be arranged by your agent to be in a lump sum or can provide regular annual amounts. As I noted above, every dollar removed from the policy is taxed at the same rate as though the entire policy had been surrendered.

Here is an example of how the ACB works in this strategy:

Let's assume you have a policy with $200,000 in cash value and a $40,000 adjusted cost basis (total premiums paid, less costs or other loans). You need $60,000 at this time.

	Total Policy Surrendered	Partial Surrender Cash Value
Cash Value	$200,000	$60,000
Adjusted Cost Basis	$40,000	$12,000
Taxable Amount	$160,000	$48,000
Percentage taxable	80%	80%

In this example, 80% of every dollar is taxable. Therefore, if you needed $60,000 now $48,000 would be taxable. The ACB would be reduced to $28,000 from $40,000. The actual taxes paid would be based on the amount taxable plus or minus the ACB, depending on the individual situation.

Collateral loan

In this method, you assign the cash value to a lending institution other than your insurance company as security for a term loan or a line of credit (by way of a moveable hypothec in Quebec). Buying insurance today with the idea of using it in the future as collateral for a loan is a great idea - if the government keeps out of it. The taxation may be different on this in the future. As this is structured, today it attracts no taxation.

Here is how the collateral loan works. Remember Chapter Six about **the power of this idea**.

The cash value of your policy grows over time. Like other assets, it can be used as security collateral to back up a loan. When you assign the policy to a lending institution, at some future date, you remain the owner of the policy but the policy is pledged to the lending company as collateral for the repayment of the loan. You cannot make any changes to your insurance policy or remove any of the cash value of your policy without the prior approval of your lending company. Some lenders will require that they be made the primary beneficiary up to the amount you borrow and owe.

The lending company provides you a line of credit or a loan. You still have to follow the same procedure with a loan application and a credit check. The lending company may not ask for any more collateral than the cash value of the policy. Since you will repay this loan either before you die, or when you die it is very important that this policy be kept up to date.

The lending institution lends you the money and you use it to supplement your annual income or for whatever your heart desires. You pay interest every month or every year. The annual growth in the cash value should pay the interest on your loan.

In a few cases, you may be allowed to capitalize the interest (add it to the loan total). In this case, you must insure that the loan balance including capitalized interest remains below the percentage required by your insurance company.

In general these percentages are roughly:
90% of the cash value for whole life
50% of the cash value for universal life

And here is the exception I mentioned above: some lenders will also allow you to use 10 to 20% of a term policy as collateral. This is not a general situation but if you have a friendly banker it is possible. There would be great limits on this loan because term life insurance expires at age 80 or 85 in most cases and does not have cash value. Term to 100 would stand a better chance of being used as collateral. However, the key for the bank is the growing cash value, so whole life is best by far.

When the insured person dies, the lending institution is paid first and the remaining money from the death benefit is distributed to the beneficiaries.

The loan must be sourced from a third party. You cannot use for example, a Manulife policy and ask Manulife Life to give you the loan. Take the Manulife Life policy to another lender; it could be another insurance company or a bank. For example, The Bank of Montreal has long experience in this type of lending.

Benefits of using the collateral loan strategy:

- Under today's tax law there is no disposition and therefore no resultant tax on the collateral loan. There is taxation on the two other methods above. Depending on the interest rates of the day, when you get the loan, it may be better to use this method as you may receive more money than using taxable withdrawals from the policy.
- You do not reduce the amount of insurance coverage you have and the tax-exempt growth within the policy continues while it is being used as collateral.
- You can arrange to receive the money in a lump sum, annually or every month to supplement your income.

The risks of Collateral loans

- The tax laws can change. There is no promise that those who wish to use this strategy in the future will not be taxed. I have noted that no money actually leaves the cash value, but governments often ignore logic and do some pretty dumb things. If that ever happen, those with existing arrangements with the lending institution would likely be "grand fathered." Anyone who wanted in after the tax change would face a different scenario. You would be unable to receive tax-free advances from the lending company.
- Here is the bigger risk. What if the lender demands repayment? This should not happen if the cash value is growing rapidly. See the example in Chapter Six. However, if the loan, in the future, because of capitalized interest or some other reason, exceeds the stipulated percentage of the cash value, the lender could demand repayment. This has not happened yet, but it could.
- You could live too long. If you live longer than the age used by the lender to calculate the maximum amount of the loan advance they could demand repayment. You could get a letter when you are 88 demanding you repay the loan, which is now much more than you can repay. That would not be good news. However, I would remind the banker that the dividends are even higher now and the cash value is growing mightily, and when you die it will all be

paid off. Sometime you have to talk to them to have them see the point.

- Banks and other lenders have been accepting insurance policies as collateral for loans for years. The recent change is that some lenders are now allowing capitalized interest. There is no guarantee that lenders will continue to honour this concept and there is no way you can bind your bank to this policy today for a loan at some future date. Capitalized interest is the only way you can get into trouble. I repeat that the cash value is growing fast and the dividends are fairly secure so there should be no need to capitalize the interest. Historically, interest rates from insurance companies have been 4% to 6%. Use 4% and work it out conservatively.

To summarize, you can use this, direct cash withdrawal or policy loans.

Whatever way you use the cash value in the policy, I hope you find this information useful.

If you own a corporation it too can benefit from insurance before any insured individual dies.

How a Corporation can profit from life insurance too

For corporations that own life insurance on key employees, executives and owners of the firm there are ways to profit from the life insurance while the employee is alive. For starters, the corporation can use the built up cash value in the same manner an individual can. The ways we just discussed apply here as well: partial surrender, a policy loan and collateral assignment.

Why do corporations buy life insurance? It is a review but I think it is a good idea to revisit this in case you are skipping around in the book. Corporations buy life insurance for these reasons:

- Funding a buy-sell agreement in the event of a death of one of the co-owners of the business.
- Key person insurance coverage.
- Funding a future capital gains tax on the shares of the corporation when the owner dies.
- Retire long-term debt when the owner dies.

Other reasons that businesses buy whole life insurance that builds up a large cash value are to:

- Provide supplemental income to the retired business owner.
- Finance the buy out of shares owned by the retired owner before he or she dies.

Whichever of the three methods a corporation uses to access the cash value, keep in mind that Revenue Canada will tax the money as it is withdrawn from the policy.

As with the personal examples above, partial surrender and policy loan will attract tax. Collateral assignment does not attract tax and it should not in a right thinking world, but there is no requirement for the tax authorities to be right thinking. Taxation of this method may happen. All the benefits and risks discussed above for an individual apply in this corporate section. There are also some other items to discuss that relate just to corporations. Let's first look at a comparison of the three methods as a business would look at them.

Partial Surrender would be used in the case of a living buy-out share redemption. It is really a cash payout of the dividend values within the policy. Let's use some numbers from an actual case for an insured co-owner of a business. Let's assume he is male and does not smoke and is 46 years old. If the corporation owns a policy that is paid off in 20 years with an annual premium of $10,000 then that would result in a total initial coverage of $327,320.

Typical Corporate Insurance Scenario

Annual Premium	$10,000
Total Premium paid over 20 years	$200,000
Cash value at 65 (20 years after retirement)	$267,027
Total death benefit at age 65	$601,892

We assume that the company wants to finance the note to pay for buying back the shares of the retiring co-owner. In other words, to finance a buy-sell agreement to pay for the owner's shares at retirement, the co-owner exchanges his or her shares for a note or a loan taken back. The payment (including principle and interest) payable over 20 years is equal to $15,000 each year to the retired owner from the company.

| Annual Payment to former co-owner | $15,000 |
| Total Payments | $300,000 |

The cash value would not be enough to repay the firm. If the co-owner lived to 85 the loan would total $600,000 and the death benefit would just pay off the loan excluding any interest. Any expense here is considered a cost of doing business and is tax deductible.

The partial surrender method would be to cash the policy at 65 or whatever date agreed. If the company totally cashed out the policy at 65 the company would receive $267,027 but that would end the corporate liability. If they waited until the co-owner was 80 the cash value would be up to $523,826. And if the co-owner died that year the death benefit would be $747,408.

Now the interest should be paid by the annual increase in cash value. What happens if the dividends are low for years? Remember dividends payments are based on three things: 1) how the insurance companies investments are doing, 2) the mortality rate among the client base, and 3) expenses of the insurance company. If one or two of these gets out of line, the policy dividends may not pay the full annual interest payments. In that remote case, you may have to surrender the policy to pay off the collateral loan. Please note that every major insurance company in Canada has always paid the full annual dividend.

If the policy was surrendered at age 85 to pay off the collateral loan, at surrender the policy may attract taxation. I would recommend you let nature take her course since death benefits are always tax-free. However, if you get near the threshold it's good to remember what they are: 90% for whole life and 50% for universal.

Remember, this should not ever happen as the cash value of whole life rises rapidly and should be more than sufficient. But it could if the firm capitalized the interest (added it to the loan) or if interest rates went sky high and you had to renew the loan under these new high rates. Again if you set it up with the bank so that the interest is paid by the cash value and there is no renewal, it is simply a loan that is paid at the death of the individual - it should be all right. With all these caveats, here is what could happen if you do not set it up right and can't wait for the former owner to pass on:

Cash surrender value at 85	**$646,498**
Less: loan balance repaid to lender	**$600,000**
Balance for company	**$146,498**
Taxable part of cash value	
(as the owner is still alive)	**$646,498**
Tax rate 45%	
Taxes payable	**$290,924**
Additional funds needed to repay	
Tax liability	**$144,426**

A business that cannot pay for this shortfall should not use this method. As with the individual collateral loan, use this method with great caution, especially if the business does not have large cash retained earnings. If the former owner lives to 85 or 95 it can be disastrous for his or her former corporation to surrender the policy. When he or she dies, the death benefit is tax-free. So my recommendation is not to panic but let the founder or whomever die in peace, collect the death benefit and pay off the loan.

The key here is to be sure the interest is tax deductible for the corporation. Many factors influence this decision by the tax authorities. Such things as the timing of the loan advances, the purpose of the loan and the overall size and structure of the company can have an impact on the decision regarding tax deductibility.

If the company uses the money to pay off legal obligations the interest should be tax deductible. For example, if the company bought any of these investments the interest would be tax deductible:

- To acquire an income producing property or business
- To earn interest from a property or business
- To buy certain annuities

One of the future uses of cash value is to fund a retirement income to a former owner of the business. If the policy was bought to fund this concept great caution must be exercised to avoid running afoul of the Income Tax Act. Within the Income Tax Act there is an arrangement called the (RCA) or retirement compensation arrangements. When an insurance policy has been purchased by the company for the purpose of funding a supplement retirement income to an employee, tax consequences could result. These can include the imposition of a refundable tax equal to the premium paid (and possibly on policy dividends as well) and the loss of the tax-free status of the life insurance death benefit.

Take great care to ensure that it is plain that the first and foremost reason for the corporation buying insurance on this employee or owner is to insure a key person or for buy-sell funding. Do not buy the policy for the purpose years from now of using it to fund your retirement by cash withdrawal. That could lead to major tax issues.

Deductibility will depend on the nature of the payments, if the payments are to redeem shares (good) or to pay a salary or retirement income (doubtful). If the corporation is the owner of the policy and all proceeds from the cash values are used within the firm then well, and good, but if the company owned insurance is assigned to a lender for a collateral loan to benefit an employee, shareholder or former owner then a taxable benefit may occur. In the same manner, if the company paid the premiums and the employee was the policy owner or beneficiary, that may also trigger a taxable benefit. The Income Tax Act is often subject to interpretation. In most cases it depends on whose ox is being gored.

Here is the one we all hate: GAAR (sounds like what it is:)

The General Anti-Avoidance Rule (GAAR)

GAAR is a provision in the Income Tax Act that may be applied in any situation where a "tax benefit' has been avoided unless the transaction involved may be reasonably considered to have been undertaken for "bona fide purposes other than to obtain a tax benefit."

This rule could be erroneously applied by Revenue Canada to collateral loans. They might argue that a collateral loan was only an attempt to avoid the taxes on a policy loan and has no other purpose. This I am sure could be successfully challenged as it is well established that taxpayers can arrange their affairs in the most tax effective manner. But rulings like this have happened and it takes many good people a lot of time and money in court to undo any foolish Revenue Canada rulings.

In summation: There are several ways for a company to arrange policy cash values to provide cash, disability income and retirement income. They all are good as they allow for cash build up without taxation. The taxes are paid only when some of the cash value is withdrawn. As with individuals, the two methods that are safest are partial surrender and policy loan. There you will pay some tax, but the risk of a large potential payment is not present. However, the collateral loan method may develop a large corporate liability. Only use this method if you are a sophisticated investor with a high-risk tolerance. Also consult with your advisors before you enter into this arrangement (financial security advisor, lawyer and accountant etc.). Deep pockets are required to cover the interest payments or the tax payment if that becomes necessary from the insured living to 99. But again, the dividends should pay the interest.

Do not enter into any of the strategies methods lightly. Consider all the tax implications and possible future tax issues. Consult with your life insurance advisors before starting this project.

Do I really need a will?

15

IF YOU HAVE children or stepchildren the answer is *you really do need a will.*

You have been looking after your children since the day they were born. You taught them not to run with suckers in their mouths and to brush their teeth at least twice a day. You have looked after them when they were young so why not look after them again now that you are older?

I have heard this attitude more than once. "I had nothing when I started and I did all right. They can start from nothing too." That attitude makes me a little sad. When most of us started out in life there were jobs for life to be had. I could have left school and joined General Motors and have been on the line since then. Yes, I could have, but I chose otherwise. Kids today do not have that choice. They are told right in first-year university to expect to have at least seven different careers! Did you ever hear that? Help them if you can no matter how old they are or how well they are doing now. Even if they are doing well now, that news can change in a heartbeat for all of us. Deep down inside you know that. Help them if you can. After all, they are still your kids and still your eternity.

You need a will for your wife or husband too. If you both die together without a will it will be a mess. If you split up remember to change you will or else you may leave all your assets to your ex!

Here are some steps to help you get organized to make your will:

1) **Make a list of what you own**. It doesn't have to be an exact list but list the big things like houses and cottages, land, rental properties, business interests, RRSPs or RRIFs, non-registered investments, boats and life insurance policies. Also add the things you really care about like grandmother's wedding ring or granddad's favourite fishing rod and reel.

113

2) **Decide who will look after the kids if you both die prematurely**. Don't think it can't happen. Read the newspaper any Monday and you'll see someone or a couple who die in some car accident or worse. Bad things do happen. In most of Canada, this position is called the legal guardian and in Quebec it is named "tutor." The simple thing is to use your parents. Don't jump to that conclusion too fast. Think about their age and health, their interests, their location, and their other responsibilities.

   Discuss this responsibility with the individual before you write up your will. Are they willing to accept responsibility? Name a backup just in case your first choice is not around when needed. Get all the addresses down clearly and ask them to let you know if they move.

3) **Who will be your beneficiaries?** When you are thinking what to give to all your beneficiaries, think about what they like. Make a list of who gets what and include in that list charities and/or organizations, if you want. Want to leave something to your old school? Make a note of it in the will. Make a special note of any unusual instructions: "To my nephew Harold, who always knew the value of a dollar, I leave a dollar. And to my niece Alice, who loved my Volkswagen as much as I did, I leave her my Volkswagen and enough money to buy 10 more if she wants ($280,000)." Something like that. Get your lawyer to help you. Most will do a simple will for $150 or $200 or if more complex up to $1,000. Don't rush this task. It can save you money if you have the answers to all these questions before you see your lawyer. Here are some questions to ponder:

   a) What will happen to your children's inheritance if your spouse remarries?

   b) If you have children from a previous marriage, what will they get if you leave it all to your second (or third, fourth, latest) spouse?

   c) What happens if your children die before you or your spouse do?

   d) What if your married children divorce? Will the former spouse be written out of the will automatically?

   e) If you are married, have a good talk with your spouse about how you want your assets divided. You may choose to leave everything to each other. Then decide what happens if you both die at the same time.

f) Think about who gets some of the small but special things: that painting, that sketch your son did, the stamp collection that belonged to your aunt. Deciding now will save disagreements later. Make the distribution to your children as even-handed as possible.

g   Can your family really manage your affairs? Do you need a trust company or advisor to handle the estate on behalf of the family?

h   Do you have any special requests for your funeral? I know people who do not want formaldehyde put in their veins when they are dead. Things like that. Better tell people close to you if you have such a request. The will may be read after you are buried. I heard of a case where a man asked not to be cremated but buried in a certain spot. The family didn't know what to do with his ashes. Tell people what you want to happen.

4) **Minimize your Estate's taxes**. Arrange your affairs to keep the income taxes and capital gains, and probate fees as low as possible. You can do this by naming your spouse as the beneficiary on your registered assets (your RRSP or RRIF). When you name them and not "estate" you can take advantage of the spousal roll-over, which is tax-free from the first spouse to die but does not apply at the second death.

Will you leave enough money to wind up your affairs?

The government believes that we all run around and sell all our assets the day we die. They say we are "deemed" to have sold everything and some things are subject to capital gains taxes at the second death. Things like the family cottage and rental properties fall into this category, but not the family home. This is a good place to use permanent insurance. Take care of the big capital gains tax on the second death by buying last to die permanent insurance (whole life or universal life) to cover the estimated tax.

If your estate is large or complicated, it's a wise idea to get professional assistance. A good place to start here is with your advisor or your lawyer.

5) **Decide who will handle all the details**. This person is generally called the executor. Sometimes this person is referred to as the liquidator or estate trustee. The executor's job is quite onerous. They have to handle all the details involved with winding up your affairs. There is a lot of paper work. Chose someone who has the inclination to handle detail. Is this person trustworthy? Does he or she have a good business sense? Do they live nearby? Do you

trust them today? How old will they be when you die? (You have to estimate here.) Do not use your stock broker because that could put him or her into an awkward conflict of interest situation and most brokerage firms will not allow that relationship except for family ties.

Chose a second executor in case the first choice has moved far away or has died. If you choose a friend, ask them first, because being an executor is a tough job. Sometimes it is best to appoint a family member and a trust company. The family member knows your wishes and the trust company knows the latest tax issues and the law. If there are no friends or family members that fill the bill you can use a trust company as your executor.

6) **Look your plan over again.** Let your first plan sit for a week or so. Then sit down and look at it again. Does it need revision? Are you truly happy with it? Are you really being fair? Do you want to be fair? Revise your plan as necessary. Then go and see your lawyer. You have done a lot of the work already and you have saved some money.

7) **Give a copy to your executor.** Let them know where they can find the original if they need it. Give a copy to your lawyer and your executor and your alternate executor. If you change your will, make sure that you replace all the copies with the new will.

8) **Then sit back and feel good.** Having been to the lawyer's office you can now sit back and feel good about what you have done. You have tackled a tough task and done it. Pat yourself on the back.

Some people never get around to this. Some die so unexpectedly that they do not have a will. Either way, dying without a will is called dying intestate (see Chapter Nine). Don't let that happen to you. Get that will done now.

The High Cost of Divorce

16

DIVORCE IS about the worst luck a man or a woman can have in life. Divorce is the number one problem for people everywhere in Canada. I mean from an investment and insurance point of view. Divorce costs all of us (and I must include myself).

Consider that over half of marriages end in divorce. Some individuals are divorced two and three times. Each divorce makes the lawyers rich and makes all of us a great deal poorer.

A lady I know is getting a divorce from her husband after a 23-year relationship. She told me that so far she has spent $26,000 with her lawyer and the two sides have only "agreed to disagree." She still has to go to court and that will cost about $7,000 a day. Multiple her experience across this nation and you can see why I claim that divorce is a huge drain on the Canadian economy. That is except for the lawyers who also spend money so the money goes around and the economy keeps going. Let me revise that statement: it does not hurt the Canadian economy but it surely hurts over half of Canadians who lose a fortune getting rid of the special one they married so many years ago.

In the last book of the Old Testament the bible quotes God as saying, "I hate divorce says, the Lord God of Israel" You can find that in Malachi 2:16. I think I understand why God hates divorce; it tears families asunder and tears their investment plans and future to shreds. So why do half of us do it?

I know that sometimes it just has to happen. I know your divorce was like that and so was mine. It got to the point where his or her _____, _____, and _____ was too much. I'm sure that most people feel that way. We had to divorce but we are all still part of the problem and not the solution.

If you are divorced what can you do now, financially? In part that depends on which side you are on. When I was divorced my lawyer advised me to get the best settlement I could since if it went to court the man almost every time gets the worst of it. He told me that the courts in Canada are the most one-sided they have ever been now regarding divorce. Men get the short end of the stick. I got a deal but it was very expensive. I know there are always two sides to every story and I suppose divorce is no exception.

My advice if you must get divorced is to have as much information as possible before you see a lawyer. Get a book and do it yourself. I remember I got a book written by a lawyer. The book gave me the forms I needed to get it started. I printed those off after I had filled them in. I then went down to the courthouse and consulted about the best move. Later, I carried my own separation papers to the courthouse and saved that way too. In the end I needed my lawyer, but I know I saved thousands doing most of it myself.

Two of the books I found useful are:
1) *Divorce Guide for Ontario* by Sandra J. Meyrick, LLB. Published by Self-Counsel Press, legal series. I used the 17th edition.
2) *Ontario: Marriage Separation and Divorce* by David I. Botnick, LLB. Published by Self-Counsel Press, legal series. I used the 10th edition.

I used those books extensively. If possible, I recommend you do too. Now there are some very complex divorces involving children, foreign property and investments for those you need a good lawyer. Even in these complex cases reading beforehand will give you the power of information. The more we know about divorce the better it will be for us if and when we go through it. For example, the courts will always decide in the best interest of any children. Know that and use it.

What does a simple divorce cost? Botnick says that most lawyers charge between $400 and $800 for an uncontested divorce with the average being about $500. I had an uncontested divorce and it cost me several times his high estimate. My lawyer charged $300 an hour. The real cost of a divorce is splitting homes that are paid off; splitting investments that took years to build up. That is why I say that divorce is the greatest cause of poverty in Canada.

Every lawyer is bound to tell the warring couples about mediation. My ex and I tried it and found it was easier to go around the corner to Starbucks and make a deal. If possible, make your own agreements without involving your lawyer. Reserve the right to review your deal with your lawyer for his or her comments. The more you do yourself, the less time you use up. Lawyers have nothing to sell but their time and they charge for every second you and I use. Keeping that time to a minimum saves us all money.

As a result of a recent Supreme Court decision whatever deal you make with your ex can now be overturned some time in the future. That is bad law, but the precedent is in the books. Do you remember the poem called the Ancient Mariner? In his classic Samuel Taylor Coleridge (1772 – 1834) has a dead albatross around our hero's neck for years. He can't take it off. Mr. Coleridge was a prophet. Be aware we can never really get away after all. Here is a small part of this great poem.

"From the Rime of the Ancient Mariner"

Part One (in part)

At length did cross an Albatross:
Thorough the fog it came;
As if it had been a Christian soul,
We hailed it in God's name.

It ate the food it ne'er had eat,
And round and round it flew.
The ice did split with a thunder-fit;
The helmsman steered us through!

And a good south wind sprung up behind;
The Albatross did follow,
And every day, for food or play,
Came to the mariners' hollo!

In mist or cloud, on mast or shroud,
It perched for vespers nine;
Whiles all the night, through fog-smoke white,
Glimmered the white Moon-shine.

"God save thee, ancient Mariner!
From the fiends, that plague thee thus!--
Why look'st thou so?"--With my cross-bow
I shot the ALBATROSS.

Part Two (in part)

And I had done an hellish thing,
And it would work 'em woe:
For all averred, I had killed the bird
That made the breeze to blow.
Ah wretch! said they, the bird to slay
That made the breeze to blow!

Nor dim nor red, like God's own head,
The glorious Sun uprist:
Then all averred, I had killed the bird
That brought the fog and mist.
'Twas right, said they, such birds to slay,
That bring the fog and mist.

And every tongue, through utter drought,
Was withered at the root;
We could not speak, no more than if
We had been choked with soot.

Ah! well a-day! what evil looks
Had I from old and young!
Instead of the cross, the Albatross
About my neck was hung.

And much later in the poem the Albatross fell off. Will people who divorce today have their albatrosses fall off one day?

Part Four (in part)

Beyond the shadow of the ship,
I watched the water-snakes:
They moved in tracks of shining white,
And when they reared, the elfish light
Fell off in hoary flakes.

Within the shadow of the ship
I watched their rich attire:
Blue, glossy green, and velvet black,
They coiled and swam; and every track
Was a flash of golden fire.

O happy living things! no tongue
Their beauty might declare:
A spring of love gushed from my heart,
And I blessed them unaware:
Sure my kind saint took pity on me,
And I blessed them unaware.

The self same moment I could pray;
And from my neck so free
The Albatross fell off, and sank
Like lead into the sea.

Something happened to me one day on the way … it was a bright summer morning, I was out door knocking about 10:00. I walked up to a wooden house with a green porch. I knocked briskly and stepped back the required eight feet. There was a scurry and a flurry behind the green door. I stayed back eight feet, there was someone there and they would answer the door soon. I waited less than minute. The door opened and a pretty little red-faced young women slipped out, closing the door behind her.

"Good morning" I said, "I'm David Campbell with Edward Jones."

"Oh she said, "I'm Susan and we are just back from our honeymoon." She was suddenly uncomfortable; something in her clothing was bothering her. "We're just back from our honeymoon", she repeated.

Finally I figured it out and asked her if that was so why did she answer the door? She looked at me and gave me a wink and darted back inside.

Disability Insurance

17

THIS IS important insurance for the self-employed people in Canada. People who work for companies may or may not be covered, and even if the company does cover you the coverage may be, and likely is, quite inadequate. Check your benefits book. You may be surprised.

Did you know that:

- One person in three will be disabled for 90 days or longer before they are 65? Think about that - one in three for over 90 days. Look at the people you work with. They did this to us at university when we were freshman.

"Look at the person on your right. Then look at the person on your left. Then look at yourself – one of you is not going to graduate from this university." It did work out that way. The girl on my left did not graduate and my wife and I did.

Disability insurance is the same. Look at your co-workers: one of three is going to be disabled for at least three months. For critical illness the stats get worse:

- One in two men and one in three women will develop heart disease in their lifetime.
- One in 2.5 men and one in 2.8 woman will develop cancer in their lifetime.

Will you be the one? Will I be the one? Time will tell. What can we do about that today?

Of course you will be the lucky one. It will never happen to you. It only happens to other people, right? I had that thought when I was younger, but now that I am a little older and a little wiser I do not share that opinion. It can and will happen to most of us. What can we do today?

As a business owner or employee your business and your livelihood depend on your being there ready and able to work every day. You expect to grow your business.

As an individual we too expect to grow. We expect that our income and our expenses will rise with time. In both cases, this happy scenario can be shattered in a second. One drunken driver, one moment of inattention on the highway, one slippery sidewalk, one space toilet seat flying down and hitting you on the head. (Ref. *Dead Like Me* a witty TV show). It can happen in a second.

The next thing you know you are injured and are in hospital. It has happened to people I know and people you know. What can we do today?

We can buy disability insurance. Here is how it can be used:

- **Pays a monthly benefit.** If you are injured or disabled, a disability policy can pay you a monthly benefit. You use this to pay your bills and look after your family. Some of the corporate plans are built to a price-point and do not pay very much. They are no use after you leave the company. Check your benefit book.
- **Business Overhead Protection**. Disability insurance pays a monthly benefit to help cover business expenses like rent, salaries, hydro and property taxes.
- **Partner Buy-Out.** If your partner gets injured you have several problems: lost effort and productivity, lost profits, increased workload for everyone else, pressure from creditors, possible damage to customer and supplier relationships. You may need to hire replacement workers while your disabled or critically ill partner recovers. You may even end up in future partnership with his wife or her husband. Not ideal is it? Partner Buy-Out insurance, a use of disability insurance, provides funds to buy out your disabled partner's share of the business.

Premiums are based on the type of work you do, where you work, your age, the insurance company's experience with this type of work and so on. As well, each company does it their way. You have to check.

This is a short chapter but a large subject. The odds are not good for any of us. So please check your benefit book and if you have inadequate disability insurance fix the problem, call your insurance agent for a quote. Much better insurance may not cost too much. You may be surprised.

Diversification 101

18

DON'T PUT all your eggs in the same basket is an ancient lesson. Why? We all know that if you slip you can lose all the eggs at once. Investing is a little like our basket of fresh eggs. If you invest in only one part of the economy you may go down when that part of the economy goes south. If you spread your investments over mutual funds, stocks, bonds, real estate, Registered and Non registered, some gold and some private mortgages (the kind you give, not the kind you get) then you can say you are well-diversified. But most of us are not that diversified. We own our homes and some investments in mutual funds and the odd stock. The average Canadian family has their home (with a mortgage) and about $80,000 in RRSP contributions and that is all.

In most cases the mutual fund manager is fulfilling his or her mandate. Be sure you are aware of the mandate of the fund managers you are investing with. That means where or what are they allowed by their firm to invest in? Are they to invest only in the Far East? If so, these mutual funds should only occupy about 2% of your portfolio. A good rule of thumb is that no investment should occupy more than 5% of your portfolio. It follows that most people should stay away from stocks and bonds until they have at least $100,000 invested. That means that with a $100,001 portfolio you can buy a stock for $5,000 and it is still less than 5% of your portfolio. Before you have $100,001, that $5,000 purchase would put you over the line.

Here is the main reason you should spread your investments over many asset classes. Can you tell me the best asset class in the last 20 years? Here they are – pick the winner if you can.

1984 – Foreign Equities +15.1%
1985 – Foreign Equities +65.1%
1986 – Foreign Equities +67.8%
1987 – Foreign Equities +17.6%
1988 – Emerging Market Equities +28.7%
1989 – Emerging Market Equities +60.1%
1990 – Canadian Bonds +7.5%
1991 – Emerging Market Equities +59.3%
1992 – US Small Caps +30.1%
1993 – Emerging Market Equities +82.3%
1994 – Foreign Equities +14.5%
1995 – U.S. Large Caps +33.9%
1996 – Canadian Large Caps +28.4%
1997 – U.S. Large Caps +39.1%
1998 – U.S. Large Caps +38.4%
1999 - Emerging Market Equities +57.2%
2000 – Canadian Bonds + 10.3%
2001 – U.S. Small Caps + 8.7%
2002 – Canadian Bonds +8.7%
2003 – Canadian Small Caps +46.3%
2004 – Emerging Market Equities +16.8%

Can you pick the one winning asset class?

What were the worst asset classes in that same 20-year period?

1984 – Canadian Large Caps +2.4%
1985 – Canadian Bonds +21.2%
1986 – U.S. Small Caps +4.4%
1987 – U.S. Small Caps –14.4%
1988 – Canadian Small Caps +5.5%
1989 – Foreign Equities +7.6%
1990 – Canadian Small Caps –27.3%
1991 – Canadian Large Caps +12.0%
1992 – Foreign Equities – 3.0%
1993 – U.S. Large Caps +14.7%
1994 – Canadian Small Caps –9.2%
1995 – Emerging Market Equities –7.8%
1996 - Emerging Market Equities +6.6%
1997 - Emerging Market Equities –7.7%

1998 – Canadian Small Caps –21.5%
1999 – Canadian Bonds –1.1%
2000 – U.S. Large Caps –28.2%
2001 – Foreign Equities –16.4%
2002 – U.S. Large Caps –23.1%
2003 – U.S. Large Caps +6.2%
2004 – U.S. Large Caps +2.8%

If you compare the lists you begin to see many of the same asset classes on each list. What does that tell you? Don't try to pick the winners - you can't do it.

In fact, if you just picked last year's winning asset class and invested $10,000 a year in that strategy over 20 years you would have invested $200,000 and have $521,601 at the end of 20 years.

If, however, you took the opposite strategy and invested in last year's loser you would have invested $200,000 and you would have $599,247 after the last 20-year period. That's better by $77,646!

But if you have invested across the Asset Classes prudently, you would have invested the same $200,000 and now have $622,720. That's better by $101,119 (Thanks to Franklin Templeton Investments for the above information).

As for Morningstar ratings of mutual funds, even that respected firm's ratings are not that sure. Yes, they get it right very often but I recall one year - if you had invested in their five top five-star funds you lost money badly. If, however, you had invested in the five two-star funds and ignored the low Morningstar rating you would have come out far ahead. I tell you this story to stop you from investing in any investment just because a rating service or a newsletter says you should.

Read widely and get a good conservative broker is still the best advice. He or she will know the great value in diversification and will steer you in the right direction. In the end, you must decide what to invest in. It's your money and you must take that responsibility.

Diversification is the best way to benefit from the two most important investing goals:

1) **Protection from undue risk**. By investing across asset classes you can manage portfolio risk.
2) **Participate wherever growth happens**. Because no one can reliably predict the markets, diversification ensures that you are constantly exposed to the top performing asset classes.

One thing about investing you have to be cold blooded to take advantage of the market. What I mean is that people get emotional about their investments and that causes them to make the wrong decisions. This is often described as an emotional roller coaster ride. If we are a little cold blooded and not on this roller coaster we will do much better. For example, we are happy when we buy the mutual fund and then it drops and we are sad. Instead of saying, "it has gone down - let's buy more," we want to sell. When the mutual fund has flown up, and we are happy, then we want to buy more, just when we should hold on and even take some profits. If we do it backwards, it is small wonder that we do poorly in the market. Get a little unemotional about it and buy when they are down. There is an old broker story about when a client is mad enough at him or her to toss a brick through the window; just remember wrap it up in a cheque as you heave that brick.

When you do sell, you have to make two decisions not just one. Before you yell, "sell" make sure you know a better place to invest the money. If you are worried about the market, you may leave your money in cash for a while but not for long. Money, like people, should be working.

Chapter Forty Five expands on this topic with Advanced Diversification. Those are strategies for the sophisticated and knowledgeable investor. Ideally, this investor is a person who has done all these things and has money he or she will not use in this lifetime.

Investing wisely in Stocks

19

THIS CHAPTER will look at the right way to invest in stocks. It will not tell you which stock, bond or mutual fund to buy right now. I will name a good stock or two later because I want to make you see your broker for timely advice. What are stocks? Stocks are common or preferred shares indicative of ownership in that company. If you are a shareholder you are an owner. You have the right to attend shareholders meetings and vote there. You can also usually vote by phone or over the Internet. Preferred shares pay dividends, and in liquidation, rank ahead of common shares. There are usually vastly fewer preferred shares on the market than common shares. Preferred shares pay regularly but do not experience the rise and fall of the common stocks. Invest in common stocks to make money and in preferred shares to keep it.

Capital Gains Tax

This is a good spot to talk about capital gains tax, as you pay it on gains in the stock market. These taxes are on financial gain on a property that when sold will lead to a increase in value or capital gain. Contrast that with business income. The capital Gains tax works like this. Suppose you invest in a stock at $10 and keep it for a while until it reaches $18. Then you sell it. You have gained $8 and now owe capital gains tax on a portion of your earnings. First reduce the amount by 50% to $4. This amount is included in your income statement on your taxes in that year. In other words, the $4 is taxed at your marginal rate.

Your marginal tax rate is the tax on the last dollar you earned in that year. For example, if you are living in Ontario and earn $70,000 in 2005, how much tax would you pay on one more dollar of income? The answer is 26% federal tax and 11.16% from Ontario that is 37.16%.

While we are on the subject of taxes, it is a good strategy to keep your gains as capital gains and your losses as business losses. Business losses are deducted directly whereas capital gains are taxed after the 50% reduction.

One of the best books on stocks, in my opinion, is Jeremy J. Siegel's *Stocks for the Long Run*, third edition, published by McGraw Hill. Jeremy Siegel has amassed 200 years of financial market returns. Once you read it you might want to only invest in stocks. That would be unwise, especially if you have less than $100,000 to invest. In fact, remember to stay away from stocks until you have $100,000 to invest. You should be diversified over at least 20 stocks and with less than $100,000 it is hard to get that kind of diversification and have a reasonable number of shares ($5000 per stock).

Here is another reason you shouldn't invest only in stocks. From 1966 to mid 1982 the stock market was negative because of Vietnam, baffling inflation, and the OPEC oil embargo. It was all those things and others, such as raising the baby boomers (our Dads and Mums had no money left to invest after my new bike and my sisters' new frocks and the famous orthodontic dentist). What if you had invested in 1966 and had the patience to wait until 1982? I mean the market went nowhere all those years, but if you stayed in the market you did very well. In 1982, inflation ended and interest rates fell sharply, and the stock market began its greatest bull market in history. With a sharp correction in October 1987, the stock market surged to new highs. From a beginning at 790, the Dow Jones Industrial Average hit 1,000 in December 1982. It surged to 3,000 just before Saddam Hussein invaded Kuwait in August 1990. After his sound defeat, the stock market ran up even higher. It was at 3,000 again in March 1991, and in 1996 broke through 6,000! Despite much professional nay saying, the Dow Jones surpassed 7,000 in February 1997 and 8,000 by July of that year. In March 1999, the Dow crossed 10,000 and hit a record high 11,722 on January 14, 2000. The bull market appeared to be unstoppable but that was not so. Alan Greenspan, Chairman of the U.S. Federal Reserve called it, "irrational exuberance" in a speech to the annual dinner of the American Enterprise Institute in Washington on December 5, 1996.

That should have cooled our collective jets but it didn't. Remember that his words slowed the market down for a few days but then it surged right on through seven and eight thousand. More than 1,300 technology companies went public between 1995 and 2000, according to Thomson Financial. The world seemed in a mass daze about tech stocks. In retrospect, it was a mania like the famous tulip craze in Holland 200 years ago. Some of these tech stocks had no products, no capital, and no prospects, but they had a great name and some hope attached to them. I remember hearing that people will buy pet food on the net and that pet foods stores were doomed. Nonsense! Would you order a large bag of dog or cat food to come by the mail or Fed Ex? The shipping charges on a 25 kg. bag would wipe out any savings. The Internet business model was hard to figure out at first on the net. eBay went through it's own teething troubles but now works well. It was hard to sort out the winners from the losers in the tech market because there was so much hype at that time.

There are many investments newsletters to help here. Some are OK but make sure they are not telling you to buy something they have an interest in. The good ones are really worth reading. But keep in mind that these sheets go to thousands of people and the stock market rewards those who get in there first. After a good new stock hits the street it is too late - the smart money has already cashed out. That is aggressive advice and is best for risky start-ups, IPO's (Initial Public Offerings) and "investing on rumour and selling on fact" ideas, which should only occupy a small fraction of your portfolio. The vast bulk of your total portfolio should be invested in conservative safe solid companies. See your conservative broker for these.

Dividends

These good conservative companies will pay you dividends on an annual or semi annual basis. Dividends are cash paid to shareholders by mature companies that are not spending that portion of profit on expansion or new equipment. Dividends are better than interest payments because of the way they are taxed. The expression is that dividends are "tax preferred." While interest is taxed the same as salary or business income, dividends are taxed differently, and that works out better for you.

This is how dividends are taxed. It is peculiar but here it is: Dividends received by individuals from Canadian corporations are taxed in an odd manner, designed to reflect the fact that the corporation paying the dividend has already paid tax on its profits. The amount included in your income is "grossed up" to reflect the total amount of pre-tax income the corporation is assumed to have earned. You will then receive a tax credit to offset the tax the corporation is presumed to have paid (at about 20%). There is no effort to find out if the corporation made a profit or not.

Canadian dividends received are grossed up by one-quarter (25%). You add 25% to the amount received and show this total as income from dividends on your tax form. The offsetting federal dividend tax credit is then two-thirds of the amount of the gross-up – two-thirds of that 25%, or if you prefer, 13.33% of the total you reported as dividend income. Provincial tax systems have similar tax-credits. In Quebec a separate dividend tax credit is available for 10.83% of the grossed-up dividend. The exact number differs from province to province. I'd check with my accountant.

Note that dividends from foreign companies are taxed just like interest. Preferred shares pay dividends rather than interest and so they may offer a better after-tax rate of return than many interest-bearing investments. Major corporations that issue preferred shares cannot guarantee these dividend payments; however, most well managed firms will pay these important dividends to the preferred shareholder even when they are operating in the red. The common shareholders may not be so lucky.

Sometimes a corporation will pay stock dividends by issuing new shares. You gross-up these dividends just like the cash dividend and apply the tax credit in the same manner even though you did not receive any cash. The amount of tax payable is based on the increase in the paid-up capital from the new shares.

Also a private corporation as opposed to a public corporation may issue capital dividends. They are tax-free. A capital dividend is usually a distribution of the untaxed one-half of capital gains. As we saw in the discussion of capital gains tax that portion of capital gains is not taxed at all. The capital dividend is used by private corporations to distribute the untaxed fraction with no tax issues for the shareholder.

Here is a comparison of how each asset class is taxed. Let's assume that we have $600,000 and we are earning 5% or $30,000 on each of the asset classes. How much tax is payable?

Investment Type	Annual Tax Payable
Bonds - Simple interest	$10,500.00
Stocks - Dividends	$5,630.63
Stocks and Real Estate - Capital Gains	$5,230.00

When you are older than 60 consider not holding any stock that does not pay a dividend. Cash flow from your investments should be king. If the stock doesn't pay income don't invest in it.

Keep as much of your investments as possible in Capital Gains. You will pay far less tax. Even bonds, which pay interest, can be in a Corporate Class income fund; in this format the gains are capital gains and are taxed accordingly. Consider this form of fund for non-registered assets. More on Corporate Class funds in Chapter Twenty-One.

DRIPs

Large corporations often offer dividend reinvestment programs. These are fine to invest in and are often a tax effective way to build your investment portfolio. DRIPs give shareholders the opportunity to automatically reinvest their dividends into common shares. Usually these shares or fractions of shares are purchased at a discount to the market price. Many of these plans permit you to purchase additional common shares and pay little or no fees at all. Keep in mind that you will be paying taxes on the dividends in the current year even though the income was directly invested in common or preferred shares. Another good thing about these plans is that as you add common shares through the DRIP program you are increasing the cost base of your investment, which will affect the average cost of the shares for capital gains purposes when you sell.

Remember stocks are a good thing to invest in but they are not the only thing.

Investing wisely in Bonds

20

BONDS ARE the opposite of stocks. With stocks and mutual funds of stocks you buy the investment and take your lumps and rewards. With bonds it's different; you lend your money to the company issuing the bond for a certain length of time. Your money grows at a predicable rate and the company pays you interest two or four times a year. When the period of time is over you get all of your principal back. Sounds ideal? Yes, except when you have to sell a bond early. Then, it depends on where the bond is on the market.

To be clearer, let me explain the life of a bond. All bonds when they are first issued are issued at par. Par is when $100 cash buys exactly $100 of the bond.

Once a bond is issued it trades either above par (over $100) for example, at $102.35 or below par, for example at $98.50. When you see a bond listed in the newspaper it reads with its price as the bid and ask prices and it reads whatever it is versus par. Today, a Bell Canada bond maturing on December 15, 2009 is listed as $126.86 for the bid price and $127.44 as the ask price. That bond is trading above par by quite a margin. On the other hand, some bonds will trade at a discount (that means a discount to par). Let's look at the listings again in the newspaper.

Most newspaper bond lists have eight headings. The headings are: Issuer, Coupon, Maturity Date, Bid Price, Ask Price, Bid Yield, Ask Yield and Yield Change.

The **issuer** is the government or corporation that issued the bond. For example, bonds can come from the Federal Government, provincial governments, large corporations and large banks.

The **Coupon** is the original interest rate the bond was issued at. For example, Bell Canada wants to raise some money so they issue a 5.5% bond at par. The coupon rate is 5.5% when the bond is at par; the interest rate is the same. Note, please, that the rate of yield is determined when you buy the bond and does not change over the life of your bond. The same bond bought a month later will have a different price and therefore a different yield (see below). If the bond is trading at a discount, you will really get more if you hold the bond to maturity, because you bought it at a discount and a bond must return to par on the maturity date. Yes, that means that even if your Whooping Fog Hole bonds were trading at $88.45 the day before maturity, they must be paid out at par at maturity. Of course, this example would never happen, as the market would have priced it at par or almost at par for weeks before maturity.

The **Bid Price** is the highest price that buyers are offering for the bond. When you buy a bond at your broker's office you either pay the market rate or you offer a lower bid. The bond floor traders will usually accept your market bid immediately and your lower bid may not be accepted at all "depending on the market". Usually the Bid price reflects the market.

The **Ask Price** is the lowest price that sellers are willing to sell the bond for.

The **Bid Yield** is the yield of the bond at the Bid price. What is yield? Good question.

Yield is the measure of the return on an investment and is calculated as a percentage. A stock yield is calculated by dividing the annual dividend by the current market price of the stock. For example, a stock selling at $25 with a dividend of $2.50 per share yields 10%. A Bond yield is a more complicated calculation, involving annual interest payments plus amortizing the difference between its current price and the par value over the life of the bond.

If you want to know at what interest rate the bond will pay always look at the Yield.

The **Ask Yield** is simply the yield on the asking price of the bond.

The **Yield Change** is the change in **ask yield** from the previous day's trading close.

Bonds are priced in a way that at first seems a little odd until we see the interaction between prices and yield. This is important so be sure to understand it. **When the price of a bond goes up, the yield of that bond (what you actually get) goes down. Conversely, when the price goes down, the yield goes up. It follows that when you buy bonds at a premium (above par) you will get a yield less than the coupon rate (the rate the bond started out with). Further, if you buy a bond at a discount (less than par) you get more at maturity.**

Suppose Bell Canada issued a ten-year bond at a coupon rate of 5%. When that bond was first issued it was a 5% bond with a par price of $100.

When the price goes up to $102 then the yield will drop to less than 5%. You have paid more and get less. If the price of this bond drops to $98 the yield will be above 5.00%. You have paid less and get more. Of course, ask yourself why the price is dropping. The ups and downs of good quality bonds are usually in relation to the interest rates of the day. In fact, interest rates drive much of the entire investment world. That is why traders are nervous when interest rates are going up. That is why the stock market falls at the same time. When interest rates are low, the economy works better. When interest rates go up, it puts the brakes on the economy. That lever is the way the central banks attempt to control inflation (see Bernanke Chapter Forty Four).

Strip Bonds

A strip bond is a good type of bond for a RRSP. Strip bonds get their name not from Sally Rand or Gypsy Rose Lee but from the old habit of stripping the coupons from the bonds. In the early part of the last century, the individual was well off if he or she was "in Florida clipping coupons."

Today that can be misconstrued but back then it meant clipping the coupons that used to surround bond certificates. The coupons were worth X dollars and you simply clipped them when the date came due and mailed them to your broker in New York. He would send you the interest money. Now it all happens by computer and electronic deposit, but it is still the same system. Strip bonds are simply bonds without coupons. Strip bonds pay you no interest on the usual twice a year pattern. Strip bonds grow by accumulating the interest and paying you the principal plus all the interest when the strip bond matures. These bonds can be used to plan for a large purchase on a certain date. For example, you may want to buy a motor home in 14 years. When you invest in a strip bond you know the exact maturity date. These bonds are great for planning to pay tuition expenses for your children. Buy an 18-year strip bond when your child is born and the money will be there when you need it. These are best used within a RRSP or RESP since the interest growth is not taxed.

If you buy them outside a registered plan you will have to pay taxes on the growth of the bond every year even though you did not receive the money. I call that "Phantom Taxation." Taxes are bad enough without "Phantom Taxation." However, if this were not the case, you would face a large capital gains tax at maturity. The other down side to strip bonds, and really all bonds these days is that we are at 40-year low interest rates, this is not the time to buy them. When rates pick up look at bonds. They are a safe investments. Generally the greater risk is in long-term corporate bonds. Will General Motors or Bell Canada be there in 28 years? For long-term bonds consider provincial or federal bonds. Ottawa will still be there in 28 years. Alberta and Ontario will still pay the interest every quarter in 28 years.

How do you buy bonds? Usually bonds are sold at a $5,000 minimum with only even thousand dollar increases after that. For example, you can buy $6,000 or $10,000 or much more but the minimum at most firms is $5,000. Many firms do not sell bonds to the public. Most prefer to trade large bond orders between firms. Often insurance companies buy large orders of bonds. One company that does sell bonds to the public in Canada is is Raymond James. I have sold millions of dollars of bonds in the last few years. Other few brokers sell to the public but many don't. I work at Raymond James Ltd. and I know we have a good selection.

Stability Rating Companies in Canada

There are two main companies that rate bonds in Canada. Use both and you will get a good sense of how strong the company that issues the bond is. One is the Dominion Bond Rating Service and their bond scale is from AAA to D. It is a bit like being back at school. AAA is very very good and Ds, well, I think you know. Here is the whole scale in detail:

AAA Long-term debt rated AAA is of the highest credit quality. Few firms rate this high, only the federal government rates AAA and that is likely because of their power to tax.

AA is of superior credit quality. Ontario and Alberta are good examples. They may differ from AAA only slightly. Most good firms are rated AA.

A means satisfactory credit quality, but these bonds may be affected by adverse economic conditions and have greater cyclical tendencies than higher rated securities.

BBB means of adequate credit quality, Bombardier bonds were BBB. This is the lowest rating for bonds called "investment grade bonds."

BB long-term debt is speculative and non-investment grade. Companies rated down here have little access to capital markets. In many cases the companies here are too small. This is the beginning of the Junk Bond level.

B long-term debt is considered highly speculative with a reasonably high level of concern as to the ability of the entity to pay interest and principal over the long term.

CCC or **CC** or **C** Companies rated down here are in danger of default and the situation is more severe than B. Sometimes these ratings are all the same with CCC used for the more senior debt of the beleaguered company.

The Rating system used by the CBRS Canadian Bond Rating Service is a little different but does the same task. Here is how they look at various types of investments:

Commercial Paper and Short Term Debt
Highest Quality A-1 +
Very Good Quality A-1
Good Quality A-1 (Low)
Medium Quality A-2
Poor Quality A-3
Rating Suspended (judgment deferred)
Un-rated

Long-Term Debt Rating (Government Debt)
Highest Quality AAA
Very Good Quality AA
Good Quality A
Medium Quality BBB
Lower Medium Quality BB
Poor Quality B
Speculative Quality C
Default D
Note CBRS uses (+) and (-) designations to indicate relative strengths within a rating category.

Long-Term Debt (Corporate Debt)
Highest Quality A++
Very Good Quality A+
Good Quality A
Medium Quality B++
Lower Quality B+
Poor Quality B
Speculative Quality C
Default D

Rating Definitions for Investment Funds
Superior Quality AAAi
High Quality AAi
Medium Quality Ai
Low Risk BBBi
Moderate Risk BBi
Speculative Ci
Rating Suspended (judgment deferred)

Preferred Shares
Credit-Enhanced Preferred Shares P-1+
Highest Quality P-1
Good Quality P-2
Medium Quality P-3
Lower Quality P-4
Poor Quality P-5
Rating Suspended: Suspended

The term suspended indicates that the company is experiencing severe financial or operating difficulties and the outcome is uncertain.

If you want to invest in bonds but can't right now invest in bond mutual funds. Often insurance companies have good bond funds as insurance companies understand bonds. I hope after this little Bond 101 you will understand them better too.

Investing wisely in Mutual Funds and Segregated Funds

21

IF YOU have less than $100,000 you should invest in mutual funds. Investing in mutual funds also works well if you have more than that and want to invest in a specific market sector like the Far East. We don't have the time to really understand all the market sectors. We can invest with good fund managers who do know these markets.

What are mutual funds? Most people I met thought they were different from stocks.

"Us? Oh, we never invest in the stock market; all our investments are in mutual funds."

A mutual fund is like a pizza. You may laugh at my simile but think about how a pizza is made. You can order pepperoni, ground beef, onions, and green peppers, anchovies, etc. on your pizza. Imagine, if you will, that all of the ingredients in your pizza represent different companies. There is the Paterson's Pepperoni Company, The Ground Beef Firm, Onions Growers and Packers International, Green Peppers and Alfalfa Sprouts Inc. and Anchorage Anchovy Limited. When the pizza is delivered you see that it is divided into slices. Each slice gets some of each ingredient or some of each company in this example.

So Mutual Funds are like a pizza in that you get a little bit of the many firms' shares in each fund. You buy units in the funds and each unit has all the holdings or names that the fund holds. This is a great example of diversification.

What mutual fund companies should you invest with? I said earlier that I would give mainly general advice. It is wise to stick with the mutual fund firms that have been through the ups and the downs of the market.

Financial Navigation

That means that the firms have been around a while. In Canada, we cannot invest in U.S. firms unless they open a branch office in Canada. Among Canadian Funds, I support ABC, AGF, AIC, Aim - Trimark, CI funds, Elliott and Page, Mackenzie, North West and Phillips Hager and North funds. Good American fund companies that can be purchased in Canada are Hartford and Putnam funds.

Canadian mutual funds I do not recommend are from banks. There is too much bad investment advice given out at banks by untrained people who are moving from branch to branch or get canned every other month. You can't go back to them and complain.

What I mean here is the advice from banks to buy GIC's even though the rate of return is minuscule. Or to invest in bank funds outside of an RRSP before you have maxed your RRSP. Nonsense. I heard all of these examples today. In one case, the woman had $19,000 in RRSP available room and $14,000 in a non-registered account at the bank. The difference in the taxes will diminish the non-registered account by almost half and the RRSP will not pay taxes until it is taken out years from now – when she turns 69, 29 years from today. She will transfer it as soon as possible and transfer the whole account from the bank. I heard this story from my colleague across the aisle. He told me that our job is to rescue investors from bad advisors. I could not agree more.

Remember to buy mutual funds across different asset classes. Have some global, some Canadian, some balanced, some growth, some growth and income, some income and some bond funds. Make sure that your funds do not match each other. I remember two Trimark funds that were almost the same. Buying both was not diversification but both did grow well under one very good fund manager.

Another key point that I will develop in greater detail later in this book is the whole notion of negative correlation. Make sure your mutual funds do not go up and down at the same time together. That is the recipe for volatility and that is the factor that drives us all a little crazy. Funds that do not go up and down at the same time are negatively correlated. There will be much more on this later, but for now have some growth funds and some income funds as a start. That is the general idea.

Tax Advantaged Funds

Do you recall the chart earlier that compared the taxes paid on $600,000 earning 5% and paying $30,000 per year in a non-registered account? I have revisited it here:

Investment Type	Annual Tax Payable
Bonds - Simple interest	$10,500.00
Stocks - Dividends	$5,630.63
Stocks and Real Estate - Capital Gains	$5,230.00

These tax-advantaged funds are fairly new to the market. They are worth looking into especially if you have a large mutual fund portfolio. Most mutual funds are structured as a trust that holds the investments. When the typical fund does well it distributes the gain to the unitholders in the form of more units. So your holdings grow BUT you pay capital gains taxes every year on the growth. After a while, the government's hand in your portfolio may get tiring.

If so, consider the tax advantages of Corporate Class Funds. These are now available from many fund companies. Mackenzie has the most experience with them. Besides the three main tax benefits (below) they have a unique feature that allows you to keep third party funds in your Corporate Class holdings. For example, suppose you really like an ABC fund. It has been good to you and you've held it for years. You want to maintain that fund. Ok fine. You can add that fund to your holdings within the Corporate Class Funds. This change is effective June 2006 so if your broker is not familiar with it tell him or her that it is coming. Right now Quadrus has this feature. Here are the three distinct tax advantages of Corporate Class funds. I will quote from a Quadrus brochure to get it correctly:

"1) The freedom to switch or rebalance among the funds without immediately triggering taxable gains or losses. When you sell one fund to buy another in Quadrus's tax-advantaged structure, **capital gains are not immediately triggered**.

2) Potentially lower distributions in any given year. The fund investments will result in gains and losses, interest income and normal fund expenses. The corporate structure allows the different funds **to pool all income with expenses** for tax purposes and all investment gains with investment losses for tax purposes, to potentially reduce the taxable distributions to investors in any given year.

3) Tax-effective income. By managing the amount of interest income the corporate structure earns and by investing part of its fixed income fund in derivative securities, investors in Quadrus tax-advantaged funds **earn capital gains or dividend income – even from the fixed income and cash management classes**. Capital

gains and dividends are more favourably taxed interest income which means lower taxes and higher after-tax returns for you."

I like these funds especially as I said for the holder of a large mutual fund portfolio. Saving tax on $1,000 is nice but doesn't mean much. However, saving tax on $500,000 or $1,000,000 can be significant.

Transfer-Out Fees

When you want to move or rebalance the account you and your broker should be able to move the holdings around within the same mutual fund company with no charge. However, if you want to transfer out of your mutual fund to another mutual fund company or to buy stocks or bonds, you may pay a fee. How and when you bought the mutual funds will determine the transfer out fee.

You can buy mutual funds front end, back end, low load or no load. When you buy them front end, you pay a 2% to 5% fee at the time of purchase. That gives you the right to move your fund out whenever you want with no exit fees. Usually paying when you buy the fund is less in total than paying the same percentage when you sell it; (one hopes and expects) the percent fee will be on more money.

If you buy it back end, you only pay when you take the money out. Here the transfer out fee depends on how long you hold the mutual funds. The longer you hold them the lower the fee. Here is a standard scale used in the industry for back end fund transfer out fees:

First Year 7%
Second Year 6%
Third Year 5%
Fourth Year 4%
Fifth Year 3%
Sixth Year 2%
Seventh Year 1%
Eighth Year and beyond transfer out is free

Make sure you buy your mutual funds wisely if you buy back end. You don't want to have to transfer out and pay fees too soon.

Low loads are not bad as they often reduce the seven-year waiting period if you want to switch out. As for no load funds, I would avoid them. No load often means no service. I know that planes can fly without a pilot. He or she is there for the rough parts. They take off and land and if something goes wrong I want someone skilled at the helm to solve it. I only want managed mutual funds. Are all no loads unmanaged? No, but they do not get the service and top drawer managers as do other funds that support the company's bottom line.

MERs

Something that you should watch with mutual funds is the Managed Expense Ratio or MER. This is the cost to run the fund. This pays for the manager and the analysts and the profit margin on the fund. Look for MERs in the 1% to 2.5% range. Note that rate of return of a mutual fund is calculated after the MERs have been deducted. People will pay more attention to MERs when the return rates are low. My advice is to watch them whenever you are thinking about buying a mutual fund and make that rate part of your decision.

ISC's

These are something new from Morningstar. It is a rating to be given to all mutual funds to discern if they are closet index funds and just how far from an index each fund rates. To explain this properly, an index fund is simply a fund that matches the growth or decline of the Toronto Stock Exchange or the New York Stock Exchange. The problem is that most funds do not match the index in the majority of years. Some managers duplicate the stock exchange and that is called mirroring. If they are mirroring the index that fund is really an Exchange Traded Fund, which charges MER's. Morningstar's new rating will at least point out which funds are really just closet index funds.

Like most things in life there is a flip side to this idea. A score of less than 7 is an index fund in disguise. A score of less than 10 is a sector neutral fund (that means that they have not over-weighted any sector of the market like resources, gold or the banking sector). A score of 10 to 25 indicates a fund that is different from the index but still sector neutral. A score of between 20 and 40 is the best spot to be in. This is a fund that can beat the index and is not taking too much risk. Funds with scores of 70 to 90 are taking too much risk. They will be sector funds like resources or gold. Fine, have them in your portfolio, but limit them to less than 5% of the whole. When your broker recommends a fund ask him or her what the ISC score is. That may rock them a little.

Dollar Cost Averaging

The best way to invest in the stock market is still dollar cost averaging. Here is how that proven system works. Suppose our friend Charlie has $500 to invest each month. He wishes to invest in the Mackenzie Ivy Growth and Income fund, for example. He will tell his broker to remove $500 from his chequeing account on the 15th of every month. It's funny but when you assign a definite sum to investing you don't seem to miss it. It just becomes a natural feeling to be investing in your future every month. It's paying yourself first.

Our friend Charlie invests and in the month of January he buys 25 units of the fund because the price of each unit is $20. In February he again invests $500 and that month be buys 22 units because the price has risen to $22 per unit. In March, he again buys 22 units, as the price is the same. In April the price has dropped so Charlie's $500 goes further. He buys 28 units since the price has dropped to $18.00. Note that there was some change left over at most of these buys. Some companies will just add the odd change from last month onto this month's contribution. Check with your broker. If you see that there are some odd bits of cash building up in your portfolio just tell your broker to invest that change every six months.

The whole point of dollar cost averaging is that you buy fewer units when the price is high and more units when the price is low. It follows that your average cost of the units over time will be lower. It is a system that makes you sort of perversely happy when your mutual fund stumbles. You can buy more units. Any system that can give you joy when your funds are down is a good system. Dollar cost averaging works for stocks, all mutual funds and segregated funds.

Dollar Cost Averaging Can Work Against You

However, please note that when you are retired and taking money out of your built up investments, then dollar cost averaging works against you. Think – you will be taking more units out when the mutual funds are low and less units when they are higher. So your total goes down faster. When you are withdrawing, if you take out a steady amount it can work against you when you are withdrawing.

The solution seems to be to take a different amount out each month. Say 10 units per month, and as the units vary in value, so varies your payment. That may be alright if you can live with a bouncing ball but most of us want something more dependable in our old age. Here is another strategy that I will call the "world's smallest lock idea."

Years ago my wife and I lived in northern California in a development called Bel Marin Keys in Marin County north of San Francisco. This development of fine homes was great as over half the homes were on the lagoon. This lagoon was kidney-shaped and not that deep. We would race Laser sailboats around a point of land across from our home. You could not see the boats when they were around the point. But if we tipped over we couldn't keep it a secret since the top three feet of the sail would be brown with mud. We would stick the mast right into the bottom. But here is the idea. The lagoon was washed every high tide and new water flowed in through the world's smallest lock. It was 12.5 feet wide and just 30 feet long. I brought a 65-foot sailboat through it by opening both ends at the high tide and riding the high wave in.

Now what does this have to do with a strategy? Well patient reader here it is:

Have your investments in a balanced fund with some conservative and some more aggressive funds. Fine, let that grow, but don't take the money out of that account every month. Let that account be like San Peblo Bay, it is rough and wide and is an offshoot of San Francisco Bay. Let it go up and down. Then once each year take a lump sum out of the main account about the size of 12 monthly payments and put that into a money market fund – from the rough bay, through the world smallest lock into a calm lagoon.

Take the money out every month from the money market account that is growing slowly, but steadily. That way you get a steady income and your funds get a chance to grow every year. You can avoid the flip side of dollar cost averaging.

I realize that the total fund is reduced by a total of 12 monthly payments and that this smaller base will not grow as fast. However, if this really effects your nest egg, perhaps the real problem is that your nest egg is too small. It takes a lot of money to retire. We all have to save to have a good retirement.

Segregated Funds

These funds are similar to mutual funds but the differences are worth considering. They are usually offered by insurance companies only and offer guarantees that mutual funds cannot. For example, segregated funds offer a maturity guarantee, a death benefit guarantee and offer some protection for creditors.

Here is the quote from a typical Segregated Fund Information booklet.

Under the heading Maturity Guarantee it reads: "On the maturity date, we'll pay you the greater of:
- the market value of all your units less any withdrawal fees; or
- the maturity guarantee of your policy based on the basic amount provided you first purchased investment funds 10 or more years before the maturity date.

For the following policies, the maturity value is guaranteed to be not less that 75% of the basic amount:
- non-registered policies if you first bought investment funds 10 years or more before the maturity of the policy;
- RRSPs purchased with 10 years or more before the maturity of the policy;
- LIFs (Life Income Funds) registered outside British Columbia, Manitoba, Nova Scotia, Quebec and New Brunswick if you first bought investment funds 10 years or more before the maturity of the LIF. (Life Income Fund – see Appendix I - Alphabet Soup).

There is no maturity guarantee for any RRIF, LRIF, or LIF, which does not have a maturity date.

If you first bought investment funds in an RRSP less than 10 years before its maturity date, there is no maturity guarantee unless the RRSP is converted to a RRIF on the maturity date of the RRSP. The maturity date of the RRSP is December 28th in the year the insured person turns 69. If you do convert to a RRIF, the maturity guarantee benefit under the RRSP does not apply upon the transfer of the RRIF but applies on December 31st of the year the insured person turns 80. For such a RRIF, the maturity benefit is guaranteed to be not less than 75% of the total of all amounts used to buy units in the RRSP (not the market value that was transferred for the RRSP to the RRIF) minus a proportional reduction for any units sold from both the RRSP and the RRIF. We calculate the proportional reduction for the basic amount."

Are you clear now? Basically the maturity guarantee is whatever the basic investment has grown to, called the market value, or at least 75% of whatever you invested. Your risk is limited.

The next guarantee that segregated funds have over mutual funds is the Death benefit. Quoting from the same information folder:

Death Benefit Guarantee

"We make a one-time, lump-sum payment of the death benefit if there insured person dies before your policy matures.

We make this payment to the beneficiary of the policy. If the is no beneficiary, we make the payment to you, the policyholder or to your estate.

The death benefit is the greater of:
- the market value of all your units; or
- the death benefit guarantee

The death benefit guarantee depends on the age of the annuitant when the contract was issued. If the annuitant was:
- under age 80, it's 100% of the basic amount
- age 80 and over, it's 75% of the basic amount.

We do not deduct early withdrawal fees for the basic death benefit.

If you have a RRIF and your spouse or common-law partner is the beneficiary, instead of receiving a one-time lump-sum payment, you may choose to have your spouse or common-law partner become the policyholder and insured person of the policy and continue to receive the regular income payments. In this case, we will pay the death benefit on the death of the final insured person.

Once your policy matures, the death benefit guarantee no longer applies."

The segregated fund is really good if you buy it before you are 80. Then the insurance company will pay the market value or if the funds were down your beneficiary would get 100% of the basic amount.

The MER's are higher on segregated funds because of the costly guarantees. Make sure that the guarantees are worth the extra fee to you. When you buy segregated funds you will receive a contract and a prospectus and a disclaimer form. Read this over – it contains good information. For example, the MER's will be quoted there. Also you'll find out about distribution and lots of other things. After that just file it, sit back and enjoy the ride.

Regarding the creditor guarantee, a segregated fund cannot be taken away in bankruptcy court. There is a caveat to that statement. If you buy the segregated funds knowing that you are going bankrupt you will get no creditor protection. The test is owning them for two years before declaring bankruptcy.

Again the best-segregated funds come from the best-known insurance companies. I think the reason is that big firms can hire the best managers and the good ones don't stay long at the smaller firms.

Income Trusts

22

WHEN I worked at Edward Jones they had a prohibition on selling income trusts. Edward Jones is very conservative and they felt that the income stream was too risky. I respected that and did not sell any of these trusts. I watched from the sidelines while my clients bought them elsewhere and got some stellar yields. That was when the prices on income trusts were down and the yields, of course, were up. Income trusts were fairly new then and nobody had much experience with them. They are still more risky than a government or quality corporate bond.

But for those who can stand a little risk I would recommend them now with the caveat that I would only suggest the ones that have a solid proven and sustainable income stream. That would leave out income trusts based on a small oil company, for example. If they have a few producing wells they are vulnerable. An oil well can run dry without notice. The expression is "depleting resources." That means your income trust could dry up as fast as a few old oil wells could stop producing.

One could question the motivation of some company owners who have converted to income trusts. They get a sudden increase in the value of their firm at the moment of conversion. On an income trust, the money is sent to the unitholders before taxes are paid and before dividends are issued. The company is now valued on a pretax basis instead of a post tax basis. It can give the firm a lift of 35%. Beware of those sudden valuation increases. It is all some investment banker's number manipulation and does not represent a sharp increase in the real value of the firm.

About 95% of the profit is sent out to the unitholders. I wonder about another issue: If 95% of the profit is going out to unitholders what is left to reinvest into the company? Will these firms suffer from corporate neglect in the future?

Income trusts react to price the same way a bond does. When the price is high the yield is low. When the price falls the yield goes up. That's important to understand. Price and Yield work together inversely. The pressure on yield from brokers who sell only yield to the exclusion of other important factors has led some income trusts to borrow money from banks to make the yield payments to subscribers. This is not a long-term strategy. Other important issues that should be looked at are the same for any stock: Price to earnings ratio, leverage, and barriers to enter the same business. Not to mention the strength of the business in the long term. It should be noted that some income trusts like REIT's and royalty trusts borrow as a standard part of their business model.

Income trusts are issued by companies that have a stable income stream, and have had that over many years; these "cash cows" are being converted into income trusts at an alarming rate. Some of these companies are not ready to become an income trust.

On the TSE, 45% of the income trusts are based on oil. That is a disturbing dominance. If the price of oil keeps on going up fine and good, but if the price of oil falls your income trust based on oil will drop in value. Remember an income trust is as risky as stock in the company. It's not really a fixed income investment.

The rule: **If you would not invest in the company's stock, then do not invest in the company's income trust.**

The reason people hold them is simple. When the banks are paying 1.8% and the Canada Savings Bonds paying a little more, people ask, "Where are the safe investments that can give me more income?" Enter income trusts. They pay income in monthly or quarterly cash distributions. When you buy an income trust you are buying a stream of income at a certain yield. The price of the unit could fall but as happens with bonds that will not affect your income. The only way to lose money is if you sell the income trust early or when the price is low or when the company has bad news.

The best ones are from pipelines, real estate, and gas companies. They have steady stable demand for their services. Those income trusts are safe; the companies will be there for years to come.

Here is the rule again: **If you would not invest in the company's stock, then do not invest in the company's income trust.**

Are they really safe? The name is so comforting. It is a Spin Doctor's dream. Think of it: INCOME and TRUST. Isn't that just so perfect? But the income is risky and the trust is all on your side. IF you buy an income trust, please understand that you are really buying a risky stock! The performance of the income trust depends on the performance of the company.

Halifax Terminals lost a large client that represented 50% of their profit. Their income trust value dropped by half. Now, they repaired the damage by doubling the units each client held but could a smaller company make it all right?

Another example, Heating Oil Partners Trust filed for bankruptcy protection on September 26, 2005. It is rather shameful being the first trust to do this; their trouble was a result of high oil prices after hurricanes Katrina and Rita.

Another reservation: The stability ratings that come from Standard & Poor's and the Dominion Bond Rating Service have only a few years experience. Compared to bonds, income trusts ratings are unproven.

Here is how the income trust ratings work:

Standard and Poor's

SR-1 highest
SR-2
SR-3
SR-4
SR-5
SR-6
SR-7 lowest

Dominion Bond Rating Service's

STA-1 highest
STA-2
STA-3
STA-4
STA-5
STA-6
STA-7 lowest

Trans Canada Power LP is rated STA-1; Pembina Pipeline Income Fund is STA-2 low; H&R Real Estate Investment Trust is STA-3

A recent change has made income trusts more attractive. Previously, if the company behind the income trust ran into trouble the people holding the trust units were liable. Now, legislation has solved that and trust holders are treated like shareholders.

In the last decade global property stocks (REITs or Real Estate Income Trusts) have out-performed global equities and bonds. Will they continue to win? As we saw in the Diversification chapter (Eighteen), last years winners seldom repeat. Nevertheless safe income trusts are a good spot for some of your hard earned investment cash.

Other real estate income trusts that are good right now are Corminar, CREIT, First Capital and Primaris Reit.

As we are going to press, Precision Drilling Corporation, PD/TSX, a Bay Street darling stock, has just announced that they will convert to an income trust. An article, in the *National Post* September 8, 2005, noted that Precision Drilling paid $131,000,000 in annual taxes. In an effort to cut that deep tax hit, the managers have elected to go this route. This could open the floodgates on this strategy. One good thing I see is that Precision will distribute 70% of its cash flow to unitholders and keep the remaining 30% to fund growth and capital spending. That sounds much better than 95%. At present, Precision has 229 drilling rigs and plans to add 20 or 30 in the next two years. They are a large company with a large number of rigs to keep busy. I think this is a good one. But keep in mind that this is was cyclical stock and it will be a cyclical income trust. That means it will be more volatile than an income stock such as bank or insurance company. As an income trust, it will have a rough ride at times.

The other thing is that Precision Drilling was at the cusp of being a huge Canadian International Company; however, to convert to an income trust they had to sell all their international positions. That is a high price to pay for converting to an income trust. At times like this, with oil flying high, it should do well. Get in early and see your broker and get his or her advice.

More late breaking news: Gordon Nixon, President of the Royal Bank mused the other day about converting part of the bank into an income trust. This is speculation, but that so scared the government at the possible loss of all the tax dollars contributed by the banks that they quickly shut down the income trust window for a few months by refusing to give tax advice to potential income trust converters. I've never seen our Liberals move so fast as when they think their tax influx will be sharply less. With huge surpluses, why attack people's income? Can we count on these people for much needed tax relief?

Apparently Canada figured the Liberals out. We wisely dumped them and put Mr. Harper on a short leash for the time being. I have hopes he will turn out to be a great leader.

As I am editing Stephen Harper is in his early days as our Prime Minister. He promises to do better - I hope he does it.

Inter Vivos Gifts

23

INTER VIVOS gifts simply mean gifts you give when you are alive. The opposite would be testament gifts; these are gifts left in your estate and delivered via your will. So when you are alive you may want to give an asset like a rental house or a stock portfolio to a son or daughter. Can you just do this and avoid all taxes? Think about that for a second. If that were true, then we could simply pass the investment assets to the kids before we die and these assets would never be taxed.

That sounds like a fine plan to me even if it is a little utopian, but the Federal Tax people beg to differ. The fundamental idea is that you give away assets so they are not part of your estate when you die and you eliminate the capital gains tax and probate on these assets. If there is any possibility that you may need the asset, do not use this strategy. It is irreversible. You need to have a substantial net worth in the first place.

It's best to quote the Income Tax Act. In "paragraph 69 (1)(b) where a person gives (or sells at less than its market value) a capital property to a non arms-length person (that means a family member) the transferor is deemed to receive proceeds of disposition equal to the property's fair market value."

Generally any accrued gain will be hit by capital gains tax. Here is how the deemed distribution rules should not be a problem:
1) * The gift is to the transferor's child but consists of farm property to which the farm rollover applies. This rollover permits a transfer of farm property from one generation to the next thereby keeping the farms of Canada going. (Why can't they think like this for the rest of us?)
2) The gift is to the transferor's spouse.

155

3) The gifted property is the principal residence. The child must live in the house.
4) The gifted property consists of cash or near-cash assets.
5) The gifted property is a capital property and has not increased in value.

To insure the gift follows common law it must meet these requirements:
1) The donor must be capable of making the gift. The donor must be mentally competent and of the age of majority.
2) The person receiving must be capable of taking the gift. In the case of a minor the gift is valid unless the receiver on reaching the age of majority rejects the gift.
3) There must be a clear and unmistakable intention on the part of the donor to irrevocably divest him or herself of the title, dominion and control of the gift.
4) There must be a delivery of the gift by the donor to the receiver.
5) There must be acceptance of the gift by the receiver.

There are specific methods of making a gift of capital property. Assuming a competent donor and recipient and the donor has an intention to give, there are three main procedures by which a gift inter vivos may be made.
1) By deed or other instrument in writing: a gift can be made by way of written deed of gift. A written formal deed of gift is the usual method of gifting land. No particular form of deed is required, although the transfer of land will require a formal written documentation under provincial land transfer legislation.
2) By delivery in cases where the recipient of the gift admits delivery. The simplest case of a gift inter vivos is the delivery of a chattel accompanied by words of gifting. The most obvious case of delivery is physical delivery, but in some circumstances constructive or symbolic delivery is sufficient. Thus chattels in a warehouse may be delivered by handing over the key to the warehouse. An automobile may be delivered by giving a bill of sale or a transfer of the ownership certificate. Shares may be given by depositing them with an agent with instructions to register them in the recipient's name and hold them for the recipient.
3) By declaration of trust: a gift may be made by the donor declaring him or herself to be a trustee of either a legal or equitable interest in property for the beneficiary. The declaration of trust need not

be formal, but for the sale of easy proof it is advisable to have it duly executed and witnessed. Once validity is established, the trust binds the property and the beneficiary receives an equitable interest therein.

* Thanks to the Estate Planner's Handbook, Robert Spenceley. Published by CCH 2002. I quoted Pages 52 & 53.

After that I think we all need a little story. That's right, it's time for a little scary story about human greed. **Yes a funny thing did happen ....**

When I was at Edward Jones we were all called to a sudden meeting at one of the local Toronto hotels. The word came at 8:30 a.m. to be there at 1:00 p.m. and if necessary, cancel or move any appointments, but be there at all costs. Needless to say I was there at 1:00. We were all warmly greeted and told to sit down somewhere in the large hall. The speaker got up and said, "Today you have been all called together and I'm sure you wonder why. You are all here because some of your clients hold Nortel. The aides will be handing out to you a copy of all the clients you have in that stock." Nortel had climbed to $108 at this point and looked like it was going to the moon.

We were then told to go back to our offices and to call every one of our clients and "tell them to sell. Insist they sell. Tell them that this stock is going to tumble and it's going to fall very very far."

I had about 30 of my more aggressive clients in that stock. I went back to the office, rolled up my sleeves and started calling. By 9:00 p.m. I had reached all but one. Everyone one of my clients told me that they liked that stock the best and that they would not sell. I urged them to sell, I got pretty firm until nearly all of them finally said, "David, it's my money and I'm not going to sell." My mother once told me that you could lead a horse to water but you can't make him drink." That night the *Toronto Star* ran an article entitled "Nortel to go to $200," nearly everyone told me about it.

Of the thirty clients, one lady called me the next day and said that she had thought about it and she was going to sell half her holdings. I sold them at $108.50 or so. I was glad I did.

A few weeks later, there was a loud honking noise outside my office. I wondered what was going on so I went outside to see. There was my client, a wonderful older lady, and her new car.

"This is my Nortel car!"

I admired her car and her wisdom and went back inside and called my clients who had Nortel again. I knew I was getting up their noses. But when Nortel fell they all came in and played back those phone calls with me.

"I remember you called. I lost ...."

They all remember. I wish I could have stopped Canadians across this land that day. But here is the sad truth. I didn't sell my Nortel either.

Exchange Traded Funds

24

HAVE YOU ever seen a day chart of the S&P 500 that looked like someone's hospital monitor after they had died? I mean a completely flat line.

Like this --------------------. There was such a day. On April 13, 1992, the New York Stock Exchange went brain dead at 11:44 a.m. Now people still traded that day in New York but because the futures market on Wacker Drive in Chicago directs the New York Stock Exchange; when Chicago went down New York didn't have a clue. Did you know that? To be clear, the Chicago Futures Market sets the tone every day for the New York Stock Exchange and the Toronto Stock Exchange gets its clues from New York. Shouldn't we be watching Chicago, too? Program trading comes from Chicago to New York to Toronto. Whenever you heard about large program trading driving the market up or down on a given day that started on Wacker Drive. On April 13, 1992 New York was brain dead while still trading because a massive flood had shorted out the Chicago Exchange and New York had no direction.

What are Exchange Traded Funds (ETFs)? They are portfolios of securities that trade like individual stocks. You can buy the whole stock exchange in one purchase when you buy a "spider," or a "cube" or "diamond." A "spider" is the ETF for Standard & Poor's Depositary Receipts and it represents a trust designed to match the performance of the S&P 500 index. Similarly a cube (QQQ) buys the top 100 firms on the Nasdaq and diamonds buy all the Dow Jones Industrial Average. These trade like regular stocks and have huge volumes. The bid and ask prices spread is usually only pennies.

They are not alone. Trading in similar funds called Index Futures dwarfs the volume of ETFs. Trading in Index Futures is often larger than all other trading on the New York Stock Exchange combined. In fact, ETFs

159

grew out of Index futures. You can buy Index Futures on the Chicago market. I do not recommend that because buying ETFs is much simpler and cheaper. More on Index Futures after we finish up discussing ETFs.

You can buy ETFs on the New York Market or Toronto market and hold them just like stocks. They are a good way to diversify your portfolio. Generally they trade for 10% of the cost of all the stocks averaged. For example, if you added up the stock prices of all the top 100 (in market size) stocks on the Nasdaq, then divided that by 10, that would be the price of QQQ.

They are different than mutual funds in several ways. One is that these funds can be traded at any hour of the day or night. The Globex futures market is open every weekday at 4:45 p.m. That is one half hour after New York closes. Globex does not have a location, no trading pit or any centralized trading area. It works on the Internet and traders can post their bids and asks directly. It is open all night and closes at 9:15 a.m., 15 minutes before the start of trading at both the Chicago trading pits and the New York Stock Exchange.

Have you ever wondered what the radio reports mean when they say, "trading was heavy overnight and it looks like the market will open higher this morning?" How do they know? From Globex and the futures market in Japan, Australia, India and China. If the Globex is trading above the fair market value of the index futures market, then the opening of the stock market will be trending up. Conversely, if the index futures market is trading below fair market then the opening will be trending down. Many financial news channels post the Globex trading in the early hours to keep viewers up to date before the market opens.

You can buy ETFs for markets such as Singapore, Hong Kong, Taiwan, Australia, and India. You can also buy many market sectors like oil, steel, or the TSE.

One good way to use ETFs is to hedge the market. ETFs are very tax efficient at hedging. Suppose you have a broad portfolio and you are fairly sure the market is going to go down. What should you do? You could just ride it out like a buy and holder or you could sell the stocks you hold. If you sold, you would trigger a capital gains tax issue and then buying them back at a lower price would cost commissions. Not a good option.

What is the best strategy? Buy ETFs short. That is, sell ETFs (that you do not own but borrow from your broker) equal to the value of the stocks you wish to hedge and keep in your stock portfolio. If you are right and the market goes down, you profit on the ETF's you shorted and that makes up the losses on your portfolio. If you are wrong and the market goes up, well, then the growth on your stocks is offset by the losses on the shorted

ETFs. It is called hedging the stock market risk and it is a way to protect your portfolio from wild rides up and down in the market.

One big difference between ETFs and stocks is that ETFs can be traded short if the market is falling. Stocks must be shorted on a market uptick and ETFs are not subject to this law. Another good thing about ETFs is that they cost very little to trade.

They do have one big disadvantage and that involves certain traders. If you try to predict the movement of the market and go in and out of ETFs you will win, far less often than you lose – it's a good way to lose a lot of money. Generally speaking, the fewer trades you do, the better you end up. Buying and Selling only makes the brokerage house rich. It's like sailboat racing – the fewer tacks and jibes you do the faster you will get to the finish line.

ETFs mirror the stock index they track. If your mutual fund manager cannot beat the index try using ETF's to do whatever the market does. They will ride up and down exactly like the market they represent. ETFs can be margined within the rules of your brokerage firm, usually up to 50%. They have many advantages and I believe they have a place in everyone's portfolio.

Now for a little bit more about Index Futures.

Futures Markets

25

THE FUTURES market that we use today began in Japan in the 1700s. It was used for the trading of silk and rice. In the 1850s the U.S. started using the futures market to buy and sell farm products such as wheat, cotton and corn.

The description and advice on futures markets is intended for Canadian farmers and producers of goods that need a way to hedge the risk of falling prices and use the futures market to do so. Speculators can also make large profits or lose enormous sums of money in this market. Unless you have a product to hedge, this market is very risky and not for the average investor.

Imagine you are a wheat farmer. (Some of us don't have to imagine; they live the following potential nightmare every spring). Our imaginary farmer decides to plant wheat in the spring. He has to know (or would sure as shooting like to know) what his price for the harvested wheat will be in the fall. If he plants in the spring and hopes for a good price, he could have a pretty grim next winter if wheat prices tumble. Or he could do very well if good markets for the wheat are established. There has to be a way to take away the guesswork and guarantee the wheat price in the fall at the time of spring planting.

Enter the futures market. The futures market uses contracts that are derivatives or financial contracts in which two parties agree to transact a set of financial instruments for physical commodities like our wheat in the fall. They agree on future delivery at a certain price. Hedging is simply guaranteeing a price in the future now. When you buy a futures contract you are agreeing to buy something that the producer has not produced yet for a set price. But does that mean that you must take delivery of the commodity? Luckily no, or else the awful vision of 1000 hog bellies arriving on your front lawn on a hot summer day could come true. Buyers and sellers in the futures market primarily use this market to hedge risk or speculate rather than exchange the actual end product.

Most investment advisors will tell you to avoid this market and I agree with them. It is too risky for the average investor. But let's go back to our wheat farmer, he has to enter into this market. He usually does it through the Canadian Wheat Board, although the usefulness of the board has been questioned in recent years.

The futures market in Chicago is the centre of all future contracts. There the trading of contracts between buyers and sellers occurs with lightning speed. The market is liquid (meaning that the money is there to handle buys and sells rapidly), risky and complex (imagine the tens of thousands of incoming orders to buy and sell). Let's look deeper into this wacky world on Wacker Drive.

The market works on an open cry or electronic bid system. The open cry is pretty much a thing of the past. (I'll miss it). The bids now come in from anywhere on earth and are matched by computer. The bids must state the price that will be paid for the product and the delivery date. I repeat just because you give a delivery date, don't worry about those high hog bellies on your front lawn. Most contracts expire long before the delivery date.

Our wheat farmer, if left to his own devices, without the help from the wheat board would have to find a bread maker somewhere to buy his wheat. Large bakeries are buyers on this market so many farmers do sell their wheat right here in Canada. Of course, tons of this life-sustaining product are exported around the world. In that case, you can see why a farmer would need to know his final price in the spring. Without that hedge, he is running the risk that there will be a no market for his wheat in the fall. Of course, by hedging, he is fixing the price at a certain level. If the wheat market takes off and prices soar he misses out on that action. In recent years, dreams of soaring wheat prices have been just that - dreams.

Before the futures market existed about 150 years ago, farmers would grow their wheat and bring it in wagons to the nearest market in high hopes of selling their crop. But with no idea of the demand, the supply often exceeded demand and the farmer went home very disappointed. Sometimes that crop just rotted. Then later in the season when the bakeries needed wheat they could not find it and the prices on bread and cakes soared.

The advent of the farmer's market in the 1850s stabilized the market. A central grain market and a central marketplace were created for farmers to sell their crops. Buyers knew where to find wheat and the system worked. These early contracts were the direct forerunners of the vast complex futures market we see today. Today, that marketplace works for Treasury bonds and securities futures. There farmers, importers and exporters, manufacturers and speculators meet in a complex marketplace. The Internet has made this market so much safer for a farmer. From Saskatchewan he can see a bid from India and he can match that bid from his den. That's a great leap forward.

Now here is the detail: In a futures contract there are two positions - the long position and the short position. The long position is the one who agrees to receive the product and the short position is the party who agrees to deliver the product. In our example, our prairie farmer would be short and the baker would be long. The key thing to remember here is that there are always two parties to a futures contact.

The futures contract contains everything: the commodity, price, and quantity, when delivered and how shipped. For example, 100,000 bushels of wheat at $4 a bushel shipped by train to Vancouver on Sept 1, 2006 and from there to Mumbai (Bombay) by Canadian Pacific ship.

When you are about to enter a contract on the market, the exchange will tell you what amount of money you have to put up. This is called the "Initial Margin" and it is a good faith amount that your winnings will be added to and your losses deducted from. Please note that "initial margin" is different than "margin" in the stock market. In the stock market, margin is buying stocks with borrowed money. In the futures market, it is the initial amount you will be asked to put down to place your contract. The ups and downs of your contract are posted daily. You know what is happening every day.

For example, if the futures contract for September 2006 wheat is $3.50 a bushel. If the price increases to $4, then the farmer has lost fifty cents a bushel and the baker's account has increased by fifty cents a bushel as he now has locked in the cheaper price of wheat. These positions will move this way and that over the life of the contract. In most cases, the farmer and the baker are only in the market to protect themselves from lower prices, in the case of the farmer, and from higher prices in the baker's side. In reality, most contracts close without delivery and both the farmer and the baker would sell and buy on the spot or cash market. Their profits or losses on the futures market help or hurt their final sale price or cost price.

If the market is extremely volatile you may be asked to increase your initial margin. These margins are under constant review. Don't be surprised if this happens to you. There is also a maintenance margin, which is the lowest amount your account can fall to without being replenished. If your account falls below that line you will be asked to increase your initial margin back to the original amount. If you get a margin call you must immediately deliver the funds to top your account up. Failure to do this will result in your brokerage selling your position to make up for any loses it has incurred on your behalf. You need to have a large amount of money to be in this market. I repeat. It is too risky for most investors.

Note that prices in the cash or spot market and the futures market move hand in hand. When a futures contract expires, the product is now valued at the spot market price.

The futures market is very useful to discover the future price. If you want to know what your wheat delivered in September will be worth, the futures market can tell you the value today. Could that change? You bet it could.

What affects the futures market? Just about everything: weather, politics, war, refugee requirements, floods, emerging countries, impoverished countries, bad debts and even land reclamation and deforestation.

The futures market tells us the sentiment of the market. Do most traders think China and India will explode with new vigorous growth? How does the high price of oil affect the market you are in? How does that effect your farm or business?

The market is so deep and diverse because information is coming in from around the world daily. A flood in Australia, Austria, or Albania or for that matter, Manitoba, can affect wheat prices dramatically.

In today's futures market there are two different types of entrants. One side is the hedgers and the other side is the speculators. Hedgers can be farmers, packers, manufacturers, importers and exporters. A hedger buys or sells in the futures market to secure a future price of a commodity that he or she intends to sell at a future date. This helps him protect against price risk. Hedgers are trying to secure the best price possible for their product. The futures market gives the hedgers price certainty when the contract is matched. This protects the hedger, our wheat farmer, from price volatility. It is intended to help him sleep better at night.

On the other hand, speculators do not aim to minimize risk, they seek to benefit from the inherently risky nature of the futures market. They try to profit from the very price changes that the hedger is trying to protect himself from. Hedgers want to minimize risk and speculators want to maximize risk to increase profits. In the futures market, a speculator buying a wheat contract low with the hope of selling it high would probably buy the contract from a farmer hedger who hopes to protect himself from lower prices. One of them will be right and the other wrong, and only time will let us know.

Perhaps a chart will help here:

	Long	**Short**
The Hedger	Secure a price now to protect against a rising future price.	Secure a price now to protect against falling prices.
The Speculator	Secure a price now in anticipation of rising prices.	Secure a price now in anticipation of declining prices.

Hedgers and speculators together make the market work. They both hope in opposite directions and there will be a winner and a loser. Usually, however, the closer the contract is to its expiration date, the firmer the data becomes. Right before the expiration dates the information will be quite dependable. That gives us an accurate reflection of market supply and demand and the price level.

I have warned you several times about the risk. Why you may ask? My warning is simply because you can make money, but you can often lose far more than you can make. Here is what I mean. Let's say that you have an initial margin of $5,000 and you enter into a long position in a futures contract for 30,000 pounds of tea valued at $50,000. That shows you the typical high leverage of this market. Highly leveraged contracts can give you one of two results: great profits or even greater losses. It is simply arithmetic. Due to leverage, if the price of the future contract moves up a little, the profit gain will be large in comparison to the initial margin. However, if the price moves down even a little the losses will be more than the initial margin. Here is an example: Suppose you enter into a future contract with an initial margin of $10,000 for an index of 1300. The value of the contract is 250 times the index. (e.g. $250 X 1300 = $325,000). With that leverage it means that for every point gained or lost is valued at $250.

If after a few weeks, the index rose 5%, to 1365 this would be a gain of $16,250 (65 X $250) or a profit of 62% (against the initial of $10,000). That is the result we want if we are long.

However, the same leverage can also work against you. If the index dropped 5% it would mean a loss of $16,250, which is much more than your initial margin. You would quickly get a margin call to pay $16,250 to repay the loss and replenish the initial margin. A few of those occurrences and many strong players are out of the game.

The good news is that prices on future contracts are limited in their movement. They can only move up or down one-quarter of a U.S. cent per day. This is known as a "tick." Suppose we have a futures contract on cotton for 3,000 bales. Every day that contract could move up or down $7.50 (0.25 cents X 3,000).

Like any regulation there are always unintended consequences. Future contracts also have a limit on their daily trading. It is the price change limit up or down. Our cotton could move up or down $7.50 with each day's losses or winnings added or subtracted from each account. If the trading gets near the daily price change limit the exchange will shut down trading in the commodity. That means if you want to liquidate a holding you may not be able to. That's another way to lose money fast in future contracts.

I remember when I first started investing I read a book by the late Dr. Morton Shulman called *How to Profit from Inflation*. The good doctor railed against playing in the futures market; he called it a fool's market place. Be careful, I think Dr. Shulman was right.

I was door-knocking one day and I met a man at the door who told me that he did not need my services because he was a futures trader. I let him brag about how much money he had made in the market. Then I asked him how many trades he had made to make that money and how he had fared on all his trades. There was an awkward silence.

Then he admitted that he had made 26 trades to date and that the first 25 had lost him money but he really made it big on the last one. I called him a year later and he was still at it. He was not any further ahead. For him it was a fool's marketplace.

Strategies for Futures Investing

I know I just told you that it is a fool's marketplace and it is. But that being said, there are Canadian farmers out there who have no choice about how to invest to protect their produce's prices. When you get down to the nitty gritty of investing in futures you are predicting the future value of an index or a commodity at some date in the future. There are three common strategies called 1) going long 2) going short and 3) spreads. Let's look at going long first.

Going Long

Going long is like a high school football quarterback in the huddle telling his favourite receiver to "Go long and I'll hit you." The boys hope for a touchdown.

When a Canadian farmer or a speculator goes long that means that he expects to profit from a rising price of the commodity. He agrees to buy and receive delivery.

Let's say the Speculator Tom Thomas is told that with an initial margin of $4,000 in March he can buy one June contract of gold at $350 per ounce for a total of 1000 ounces or $350,000. By buying in March, Tom is going long as a strategy and he expects gold to climb higher by June when his contract expires.

In May Tom notes that the price of gold has risen to $354.00 per ounce. He decides it is time to sell the contract in order to take his profit. The 1,000-ounce contract would now be worth $354,000 and his profit would be $4,000. Given the very high leverage by going long, Tom Thomas made $4,000 or 100%. Recall that his initial margin was $4,000.

Before you get to excited about the easy way to double your investments, what if gold had dropped to $346,000 on the 1000-ounce contract? This is only a drop of $4 an ounce. What then? Our speculator would have lost his entire initial margin and as his contract fell below the maintenance margin level he would have had to respond to several margin calls. Going long is called a naked strategy. So is the opposite, going short.

Going Short

Going short is, of course, the exact opposite of going long. Here Tom enters into a futures contract by agreeing to sell and deliver (vs. buy and receive). He is hoping to make a profit from falling prices. By selling high now, the contract can be repurchased in the future at a lower price, giving our speculator his profit.

Let's go short on oil. That is a risky idea now with oil shooting above $60 a barrel with predictions of $100 oil around the corner. But even the strongest tide has back eddies (that's where the tide moves against the main current). Let's say that George the Genius had concluded that all that stuff about China booming and needing lots of oil was all wrong and that the millions of cars that suddenly affluent Chinese will buy and drive will not even use oil. (Some people may even really think this way!) Ok, so George with an initial margin of $3,000 sold one oil future contract for May in November at $60 per barrel. The contract was for $60,000. By March, the price of oil had dropped at least in the short term to $55 per barrel. George was watching the price of oil like an eagle and decided to buy his contract back. The contract price is now $55 per barrel or $55,000. By going short he has made $5,000 profit.

However, what if the price of oil zoomed to $75 a barrel or higher. Invest in bicycles? George has lost his initial margin and had to endure margin calls. It would be painful.

Both Going Long and Going Short are examples of "Naked" futures contracts and they are the most risky contracts there are. There is a better way.

Spreads

Spreads take advantage of the price difference between two different contracts on the same product. Spreading is one of the safest strategies especially when compared and contrasted with naked futures contracts.

1) Inter-Market Spread. Here a speculator, with contracts for the same month, goes long in one market and short in another market. For example, long March corn and short March wheat.

2) Calendar Spread. Here the trader simultaneously purchases and sells two futures contracts of the same product, having the same price, but having different delivery dates.

3) Inter-Exchange Spread. Here the trader invests in a position in two different markets. For example, the Chicago market and the London market. (The Chicago Board of Trade and the London International Financial Futures and Options Exchange.)

I am not kidding about the risk of these strategies. They are not for everyone. I know I am repeating myself, but the risks are high and you can lose a lot of money. On the other hand, a few people do make very good money using these strategies. The key is to have enough time, attention and money to withstand the reverses.

Fortunately there are safer ways to invest.

Here are some options on how to trade futures:

1) **Go it alone**. As an investor you trade your own account without the help of a broker. You are responsible for managing your money, making trades, maintaining margins, getting research (from several sources) and analyzing the market yourself. You must have the time to focus on the market. I recommend you subscribe to several good newsletters in the market you are going to focus on. I would not follow just one man's ideas unless he had proven his acumen to me long before.

2) **Open a Managed Account**. This is similar to an equity account at a broker's office. Your broker has the authority to trade on your behalf following written instructions from you. This should lessen your risk but you are still responsible for any losses and margin calls. Plus you would likely have to pay a management fee. This could be a safer way to go. Be sure your broker is experienced and sharp.

3) **A Commodity Pool.** This is the safest way of all to invest in futures contracts. It has the smallest risk and is similar to a mutual fund. The commodity pool is a group of commodities that everyone invests in. You cannot have an individual account with the pool. You invest as part of a group. The funds are combined together and traded as one. The profits and losses are directly proportional to the amount of money you invested. Pools give you access to other products that you may not know enough about to invest in. You will not pay any margin calls. However the risks of commodity investing are still present even with a commodity pool. Ensure you have a skilled manager.

The futures market is not for everyone, but some people do make it work using the strategies above. If you want to know more, buy another book, on futures trading and after you read it, see a good broker. Or conversely, after you read it, put it on the shelf and never think of investing in futures again.

Options

But options are a little different. With good advice and lots of experience you can make a good profit. This is for more aggressive investors. Options consist of either puts or calls. Both of which need some definition.

A call option is: An option, which gives the holder the right, but not the obligation, to buy a fixed amount of a certain stock at a specified price with a specified time. Calls are purchased by investors who expect a price increase.

A put option is: An option, which gives the right, but not the obligation, to sell a fixed amount of stock and a specified price within a specified time. Puts are purchased by investors who think a stock may go down in price.

Please consider calling me. I have a Monday morning, "Campbell's Put and Call Option Service." It's a weekly option advice ser-

vice. **Early every Monday morning, I will send you an email with that week's option play. It is mainly large American corporations. You can sign up and then proof test it for a few weeks and then, when you see how good it is, start to trade. I hope you would trade with me. I charge for the service. Options are not for the faint hearted. Remember they are risky.**

How do I know which options are right every week? Call me and I will let you in on my method. Contact information is in the Conclusion.

What are Double and Triple Witching Days?

At times to the uninitiated, the stock market can seem haunted, especially on certain days. In medieval times, it was believed that little children out wandering about on their own could be snatched up by witches flying by on their broomsticks. I assume that is how these days got their name. I haven't heard these terms double and triple witching days for a while now but there was a time when the market would go through strange gyrations on one of these Fridays. It has to do with Index Futures.

Recall in the last chapter I mentioned the high volumes of index futures. All those contacts are based in the world of index arbitrage, which is the simultaneous buying and selling of stocks against futures contracts. These contracts expire on the third Friday of the last month in each quarter. That means the third Friday of March, June, September and December. On these days, the arbitrage boys and girls sell their future positions at the same time their options expire. That's two things expiring at the same time - futures and options. That is called a double witching day.

The plot thickens because on the third Friday of every month something else happens. The options on Index, commodity and individual stock options expire on these days. If we put the whole situation together we note that on the third Friday of the months above, all the future contracts, all index options, and all stock options, trade at once. The triple convergence has caused some spectacular gains and losses. The market can be quite volatile. That's a triple witching day.

If the incoming buy orders overwhelm the incoming sell orders the market will shoot up. If there is an imbalance of sell orders, the opposite happens.

The definition of a triple witching day is the third Friday of the last month of each quarter when future contracts, index options and regular stock options all trade at once. That happens four times a year.

A double witching day is the third Friday of every month when no future contracts are wound up and just the index options and regular stock options are traded.

The strange gyrations caused by these days have diminished substantially because the New York Stock Exchange requested that the Chicago Mercantile Exchange change their procedures. Now future trading ends with the close of business on Thursday and the contracts are settled with the opening prices on Friday morning. This gives the market specialists more time to find balancing bids. This change has smoothed out the entire process. It does show the power of the Chicago Mercantile Exchange. Because of that market, we just don't hear that much anymore about Triple and Double Witching Days.

Hedge Funds

26

IN 2005, the papers were filled with the Portus story. Portus was a "fund of hedge funds." The authorities are still investigating. It seems many Canadians lost their life savings. The money was sucked through 16 banks and got lost along the way. My sources tell me that a lot of those life savings ended up with one of the partners in Tel Aviv. That was nothing short of robbery on a grand scale. Portus had 26,000 investors and more than $730,000,000 in assets under management before being shut down in February 2004.

Manulife says they will make up the losses. Manulife didn't have to take the heat. They backed a bad horse but they shouldered the blame for all the losses. That was a noble deed indeed. I was proud of Manulife for the principled stand. However, many other firms sold those "funds of hedge funds" too. Recently, led by Berkshire Group, other dealers have created a large pool of cash to repay their clients as well. Good on them. The worst will come out in the press later.

Does that mean that all hedge funds are bad? No, any more than backing a bad horse makes all thoroughbred horses somehow suspect. A person's character is the key. The lessons are old ones: if it sounds too good to be true it probably is, and be careful about the people you go into business with.

However, some U.S. hedge funds have been run for years and are quietly making their clients large profits. The take-home pay of some hedge fund managers is stupendous. According to Institutional Investor Alpha magazine, the top 25 American hedge fund managers average income in 2004, was an amazing $251,000,000. That is 251 million dollars on *average* for the top 25 managers for the year 2004. Hedge funds are generally run by rich people for rich people. The authorities feel that these people should know enough about investing to not need regulation. Perhaps they should be more careful. Hedge funds can severely damage the whole market if they run amok.

What exactly is a hedge fund? A hedge fund is simply a private, largely unregulated pool of capital that can purchase stocks, sell stocks and do anything else it wants. The major investors are institutional investors such as company pension plans, union pensions and university endowments. These funds are useful. Are they right for Canadian investors?

According to the *New York Times*, there are 8,000 hedge funds in the United States and 40 percent of them have opened in the last four years. Business school graduates who once flocked to venture capital firms, private equity or dot.coms, now all want to work for hedge funds. It all seems a little too much, too fast.

This mania about hedge funds in the U.S. could end the same way as did the mania for mutual funds in the late 60s, or junk bonds in the 80s, or more recently the dot.coms of the late 90s. When the bubble bursts, some good ones will be left after the weak ones are weeded out. Right now I would not invest in any U.S. hedge fund - even if Canadian laws allowed it.

Like American dollar mutual funds, Canadians cannot invest in those U.S. hedge funds from Canada. In this case, that's a good thing. From up here it's going to be hard to pick the eventual winners. Like the dot.coms, there will be good ones left after the carnage to come. I understand the authorities wish to protect the local mutual fund and hedge fund industries.

Canada now has thousands of mutual funds and it is getting harder to find the clear winners here, let alone for American hedge funds. This time out I'm glad we cannot invest in American hedge funds. At least Canadians can sit this bubble out and be better off for the restriction.

That being said, American hedge funds do impact the Canadian market as they exercise such a huge impact on New York. When a number of hedge funds get excited about a certain stock they will together (of course unintentionally) bid that stock up. We can see the uptick and buy in only to have the hedge funds get out and collectively drive that stock down. Call it the hedge fund bounce. One wag likened it to an elephant jumping into your backyard pool. They jump in and lots of water splashes out. The level of the water rises and spills over the edge. When they climb up the ladder and get out of the pool, the water level is much lower.

The real reason hedge funds are booming is that institutional money is flowing into them. University pension funds by the hundred are investing in hedge funds. That goes for large corporate pension plans, too. How else do we fund the retirement of so many baby boomers?

Understand the North West Quadrant and its relation to the full Efficient Market Theory.

This hedge fund business began back in 1949, when a former writer for *Fortune Magazine* started up the first hedge fund. Alfred Winslow Jones started up his new business with $100,000 in capital and a new business model. His new idea was to invest aggressively while protecting his client's capital. At first glance, that seems quite contrary. Invest aggressively and protect capital? His idea was to have 40% of his investments going short and 60% going long. (If those terms don't make sense go back and read the last chapter). This gave Mr. Jones protection: when his longs went down, his shorted stocks held his investments up. It was brilliant and Jones made piles of money for his clients. Between May 1955 and May 1965, his hedge fund returned 670 percent, according to *Fortune Magazine*. He also kept his wealthy clients below 100 in number, which kept him from excessive regulation. His fees were 20% of any profit. He became very wealthy.

Hedge funds today still use his model. It has been proven to work most of the time. What happened in the late 90s when several very large American hedge funds got into big trouble was that they forgot to hedge. This scandal was called the LTCM Hedge Fund Crisis. The last great bull market lasted from August 1982 to March 2000. With every stock going up, it seemed like a bad idea to deliberately lose money going short. So they forgot to hedge and when the market turned south. Wham! They appealed for government assistance. It seems like a simple idea: Hedge funds should (wait for it) *hedge* their investments.

As an aside: That reminds me of a great California bumper sticker I saw last month. It reads "Please God just one more bubble."

Hedge funds are now paid on the Alfred Winslow Jones model: 20% of any profits with one addition: like mutual funds they are now also charging an additional 2% on assets under management. That's how they make such great profits. An $8 billion fund that gains 10 percent in a year and charges "2 and 20" has generated $320 million for its owners. An $8,000,000,000 fund that fails to make its clients one thin dime still makes $160 million on asset fees alone that year. Of course, if that year is repeated, clients and staff will head for the exits.

There are many different kinds of hedge funds; there are managers of hedge funds that only invest in various derivative securities, some only in distressed securities, some others that specialize in short selling and some invest in specific geographical areas. A few are market neutral (50% short and 50% long). However the hedge funds invest, the one thing they have in common is those incredible fees.

The dominant theory of stock market investing is called the efficient market theory. This theory is the foundation of many hedge funds today.

The father of this theory is Dr. Eugene Fama of the University of Chicago. He wrote a number of papers in the 60s and 70s that made his idea popular. He also noted that the theory needed to be tested.

They did test it. Looking at data as far back as 1927, Fama showed that if you divided the stocks into thirds and put the least expensive stocks into the "value basket" and the most costly in the "growth basket," they showed that the value stocks outperformed the growth stocks in *more than two-thirds* of the years. Does that mean that only investing in value stocks is a guaranteed way to invest? No, there are no perfect methods. Markets are really people investing and selling for all kinds of business and personal reasons. Fama did show that history was your friend if you invested this way. More importantly, he showed that if growth stocks went down, value stocks went up. Even if the overall market rose, value stocks still went up.

Recently Fama's theory has come into some question in academic circles. We have come to a better understanding of risk, they tell us. Now the newer theory shows that cheap will beat expensive more than it should according to the "efficient market theory." Another theory showed that a large group of diverse momentum stocks also outperformed the "efficient market theory". Why did that happen? One theory is that stock investors "over extrapolate". That is they know that some bad things will happen to value stocks at times so they do not invest in them at all. Also, they get more optimistic about growth stocks than they should and invest too heavily in them. Often enthusiasm will push a stock higher but when investors tire of it, the stock falls off sharply. Fama still clings to the efficient market theory saying that we need to measure risk even better.

Some hedge fund managers have found that within these theories there are little anomalies – that the efficient market theory is not perfect. Some hedge funds have built a good business by exploiting these anomalies. That perhaps is why no one really understands hedge funds investing. It is built on market models and powerful computers that find the up-to-the-minute data and buy growth stocks and also short value stocks that are about to fall. It all happens at the speed of summer lightning and it cannot be duplicated at home. It's a complex quantitative approach.

It is worth noting that this theory did not work during the tech stock and Internet bubble. At that time, expensive absolutely crushed cheap. But when the dust of dead dot.coms had cleared, the theory returned to form.

Sometimes a theory starts off strong and over the years gets so diluted and watered down though the telling that it comes down to a bare shadow of itself. This has happened in Canada with the Efficient Market Theory becoming simply the North West Theory. The North West Theory says that

we should invest in mutual funds or stocks that [a...] of a grid chart: If the y axis (going up the left s[...] the investment and the x-axis (going horizontal[...] resents **risk.**

The North West Theory is simply to inves[...] are low in risk and high in return. (DUH!). Fam[...] "efficient market theory" which is discussed in [...] Eight. That simplification is not the whole Effici[...] that Jones uses shorts and longs to balance risk. [...] Do not be fooled; some firms use the term "Effi[...] then give you the North West idea. That's weak [...] Twenty Eight for more on The Efficient Market [...]

Here are two other problems with American [...] are over 8,000 American hedge funds. Are there [...] hedge fund managers? Being a good fund manage[...] impossible. Many hedge funds will dilute the m[...] ners will be again hard to find.

Secondly, when some hedge funds work by e[...] alies, what happens when many of the 8,000 fir[...] inefficiencies? I'll bet they will return to the no[...] magic bullet or perfect panacea for investing. The[...] invest wisely and diversify your portfolio over 20[...] ferent mutual funds.

That means that with the eventual dilution of [...] pool and the normalizing of the little anomalies t[...] of institutional dissatisfaction with American hed[...] out of the mess to come.

What do I expect you to take away from thi[...] hedge funds?

1) I want you to know they are out there and t[...] dian market by their size alone.

2) I want you to consider selling short even [...] that some companies fail. Some companies[...]

3) I want you to see that another way of using[...] possible.

4) When the next Portus comes along and is a[...] you to know a little bit more about hedge fu[...] until I have seen the number of U.S. hedge [...] to 4,000 or less.

Canadian Hedge Funds

27

GENERALLY, CANADIANS do not understand hedge funds. "My hedge is in my garden." This is not an unusual comment.

Many Canadians have been looking for an alternate investment because the safe investments like GICs and medium term bonds have very poor returns. This is a 40-year low in interest rates and people still need steady income. Is the risk of Canadian hedge funds worth it? All the potential problems of American hedge funds exist here in Canada, too.

People are looking for better returns and some sly hedge funds are promising 8%. That sounds so good, but please STOP and look very carefully. In a nutshell, I do not think hedge funds are good for the average investor. Many Canadian hedge funds are aimed at this very market. Portus had almost 30,000 clients in just six months existence. That shows a great demand. In a Decima poll of 1,018 people quoted in *The Globe and Mail*, June 1, 2005: fully 33% of Canadians want to put some money into some kind of alternative investment, 6% already hold some hedge funds in their portfolio, 17% do not own hedge funds but might this year and 66% of Canadians are not confident in the level of regulatory oversight of hedge funds. That is significantly higher than the 47% who are not confident in the regulatory oversight of income trusts.

These numbers are scary in the sense that there is both interest and ignorance out there. Poor advisors will just tell unwary investors the top line and quote some figures, and then promise safe returns with graphs of past performance. If that is what you hear, Run!

Today Canadians can get into hedge funds for as little as $500. That opens the door to a lot of small investors, some of whom will lose all their money. This investment is not a safe alternative to GICs and medium bonds with good ratings. The same article in *The Globe and Mail*, quoted Adrian

Mastracci, President of Vancouver-based KCM Wealth Management Inc, "Anything can go wrong with hedge funds – the volatility is simply much higher… If you can't stand the heat, you've got to get the heck out of the kitchen." (Harry Truman said it better). Mr. Mastracci continued, "I know some of them are going to blow up; I just don't know which ones."

How about those promises of 8%? Can the hedge funds of Canada really deliver? The same article from *The Globe and Mail*, quoted a survey done for the Analysis Group, a Washington-based research organization. "We conclude that hedge funds are far riskier and provide much lower returns than is commonly supposed." The researcher, Atanu Saha, told *The Globe and Mail* that, "the funds called funds of hedge funds, do even worse. These funds are popular with average investors because they are supposed to spread the risk." According to Mr. Saha's research, they under-performed the S&P 500 (Standard and Poor's index of the top 500 companies in the U.S.) by almost 5%.

Another concern is the high fees. The aforementioned hedge fund fees of 2% & 20% program works here too but a "fund of funds" charges even more. For example, some of the Portus funds had to earn almost 13% before they covered all the fees. If they couldn't earn 8%, how in the world did they expect to earn 13 per cent for fees plus 8 per cent for you? 21% percent is near impossible most years.

One fast growing feature of Canadian hedge funds has been the "principal protected note." Let's look at that little wrinkle carefully, too. Who is backing the note? Usually it is a bank. The French banks Society General and BNP Paribas are the dominant backers of these notes. Wouldn't any Canadian banks back these notes? The "principal protected note" offers investors a guarantee that their initial investment in the hedge fund will be paid back when the note matures, usually within 5 to 11 years. There is no guarantee that the investor will earn any positive return on the original investment.

Think about that guarantee for a moment: I come to you and I offer to take your money with a promise to give it back in eleven years? I might tell you that you will get a return but I can't guarantee that, only that you will get the original investment back. *Run,* don't walk, from a non-promise like that.

This year (2005) Canadian hedge funds have been making less than one per cent for their clients. These investments are simply not for the average investor. The oddly dangerous combination of low returns and high risk is just not a place to invest hard-earned life savings.

The Modern Portfolio theories or (Markowitz and Fama revisited.)

28

WHO ARE these men? Some companies speak of Harry Markowitz as though he was born yesterday and had some great idea. Well, Harry did have a great idea, but it was published in 1952 and a lot of water has passed under the bridge since then. Fama had good ideas too. They were both big thinkers. But I'm getting ahead of myself here.

Decades after these two, when I worked at Edward Jones, we could pick stocks and mutual funds any way we wanted. Some advisors had their clients in 50 or 80 different mutual funds, some in very few. I ran my business on very few because I realized that understanding 10 mutual funds was enough and properly understanding 80 nearly impossible. We did not have a model to work with but we did have a short list of "Recommended" and a broader, but limited, list of "Approved" mutual funds to chose from for our clients. We just did not have an overriding theory to frame our work. That is the American model in the land of the brave and the free.

But there has been order, if not law, in the land since 1952 when Harry Markowitz published his paper called "Portfolio Selection" in the *Journal of Finance.* Thirty-eight years later he won the Nobel Prize for his good work.

In essence, Harry Markowitz said that buying stocks with the best opportunities for gain with the least risk was foolish. One could think that about railroad stocks and then construct a portfolio of nothing but railroad companies. He recommended that investors buy portfolios and not individual mutual funds or stocks. Remember, I called the simple North West idea "weak tea" two chapters ago? Here is why:

This is what Harry Markowitz wrote in 1952: "If we treat single-period returns for various securities as random variables, we can assign the expected values, standard deviations and <u>correlations</u>. Based on these, we can calculate the expected return and volatility of *any portfolio* constructed with those securities. We may treat volatility and expected return as proxies for risk and reward. Out of the entire universe of possible portfolios, certain ones will optimally balance risk and reward."

These comprise what Harry called an efficient frontier of *portfolios*. "An investor", he said, "should select a *portfolio* that lies on the efficient frontier."

Did you get that? An investor should select a portfolio that "lies on the efficient frontier." That is the North West idea more fully explained. I think I know why companies water down the wisdom of men. They believe that their market or their people in general cannot understand it. So they water it down and somehow miss the central idea. I believe you have read this far because you are interested in investing and want to know how to do it right.

Harry Markowitz was a great thinker and deserved the Nobel Prize. It should be noted that he built on the work of James Tobin of Yale who taught earlier and wrote about diversification of risk though balanced portfolios. The Nobel committee honoured Mr. Tobin in 1981.

In the year that Harry Markowitz was awarded the Nobel Prize (1990), the committee also honoured Merton Miller for his work. Mr. Miller was honoured for work on how a firm's capital structure and dividend policy affected the market price. He was a Boston Latin graduate and a member of Harvard College Class of 1944. Miller once quipped that he "spent his war years in the Treasury Department trying to think up new taxes."

William Sharpe was also hailed as the author of the capital asset pricing model, which gave Wall Street and Wacker Drive the idea of the beta, which represented risk. As Mr. Sharpe put it "beta – a coefficient designed to measure its riskiness and volatility relative of a particular stock, relative to the performance of the stock market as a whole." In other words, Sharpe's "beta" measured risk versus the market (See Chapter Thirty Six).

Each of these men deserved the Nobel Prize and each of them won. Why did the Nobel committee issue three Nobel prizes in 1990? In my opinion, it was because the main idea stands and falls on all three men's work. You need to combine Markowitz, Miller and Sharpe's concepts to get the idea of low risk portfolio selection. Indeed, Swedish economist

Vassar Lind Beck, secretary to the Swedish Academy, said, "Each of them gave one building block. The theory would have been incomplete if any of them had been missing. Together they created a complete picture of theory for the financial markets which has had great importance." It's odd, but the three did not work much together. They built on each other's work in the financial journals over a period of 10 years.

What stands out today that is Harry Markowitz's Modern Portfolio Theory has been proven. Remember to invest in portfolios on the efficient frontier and not just mutual funds or individual stocks in the North West quadrant. You see the efficient frontier is a curved line.

Like this:

Efficient Frontier

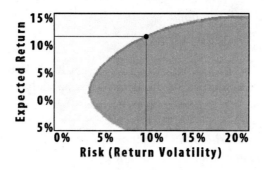

This a common chart, I sourced it from *Investopedia.com* and changed it. Please note that an all bonds portfolio is more risky than a bonds portfolio with 20% equities and 80% bonds. This portfolio would be at the start of the small line at the sharp bend. Do you see that expected returns of all bonds is somewhere on the lower limb but when you add stocks the return goes up and the risk goes down. Here's the essence of Harry Markowitz's theory: construct a portfolio and make sure it is somewhere on the upper limb of the efficient frontier.

Correlation

Do you recall the word used previously - correlation? It was in the scholarly quote of Harry's on the last page. I underlined it for a reason. Correlations with mutual funds are a key strategy. Correlations are the modern wrinkle on Harry's theory. Turned out he knew it all along.

Most people's portfolios are built on the idea of positive correlation. That means all your mutual funds are fair weather funds. When times are good your whole portfolio is up, up, up. But when times are bad, your whole portfolio is down, down, down. Positive correlation means that all your funds move up and down together. That, friends is called volatility, and volatility is what makes us all sweat and lose sleep at night. It gives us anxiety to see all our mutual funds go down together. That is why I sold bonds with mutual funds, but there is a better way.

The better way is "negative correlation" in which some of our funds are up and some are down at any time in the market cycle. Use bond funds, value funds and growth funds. This gives the whole portfolio little or no volatility; it yields a gentle slope up or a gentle slope down. Over time it gets you where you want to go. Look for negative correlation and sleep well at night.

In a 1997 interview by Peter Tanous with Eugene Fama, Fama talked about his theory of efficient market. I will quote bits of this interview, which appeared in *Institutional Investor*, but first let's define some of the terms you will read:

Efficient Market Theory: The theory that holds that stocks are always correctly priced as everything that is publicly known about the stock is reflected in its market price.

Random Walk Theory: One element of the efficient market theory. The thesis is that stock price variations are not predictable.

Active Management: The practice of picking individual stocks based on fundamental research and analysis in the expectation that a portfolio of selected stocks can consistently outperform the market averages. Mutual funds are good examples of active management.

Passive Management: The practice of buying a portfolio that is the proxy for the market as a whole on the theory that it is so difficult to outperform the market that it is cheaper and less risky to just buy the whole market. Good example here are ETFs or Exchange Traded Funds like Diamonds and Cubes.

Outliers and Fat Tails: In a normal, bell-shaped distribution of returns on investment portfolios, the majority of the returns, or data, can be found in the "bell," or bulge, which centers around the weighted average return for the entire market. At the ends, both right and left, we find what are known as "outliers," those returns which are either very bad (left side) or very good (right side). Of course, few mangers are either very good or very bad. Those returns on the right and left tails are known as "outliers" because they live on the outlying fringes of the [bell] curve.

Similarly, "fat tails" refers to larger than normal tails of the curve, meaning that there is more data on the extremes than you might expect.

Interviewer (Peter Tanous): Okay, let's get into it. You are known for your work on efficient capital markets. In fact, on Wall Street, the phrase "efficient market" is often attributed to you. I believe you … made the point that stock market returns are, in fact, predictable over time. How does that jibe with the random walk theory?

Eugene Fama: The efficient market theory and the random walk theory aren't the same thing. The efficient market theory is much more powerful than the random walk theory, which postulates that the future price movements can't be predicted from past price movements alone. One extreme version of the efficient market theory says, not only is the market continually adjusting all prices to reflect new information but, for whatever reasons, the expected returns – the returns investors require to hold stocks – are constant through time. [For example, we know that, since the 20s, returns on the New York Stock Exchange common stocks have *averaged* a little over 10% per year: Author] I don't believe that. Economically, there is no reason why the expected return on the stock market has to be the same through time. It could be higher in bad times if people became more risk-averse; it could be lower in good times when people become less risk-averse.

[Small talk here not printed. We pick it up again after that.]

Interviewer: But, in one of your papers, you did refer to the predictability of returns over time. Is that just the investor getting paid for the risk he was willing to take? Is that the point?

Fama: It could be that or it could be that people are simply more risk-averse in bad times.

Interviewer: On a related subject, I think you also said that fundamental analysis is of value only when the analyst has new information, which was not fully considered in forming the current market prices. When I hear that I say: Hey Gene, that's the point! The analyst believes he knows something or infers something, which other analysts don't see. He sees an evolution-taking place or he believes this company is doing better than people think, and that's why he gets paid millions of dollars on Wall Street to pick stocks. What's wrong with this thesis?

Fama: Well, not everybody can have that talent. In fact, as far as I can tell, not many do. The system is designed to make that very difficult. By that, I mean under U.S. accounting [and regulatory] systems, if you reveal anything, you have to reveal it to everybody.

Interviewer: Fair enough, but what if the analyst is making a judgment on the future prospects of the company. For example, the analyst might say, "The Street says this company is going to earn $0.82 per share and I say it's going to earn $1.10 because I see order flow, consumer demand, customers' tastes for the product and what have you. Now, if the analyst is right, he's worth the millions he gets paid. My question is: in your thesis, if he's right, is he right because he's so smart or just because he's lucky?

Fama: For the most part, I think it is luck. The evidence is pretty strong that active management doesn't really do better than passive management.

Interviewer: Except, of course, when we start talking about the so-called outliers, those managers, … who have persistently outperformed the market. That, in turn, leads to the other great exercise in our business, particularly with mutual funds, which is the predictability of future investment success based on past success. I know you've done some work on that, too.

Fama: One of my students just finished his thesis on that subject, actually. What he found was that performance does repeat when it's on the negative end! In other words, funds that do poorly, tend to do poorly persistently.

Interviewer: Why couldn't one postulate that the same would be true at the other end of the spectrum?

Fama: One could postulate it, but it doesn't seem to be true. On the negative end of the spectrum, you have things like turnover and fees and all that kind of stuff, which can explain why you have negative persistence in poor returns.

Interviewer: Yes, but good managers trade and charge fees, too. They might even deserve them more!

Fama: Poorly performing funds tend to be higher fee and higher expense funds. In fact, when my student adjusted for fees and expenses he could explain most of the persistent under-performance.

One thing I {Fama} did a couple of years back was take all the funds that survived from the beginning of the Morningstar tapes, which is 1976. Now, funds that survive that long have survivor bias built into the test, because only the successful funds survive. So I split the sample period in half and took the 20 biggest winners of the first 10 years, or the first half of the period, and I asked how did they do in the second half of the period? Well, in the second half of the period, half of them were up and half of them were down.

Interviewer: Wow. Half were up and half were down? [That indicates that there was no predictive value in the fact that these managers all finished in the top half in the first ten-year period: Author]. So even risk tested, the data came out 50/50, which means that mutual funds that did the best for ten years only had a 50/50 chance of repeating their success.

Another issue you have addressed: that old subject, value stocks versus growth stocks. Are stocks of good companies good stocks to invest in?

Fama: They're good stocks, they just don't have high expected returns.

Interviewer: Then growth stocks are stocks of good companies, not good stocks, right?

Fama: To me stock prices are just the prices that produce the expected returns that people require to hold them. If they are growth companies, people are willing to hold them at a lower expected return.

Interviewer: As we get into this, I think our readers are going to be surprised to read that value stocks are riskier than growth stocks. That is counterintuitive.

Fama: I don't know why it is counterintuitive.

Interviewer: Well, we used to think of value stocks as stocks that may have already had a decline that are languishing. We believe we're buying value stocks at the bottom and waiting for them to go back up again.

Fama: Value stocks may continue to take their knocks. Their prices reflect the fact that they are in poor times. As a result, because people don't want to hold them – in our view because they are riskier – they have higher expected returns. The way we define risk, it has to be associated with something that can't be diversified away. Everybody relates to a market risk. If you hold stocks, you bear stock market risk. But the stock market is more complicated than that. There are multiple sources of risk.

Interviewer: In our business, we usually associate growth stocks with high earnings multiples, and value stocks with low earnings multiples. Multiples are themselves usually an element of risk. So, if a growth stock falters on its anticipated growth path, it declines precipitously because it no longer deserves the multiple that had previously been awarded to it when its prospects were better. Therefore, a lot of people think that growth stocks, in fact, are riskier. What is wrong with that thesis?

Fama: Just look at the data. It's true that growth stocks vary together, and it's true that value stocks vary together. In other words, their returns tend to vary together, which means that there is a common element or risk there. [positive correlation]. Now, for growth stocks that seems to be a risk people are willing to bear at a lesser return that the return they require for the market as a whole. Whereas, if I look at the value stocks, which we also call distressed stocks, their returns vary together, but people aren't willing to hold them except at a premium to market returns.

Interviewer: So you're saying that I expect to make more money when I buy value stocks than when I buy growth stocks.

Fama: Right. On average . Of course, sometimes you get clobbered. ...

The article goes on. I wanted you to see that Fama was quite humble in his analysis. He said that could be so but it could also be that people just are simply more risk-averse in bad times. I also wanted you to see that the big winner mutual funds have only a 50% chance of repeating as champs. I wanted you to see the value of passive management and something about the relationship between value and growth stocks. I hope you enjoyed it and learned something new.

What stocks are right for real Widows and Orphans?

29

MANY PEOPLE can't afford to lose their money. They have retired on a certain sum and it has to last the rest of their lives. For these people please re-read the chapter on annuities (Chapter Four). They can guarantee that you will not outlive your money. For those with a little risk in their bones and yet still wanting safety and income, there are stocks that fill that bill. Rob Carrick, of *The Globe and Mail*, wrote an article March 5, 2005, which I will quote from. For their computer search for safe Canadian stocks, Rob and his researcher, Pierre Javad, used eight different criteria all of which concerned safety and stability. They applied these criteria against all Canadian stocks. This exhaustive computer search turned up an interesting list of 13 companies, some of which you would not expect to be too safe and stable. These are mostly conservative blue-chip companies. Now there is not a guarantee that these stocks will be solid and stay out of trouble in the future and past performance IS NOT an indicator of future performance. Caveats aside, here is the list. My thanks for this to *The Globe and Mail*:

Company	Symbol	Current Dividend	5year Dividend average	Market Cap (In millions $)
Fortis	FTS	3.11%	3.92%	1,749
Emera	EMA	4.68%	4.92%	2,072
Reitmans (Can)	RET.NV.A	1.99%	3.03%	973

Company	Symbol	Current Dividend	5year Dividend average	Market Cap (In millions $)
Canadian Utilities	CU.NV	3.61%	3.64%	3,867
St. Lawrence Cement	ST.SV.A	2.04%	2.41%	1,162
Great-West Lifeco	GWO	2.68%	2.32%	25,961
Magna International	MG.SV.A	2.04%	2.24%	8,836
Royal Bank	RY	3.04%	2.80%	46,221
Thomson	TOC	2.22%	2.23%	27,477
National Bank	NA	3.17%	3.02%	8,908
Bank of Nova Scotia	BNS	3.20%	2.73%	40,340
Dofasco	DFS	3.29%	3.88%	3,095
IGM Financial	IGM	3.43%	2.95%	9,944

Check with your broker about these recommendations. Right now (2005) Great-West Lifeco, Royal Bank, Scotia Bank, and IGM look like good investments due to their market capital and dividends. NO stock is good all the time. Here is a good place to start if you can stand a wee bit of risk. If not, stay away and go to the safety of annuities. Remember to put life guarantees on those annuities.

One thing about this stock list is that it is well diversified within Canadian stocks. That being said, Canadian stocks represent about 2.5% of the world economy. That leaves 97.5% of the world's economy left to invest in. Where would I go out there?

When you invest please think hard. It is so easy to follow the crowd. Your neighbour tells you about Nortel and you called your broker (OK, maybe you were wiser). Most Canadians buy the stocks when they are on the way up and sell for some emotional reason when the stocks are low. History has shown that this is human nature. We are supposed to buy low and sell high; yet most of us do the exact reverse. We buy high and sell low. Be honest, haven't you done that? I'll admit it I have done that, too. I already told you my Nortel story.

Here is where I would invest right now. Buying straw hats in winter is a good rule of investing.

At this time I do not believe we should invest in America. The dollar will one day come to a large cliff and fall over. After that there will be bargains. Then and only then, I would invest in these American companies. Within the United States there are many good firms and some I would not touch. I'd stay away from the major American Banks (City Group, Bank of America) because they may have big derivative problems in the near future. I would stay away from American property insurance companies because Katrina and her sisters are huge problems for these firms.

But I would look at some of the big life insurance companies like MET Life. I would also look at a well-diversified company in health care like Johnson and Johnson. The health care sector has had some rough days recently, but JNJ is a good company. Stay away from Fannie Mae and Freddie Mac; these mortgage pool firms will be hard hit when the dollar falls. (read more on this in Chapter Forty Four).

Look at the timber sector, too. They have not lost money in years. Trees grow every year and don't know about any war, the Nasdaq or Alan Greenspan. Trees just keep on growing. Consider Plum Creek Timber (PCL – NYSE). They own 8 million acres of timber with 1.3 million of the lands designated as "higher or better use lands" meaning the land will be sold to a developer one day at much higher values than the value of the trees alone. Their land is in Mississippi, Maine and Wisconsin.

Remember, buy straw hats in the winter and snowshoes in the summer.

In the rest of the world, consider these ideas. BHP Billiton, is the world's biggest mining company based in Australia, with a pipeline to China's many steel mills. Newmont Mining, based in Denver, Colorado, is an international un-hedged gold producer. If you own it, hold on to it. In Korea, put a little money in KEPCO, the Korea Electrical Power Corp. For an ETF try symbol EWM; that is the Malaysia (Free) index. Also India is a rising power. Their ETF symbol is IFN.

Those are a few stock ideas. Keep in mind that time may turn the tide against any good company. Right now these are good investments. (July 2005). Be sure to check with your broker for up-to-date recommendations. Of course, if you live in Ontario you can call me. (See the Conclusion for contact information).

Something happened to me while walking in the midday sun. I remember one day in particular when I was out knocking on doors for Edward Jones. One home I knocked at was elated about a newborn baby. I congratulated them and moved on down the street. When I rounded the corner I saw many cars converging on one house. I watched a while and noticed most people who got out were dressed in black. It was funeral reception and of course I did not bother them. It struck me that we come in and we go out and only God knows when. That's why I sell life insurance.

Will the Canada Pension Plan really be there for you?

30

THIS BOOK is being written during the early spring of 2005. In the news these days is the fact that both General Motors and Ford have been downgraded to junk bond status. That makes them a C level bond. Most companies that issue C level debt go under. I say most but not all. Why are these large companies in trouble with the bond rating services? There is a problem with the company's pensions. I am, of course, not privy to the details, but likely they cannot completely fund the pension payments to all the men and women who worked at Ford or GM all their working days. That is a big problem for the companies and for their retired workers and for those employees who will retire one day soon. I hope they have saved aggressively and have really built up their RRSPs and Non – Registered investments. If they haven't done that, one day they could be in for a sad surprise.

How about your pension? You know the one we all get if we are over 65? Yes, I am speaking of the Old Age Security Benefits (OAS); it used to be called the Old Age Pension. Recently it has become fashionable to say, "the Old Age Pension will not be there for me." I must admit I thought that, too. But I was wrong and so are you if you think it will not be there. Personally, I hope I never get it. What does that mean?

You can start the OAS anytime between your 60th birthday and your 70th birthday. You can start it early, perhaps at 60, if your circumstances tell you to that. There is a cost to starting before age 65: that will reduce the monthly payment by 0.5% per month you start before age 65. That is the same as saying that your pension will be reduced 6% for every year you start before 65. The inverse is also true. If you wait until after your 65 birthday your pension goes up by the same factor. That is great if you are planning to work until you are older than 65. You can see the government's gambit here, can't you? If you wait until you are over 65 many of us will not collect very long. You have to make the call you need to make.

I mentioned I hope I never get the OAS. Have I lost my mind? Why not? The OAS is clawed back starting at $59,790 of yearly earnings. It is completely clawed back (lovely term, isn't it?) at $96, 843. Why I hope I don't get the OAS is I hope and expect to be making more than that every year.

But I do expect to get some pension in my old age. What is the reason for my relative optimism? Right now the OAS is fully funded and expects to be fully funded for years to come. Here I will quote directly from an article in the *Advisors Edge Report* dated April 2005 by Scot Blythe. I'll pick up Scot's fine article in the third paragraph. At the start he writes concerning the other pension, the Canada Pension Plan. That is the one we all get if we have worked in Canada 40 years. He gets to the OAS later on:

"In the public sector, however, the Canada Pension Plan looks hale and hearty. In a presentation to the Watson Wyatt / Conference Board conference, Jean-Claude Menard, chief actuary for the Office of the Superintendent of Financial Institutions, the federal banking, insurance, and pension regulator, said that the steady-state contribution rate, currently 9.9%, should be sufficient to ensure a surplus of contributions over benefits paid out until 2021.

That's based on a number of demographic and economic assumptions, including an inflation rate of 2% to 2.7% after 2015. Another assumption is that CPP assets will be 65% equities and 35% fixed income until 2020, before falling to 55% equities as payouts exceed contributions.

The long-term real rate of return on plan assets is assumed to be 4.1%"...

In a supplemental actuarial report released later in April (2005) the chief actuary's office looked at the funding status of Canada's old age security programs: old age security (OAS), and the guaranteed income supplement for poor seniors (GIS) and the allowance for survivor's benefits.

The impetus was a government bill to raise the GIS benefits by $36 for singles, and $29 for couples, with half of the increase slated for January 2006 and half for January 2007. That would lead to a $325 million increase in expenditures in 2006, which will more than double by 2010. By 2050, the extra expenses with be ten times that amount.

At the same time, the number of people drawing OAS will rise from 4.2 million in 2006 to 9.6 million in 2050, while an additional 500,000 will be eligible for GIS, or 2.1 million people in total. Old age benefits currently represent 2.41% of the economy and will rise to 2.75% of GDP in 2050. However, the additional benefits will amount to only 0.04% of GDP (Gross Domestic Product) by 2050. ...

At this point the article gets a little foggy for this book. The essence of the article is that the OAS is not difficult to fund given its size compared to the overall Gross Domestic Product of Canada. In other words, we can afford it. Scot backs up his claim quite well. The CPP is and will be "hale and hearty." In addition, I believe that the CPP has some room in their model that should allow it to handle many unforeseen events. What if we have rampant inflation again or the bird flu proves as bad as the news people are saying? Inflation could wipe out years of savings. There are lots of things we cannot predict in the future so it's best to err on the side of caution. I would not count on my CPP and OAS and would make sure I had other investments to carry me through old age. If the CPP and OAS are there fine and grand, I think they will be there, after all, for many of us.

How much would you get if you do get CPP and OAS? Here are the 2005 up-to-date numbers.

Canada Pension Plan rates are adjusted every January if there are increases in the cost of living as measured by the Consumer Price Index (CPI). The following rates apply in 2005:

Canada Pension Plan	Monthly Maximum Benefit
Disability Benefit	$1,010.23
Retirement Benefit (Age 65 in 2005)	**$828.75**
Survivors Benefit (under age 65)	$462.42
Survivors Benefit (Age 65 and over)	$497.25
Children of Disabled Contributors Benefit	$195.96
Children of Deceased Contributors Benefit	$195.96
Combined Survivors & Retirement Benefit	$828.75
Combined Survivors and Disability Benefit	$1,010.23
Death Benefit (maximum lump sum)	$2,500.00
Maximum Employee Contribution	**$1,861.20**
Maximum Self-Employed Contribution	**$3,722.40**
Basic Exemption Amount	**$3,500.00**
Pensionable Earnings Ceiling	**$41,100.00**

Old Age Security (OAS)	Monthly Maximum Benefit
Retirement pension (Age 65 or older)	$476.97
Guaranteed Income Supplement (GIS)	$566.87
• Spouse of Non-Pensioner	$566.87
• Spouse of Pensioner	$369.24
• Spouse of Allowance Recipient	$369.24
Widowed Spousal Allowance	$934.24

If you think you can live on this money, I urge you to think again.

Pay Yourself First
or Maybe Second

31

I EXPECT you have read a lot about paying yourself first. I can't be sure about you, but I know it's true for me. I have read in investment books, time after time, about paying myself first. There is nothing wrong with paying yourself first. This chapter will be different and will show you another way.

Paying yourself 10% first is a very good idea. It gives you a quick start on saving and really doesn't hurt much at all. Truth is it doesn't hurt you at all. But hardly anyone does it. As the kids say, "What's up with this?"

When we use our computers we have to save our work or we may lose it. In the same manner we have to save for our future or we may be destitute. If you and I plan a quick budget and I say, "Good now take 10% out and save it." I know some will say,

"It can't be done."

"I am tight as the paper on the wall – impossible."

To that I say, "Right, just do it anyway." I say go further, save a total of 20%! So set up your quick budget and get started with the next paycheque. Here is where my advice will differ from any book you have read on this subject: I say don't pay yourself first; I say pay yourself second! Pay God or Allah or whatever you call the One who created the universe. Pay Him first and yourself second. That is, paying your first 10% to your church or favourite charity and the second 10% to yourself.

Good things happen when you do. I know that is true and I think I may know the reason why. It seems when we do the right thing it moves in harmony with what pleases our Creator and good things happen.

There is evidence in the Bible that backs this up in Malachi Chapter 3 (last book in the Old Testament) using the NIV (New International Version):

Here is part of the promises in that passage:

V:8 *"Will a man rob God? Yet you rob me.*
But you ask, how do we rob God.
In tithes and offerings…

V: 10 *Bring the whole tithe into the storehouse, that there may be*
food in my house. Test me in this", say the Lord Almighty, "and
see if I will not throw open the floodgates of heaven and pour out
so much blessing that you will not have room enough for it." (Mal.
3: 8, 10).

See God says, test or prove me in this. He is challenging us to do it his way and to see if his blessings don't pour out. Now I'm not preaching a do well and get blessed idea. That is too simple and the righteous poor man is a common sight, so what do I really mean here?

Is it impossible to save 20%? Is that really what I am speaking about? Let me be clearer. Pay the first 10% to your church or, if religion is not your thing, to a charity of your choice, Get that first 10% working for the betterment of mankind. Then pay yourself that second 10% as a reward for doing the right thing. Did you know that famous people in the past used this principle? Men like the Rockefellers and Andrew Carnegie.

I know that life works better when you are more concerned with the betterment of humankind than yourself. It seems to put your mind on a higher plane. It makes you reach beyond yourself. And, as Martha Stewart would say, "That's a good thing."

I can guess what you are saying now. "Is he nuts?" Well, the answer is that I've tried this advice out. I have practiced it for 17 years and I can tell you it works. When I did this I traveled the world every year. I had a great job and life seemed to work better. I stopped a few years ago and life became very difficult. Perhaps that is too simplistic, the effect is not that direct. I know it works. I am back on the program again now.

I must also admit I tried 30% and that did not work well. But 10% to a charity or church and 10% to you and your family does work and works well.

It seems that God is as good as His word. Blessings do seem to pour out on us when we live this way. What should you do with the 10 percent that you pay yourself second? Save it up and then invest the money conservatively. Invest in conservative mutual funds until you have $100,000 and then invest in stocks. Professional money managers manage mutual funds, and they live and die by the growth of their funds. They must succeed, and you can ride their coattails, and grow your money slowly but surely.

Buy a good conservative mutual fund from a broker; some of the bank funds also work well here. I do not mean a money market fund. In those you have a hard time NOT going backwards.

Consider what we are doing when we invest in a money market fund. We are limiting the growth and over-increasing the safety. Right now banks are paying less than 2% on money market funds. So you get 2% or less and then are subject to taxes and inflation. It is easy to see how both of those will be over 2%. You are going backwards fast in a money market fund.

If you have room in your RRSP (and most of us have quite a bit of room) then use it. Save it within a RRSP. That will defer the taxes you must pay. But if your room is small every year because of your corporate or government pension, then save it all in a non-registered account. Some of the funds I like are Aim Trimark Growth and Income, a bond fund from Hartford and the Mackenzie Dividend fund among others. Make negatively correlated quality mutual funds part of your broadly diversified portfolio. Here you should check with your broker to ensure that these funds match your risk tolerance.

Save, Save and Save again. Do not be tempted to use it for a new car or something similar. If someone asks you to borrow some money do not lend him this money. Keep this money safe from too much risk. If you must risk other capital, just do not touch this pay yourself saving fund. This can be a challenge – work at it.

This is money you are saving for your old age so you can sit under your fig tree with your grandchildren at your feet.

Saving for your child's education

32

SPEAKING OF children and grandchildren, do you know how fast the cost of educating them is going up? Here are the shocking numbers that we hear over and over on news shows, in magazine articles and television shows: The cost of post secondary education is rising dramatically. Tuition has risen an average of 86% since 1984, 62% since 1990 alone. These numbers tell me that with less government funding we all have to save aggressively for the education of our children. **A baby born in this year will pay almost $100,000 for a four-year undergrad degree.** That is not considering housing, living expenses, books, social activities and fees for gym, football, field hockey or whatever sport. Educating your children is very expensive, but worth it.

University enrollment is up as more and more young students see the need for higher education. When they graduate they will start off their working careers with massive student debt currently estimated at $25,000. That is a national shame. How can a parent help? There are four ways:

- Registered Educational Savings Plan
- In-Trust Account for the Student
- Permanent Life insurance
- Scholarships or Bursaries

RESP

What is an RESP? A Registered Educational Savings Plan is a federal government plan. It allows parents, grandparents and interested others to contribute to a registered savings plan on behalf of a beneficiary who will be attending post secondary school in the future. The contributions are not tax deductible. The income on the contributions grows tax-free until withdrawn to fund the post secondary education. The good news is that it is taxed in the hands of the student, usually at a much lower rate than it would be for the contributor. As the beneficiary is a student, and is not working beyond a summer job, there may be no tax payable on withdrawal to fund tuition.

You can use a RESP at virtually every post secondary school in Canada. You can even use it outside of Canada as long as the beneficiary is enrolled full time for 13 or more consecutive weeks. Here are some rules about the RESP. There are a lot of details you should know:

1) There are self-directed RESP and Scholarship RESPs, which pool your funds with others and invest it for you. In a self-directed RESP you plan the investments with the help of your financial security advisor.

2) Universities, colleges, CEGEPS, vocational and technical schools are now included.

3) The maximum contribution is $4,000 per year. The total you can invest in a single child's RESP is $42,000.

4) The federal government grants you up to $400 per year in the Canada Education Savings Grant (CESG).

5) To receive the CESG the student must have a Social Insurance Number. Your financial advisor has applications for the number. These are useful forms if the beneficiary is young and has not worked yet.

6) The plan can continue for 25 years, after which it must be wrapped up.

7) Grants are available up to and including the year the student turns 17. There are some restrictions to this rule. You must have contributed at least $2,000 before the student turned 16 or there must have been contributions of at least $100 per year for the four years before the student turned 16. I think they want people to save long-term – so do I.

8) Grants are based on 20% of the first $2,000. If you contribute a minimum of $2,000 per year you will attract the maximum CESG of $400.

9) If you contribute a minimum of $2,000 per year from the day your child is born the government grant will total $7,200. If it grows at 5% for 20 years that could put an extra $13,000 towards your child's education.

10) You can invest across a broad range of investments within a RESP. You can invest in cash, GICs, bonds, Canadian and International mutual or bond funds or stocks. In the case of a RESP offered by a mutual fund company, you may be limited to investing in the mutual funds that company offers. For example, Mackenzie offers RESPs and you can invest in their many funds.

11) You can purchase a single child's plan or a family plan to cover several children. These are useful if the beneficiary chooses not to attend post secondary school. You can transfer the RESP to another child related by blood or adoption. Ideally, you would have RESPs for all your children.

12) If the beneficiary does not attend post secondary school you have seven options:
   a) Name a new beneficiary under the same plan.
   b) Allocate the money to other children already in the Family Plan.
   c) Transfer the assets to a different RESP for other beneficiaries. Remember there is a 25-year limit to the plan.
   d) Transfer up to $50,000 of RESP assets to your own RRSP if you have contribution room within your RRSP.
   e) Donate the accumulated income to a university or college.
   f) Donate the accumulated income to a registered charity and get a tax deduction for your efforts. Note: most universities are not registered charities.
   g) Last and least option is to withdraw the contributions (a refund of the payments) and withdraw the accumulated income (accumulated income payments). The accumulated income payments represent the tax-free growth and are fully taxable to the subscriber and a 20% tax on top of all that also applies.

13) To expand of the last point g): If you want to get out of the plan before it is used for higher education or if it won't be used for higher education. You can get all the money you have put in back tax-free, as you paid it into the plan with after-tax dollars. There is no tax on withdrawals; however, some operators of RESP plans may place restrictions on withdrawing the money.

There is no tax on contributions you withdraw, but there is a tax on the accumulated income. First there is regular income tax and then a special 20% federal tax to get back the grants. This tax can be reduced if the proceeds are transferred to a RRSP belonging to the subscriber or spouse or common law partner with the following conditions: The transfer must be made in the year the

RESP is wrapped up or within the first 60 days of the following year. You could max your RRSP over two RRSP seasons by taking the RESP assets part in February and the other part in March. All this assumes that there is contribution room in your RRSP.

14) You can carry forward the contribution and CESG room. Here is an example of what I mean: If you miss the contribution one year, you can double the contribution and grant the next year. The plan must already be established. You can't start off and claim for all the years you have missed. Those opportunities have gone.

15) Here is a good strategy if you want to maximize the RESP: contribute $4,000 for the first three years; then contribute $2,000 per year for the next 15 years. That will maximize the government grants and hit the lifetime limits of $42,000 contributions and maximize the effects of compound interest.

16) Here is another strategy: If you are in the 40% tax bracket you can make a $5,000 contribution to your RRSP and get back a tax refund of $2,000. If you put this refund into a RESP it will attract a grant of $400. You will have turned $5,000 into $7,400 of total assets.

17) Advisor fees on RESPs are not tax deductible.

18) The capital within an RESP is not guaranteed. Any investment will go up and down over the years. Be especially conservative in your investment choices as you near the time to use the proceeds for your child's education.

In-Trust Accounts

Let's now look at the second option, which is In-Trust Accounts for the student. These informal in-trust accounts, also called "bare trusts," can be set up without a lawyer; your investment advisor can arrange them. There are some strict rules to observe. In most cases, relatives or legal guardians of the student can contribute to this plan. The intention is that the child pays the taxes on the trust because his or her income will be so low there will likely be no taxes paid. However, any interest or dividends earned by the investment will be taxed in the hands of the adult under the "Attribution Rules." (Attribution Rules are part of Canadian tax law. These rules say that, when you attempt to transfer income to your spouse, children, in-laws, nieces or nephews by transferring income-producing assets or property to them, *you* will be taxed on the income, not the person you intended to pay the tax.)

So the best strategy is to invest in mutual funds and securities that generate primarily capital gains. There will be some dividend taxes owing on the distributions of the mutual fund if there are dividends paid.

1) You can invest in cash, GIC's, bonds, Canadian and International mutual and bond funds and stocks.

2) There are no government grants.

3) There are no contribution limits. The contribution is considered a gift and is held in-trust for the named beneficiary. This is a good way to make a large contribution of, for example, $15,000 or $60,000 and let it grow over the years. That is a great idea for grandparents who want to help their grandchildren prosper.

4) There are no age limits. That means these are not just for young students or just for school uses. This idea can be used to help any-one you care about.

5) You must set these in-trust accounts up correctly or you could have tax trouble. The law says that there must be a real and ir-revocable transfer of property to the child or other beneficiary. Revenue Canada uses words like, "dispossess," "divest" and " de-prive," get the picture? If you set this up with the idea of some day pulling the cash out – for a new car or boat – you are in for a nasty surprise. If you don't make this kind of complete transfer you are treated like you still own the investment, and guess what. You are taxed on every dollar that investment earns and that includes capi-tal gains.

6) The informal in-trust really means that the money is the child's and when he or she reaches the age of majority can do anything with that money - use it for education or buy a fancy new sports car. Think about that possibility with these trusts.

7) If you want to be very sure you will not be in trouble with the taxman, simply spend the money on education. If you want to be double sure, open a Living Trust. Living Trusts are like informal trusts except they are set up by a lawyer and are expensive. It is an inter Vivos trust.

Both the RESP and the informal trust have a place in planning for your child's education. The RESP because of the CESG; and the informal trust because the restrictions of the RESP. I mean even if you build it to $42,000, there will not be enough money available to pay for university in the future.

Permanent Insurance

The parents can use the cash value of their insurance policy to pay for their child's education or add the cash value to an RESP, if the RESP is not going to be large enough. If the insurance is in Dad or Mom's name they can cash it in and pay for university directly. If the insurance is in the child's name they can cash in some of the cash value for university with their parent's approval and understanding. It is not a great strategy, as it will negate the insurance protection. There will be taxes owing on the cash withdrawal from the insurance policy. It is a way to finance the education of a child, but it is not the best one, unless the policy was bought with the education of Johnny and Jill in mind in the first place.

Scholarships and Bursaries

Look in the calendars that come from the universities your son or daughter is investigating, and you will find lists of scholarships and bursaries. You should apply for these at least 12 months before school starts. This is money to be used for post secondary education that does not have to be repaid. It is a grant. Most times these grants are based on excellence in high school grades, sports or community work. Sometimes the award is granted because of financial need and good marks. Usually you have to write an essay to be considered – that essay can make all the difference. Universities don't just want super smart people to go there; they want good all-round students who can be student leaders and nation leaders later. People who can organize are highly prized at university. So write a great essay and send it on to the university of your choice. The prizes range from $500 to well over $2,000. You can also search the web to find more Canadian Scholarships and Bursaries. There are hundreds out there. Good luck in your search.

Use the RESP, informal trusts and scholarships and you will get the job done and be able to look forward to your child's graduation day.

Famous Frauds and other ways to lose money

33

THERE IS a web site called bestfrauds. com that should be required reading for all of us. I have been getting emails from Nigerian con men now for four years. I'm sure most of us have had something from them. It seems to happen if you advertise on the net that you have something for sale. I had an old dinghy for sale on a local yacht club's website. I had purchased a new dinghy for my boat, and I simply wanted to sell the 6 hp Johnson motor and the little craft as well. I got an offer right away from some person who didn't pass his English grammar lessons. His email was littered with errors but he wanted me to respond to him listing the condition of the boat and my lowest price. Dumbly I emailed him back with the information.

After that I was inundated with con jobs and offers from these damn Nigerian con men. In addition, once I "won a Dutch lottery," which I didn't enter, next I have to help get "some money out of South Africa or The Middle East" and so on. The same old frauds over and over again. They vary the pitch but it is all the same nonsense. It is all a gigantic fraud being perpetrated on the world by the worst sort of thieves. They prey on frail trusting old ladies and old men and the simple of this world. They promise the moon, but ask you to send them $5,000 to pay for government fees and the like. If a website, snail mail or email asks you to send money to get money, forget it. As soon as you do you will never hear from them again. I finally wrote back threatening legal action and it all stopped. That is one of the problems of the Internet, fraud is more prevalent today than ever and it can reach more people than ever. It literally reaches around the world. No local government is able to stop it. If the Nigerian government clamps down and tries to nab these bad guys, the base of Internet fraud just moves location. I understand now that they are operating out of Spain. As soon as the Spanish authorities try to arrest them they will move somewhere else.

Canada is a hot bed for another kind of nasty fraud. Some of our citizens are selling credit cards with ridiculous rates to unsuspecting Americans. They lie about the rate with phrases like "introductory rate of only 4%;" they don't tell you about the 28% rates that come after that short introductory period.

Some of our good Canadian banks are just as bad in this area. They are charging 18% on credit cards balances with the prime rate is now 5.25%. That is part of the reason I am generally against banks. They are ripping their own customers off every month. See if your cards are like this and if they are, switch to a low interest rate. The Royal Bank and TD Canada Trust "low" interest rate cards are 11%! (More on this next chapter). In my opinion, the market is wide open for a truly low rate credit card. Canadian banks are too greedy in this area. But I'm talking about frauds here and what the banks are doing is not illegal, but that doesn't change the fact it is greedy and part of the reason Canadians generally hold the banks in disrespect. I say this despite the Royal Bank claiming to be "Canada's Most Respected Company."

Banks are concerned about one fraud that will hurt their consumers. This is a quote from the TD Canada Trust web site July 2005 (tdbank. com):

"Currently, there are various emails in circulation claiming to have been issued by Canadian Banks, requesting customers to verify their personal and/or banking information. Customers are asked to click on a link in the email that directs them to a pop-up window or modified online banking login page to enter their respective Bank's login ID and password.

Banks and any financial company in Canada will not ever ask you for your banking information in any email. TD Canada Trust has not sent and will not send email messages to customers requesting confidential information."

They are concerned and rightly so. Some con men or con women have built a counterfeit Internet site faking a bank web site. That is too much. For all the good the Internet does, it is just as bad as the worst of mankind as well. It has this kind of fraud and more garbage on it, porn sites by the hundreds of thousands, fraud of all types and now telephone fraud.

This is a form of telephone fraud. If you are asked to call an 809 area code do not do it. That call ends up in the Dominican Republic and they can and have charged unsuspecting people up to $24,100 for a simple call of a few minutes. There is apparently no limit to what they can charge for calls to that country!

On that web site I mentioned they list many frauds by American companies. They are after the major airlines, Sears (credit card issue), AT&T, Radio Shack and Topp Telecom, the discount airlines and lawyers. They claim that each of these firms is breaking some laws and they aim to stop it. As I said, it should be required reading for all of us. Check out **http://www.bestfrauds.com** and see what I mean. There is no sense in repeating all that here - have a look for yourself.

There is another kind of "fraud" that is not really a fraud but it has the same result. We can lose our money following the crowd in investing. Do you remember how we all stampeded after Nortel? Does that memory hurt a little? Does a similar pain happen if I mention JDS Uniphase? These are stocks that are, at heart, good companies. It is just that we all invested at the same time and blew them sky-high and they were not worthy of that lofty price. There is a good theory you need to know about at work here. It is called "the greater fool theory."

It happened with Nortel quite clearly. Nortel reached a high of $124.50. That means that some fools bought Nortel at that level and then the market ran out of fools who would pay that much or any more. There were no greater fools out there. The stock, based on that information, had to fall and once it started falling there was no floor until it hit $0.69. What a waste of investor's money! Their (OK, mine, too) money just evaporated like mist on a lake burned off by the morning sun. In the tech meltdown, trillions of investors' dollars were lost. Many lifetime savings were eliminated. It was not a fraud, but we still lost our money.

I think there is great mileage in being a contrarian. If you look up "contrary" in the dictionary you see that it has synonyms such as: *Perverse* (not the one I mean), *Restive* (yes, that's sort of the idea) and *Balky*. Balky suggests a refusal to proceed in a desired direction or course of action. I like balky best. I want you to refuse to follow the crowd again. That means getting a good broker who knows enough not to follow the crowd. Most brokers don't know that they are the crowd.

Being a contrarian means you invest in companies early when no one else is investing and it means you skip investing in something everybody wants. Remember that story about the late President John Fitzgerald Kennedy's grandfather, in the year 1929. The well-known story is that Joseph Kennedy heard from his favourite shoeshine boy that he should invest in some stock. Mr. Kennedy knew about investing, he knew the market and he knew then that the crowd was in the market. He got out of the market that afternoon, missing the crash that followed.

What is the problem with the crowd? It seems that when everyone invests in a stock, that equally, everyone can get tired of the same stock all at the same time. So we buy in well after everyone else is in and we sell after it gets so low we can't stand it anymore. The crowd operates in the arena of emotion and emotion has no place in investing. If you feel that you have to invest in some company because you have heard that everyone is doing it, STOP right there and save your investment dollars. Avoid that crowd and get out if everyone else is getting in. That is the essence of buying low and selling high. That is how to do it.

If you asked me to sum up my investment philosophy I would tell you that I am a conservative contrarian. I will readily admit that when I stray from that position I lose money. I will invest in an aggressive fund or similar, but only to a strict limit of less than 5% of my portfolio. I know that many of us "want to take a flyer" on a certain stock. I say go ahead, but limit your money to money you can afford to lose because probably you will lose it.

A good strategy is stop loss orders. They will sell your stock if it drops 15% or 20% or 40%. You set the level. They can stop you chasing a stock like Nortel right down the toilet. Ask your broker for these. Set the sell level not so low so that on a market dip you are sold out of the stock. Set it at 20% ,as an example, higher if the stock is under $5 and could drop before it goes higher.

It reminds me of going to a gambling casino. If you play, you only play with money you can afford to lose. Not a cent more. Then you are playing safe.

Years ago, I was in Las Vegas (or "Lost Wages") with a company for whom I handled most of the advertising. They invited me to their annual sales convention to speak and so forth. Late one night after we had seen disappearing elephants and white tigers I could not sleep, I got up and decided to go downstairs to play a little Blackjack. I know that game fairly well. But I told myself to take $100 with me and not a cent more. I could afford to lose $100 back then and not a cent more. Armed with my $100, I went downstairs at 2:30 a.m.

The Black Jack area was almost deserted. I bought my chips, picked a table and sat down to play. If you know Black Jack, you know that if you get a pair in the first two cards you are dealt you can play two hands. It is called "riding the bicycle." I was dealt two eights and I rode those cards and won both hands. In a few minutes my chips had increased to almost $500. I should have quit then.

That was when the casino played their hand. A beautiful, buxom blonde bombshell came over to me, leaned well forward and asked me in a deep husky voice if I would like a drink. Being a Canadian, I wanted to be polite so I asked for a small scotch on the rocks. In an instant she was back with a bucket of the stuff. I sipped and the more I sipped the worse I played cards. She distracted me and the booze was not a good idea. Soon my $500 had dropped to $100. I realized that it was well past time to go back to bed. I took my $100 and went back upstairs.

It is the same with investing in risky stocks; which are tips you hear about at work, pet ideas and theories, and stocks that are pumped on the net. If you can afford it, go ahead if you must. I wouldn't and I'll bet your broker wouldn't either.

However, if you must, then limit it to only a sum you can afford to lose. Never do it with the money you have saved in your pay yourself fund. Never gamble the mortgage or rent money. Put some limit on yourself as I did with the 100 U.S. dollars. I was prepared to lose the hundred bucks but I didn't, and I got a pretty good story to tell afterwards. Make that aggressive speculative stock trade if you must, but know that likely you are kissing that cash away.

I really think that conservative contrarian is the way to go.

The Care and Feeding of Credit Cards

34

CREDIT CARDS are a necessary evil. They are required to order anything on line, to order tickets for the Shaw Festival, to rent a van, to book a vacation or hotel. You get the picture - we all need and must have credit cards to live a good prosperous life in Canada today.

The debt that Canadians carry on their cards is appalling. One newspaper story has it well over $8,000 for every family. I have reason to believe it is even higher. When I spoke to the 5,000 people over those five years I heard a lot about higher credit card debt as a reason people used for not investing. Sad but true, credit card debt keeps many people from paying themselves second or saving for their old age.

I have a client who has this problem. He owes about $30,000 on several cards, which he built up buying, and selling on the net. He collects and sells antiques. He is paying interest of about 18% on these cards and keeps making payments only to stay even. He went to a bank for a loan to pay off these credit cards and of course they told him his credit was too bad because he has all these credit cards. It's a Catch 22 problem. He can't get the loan to pay off the problem because of the problem. He is staying even with them and still owes $30,000 on his credit cards. He has a good job and works hard. Right now the story does not have a happy ending. If the situation changes before this book goes to print I will change the story here to the hoped for happy ending.

Credit Card offers come in the mail or phone almost every week. There is something from MBNA, or Citibank, or RBC, etc. I'm sure we all get them. The banks push these cards because it is a very profitable business for them. They have the budgets to market these cards aggressively.

And why not? Any business that makes a gross profit of 18% to 28% on a huge volume is a great business, from the bank's point of view at least. From the customer's point of view it is a different story. Over the years, credit card misuse has caused a lot of family problems in Canada. Family disagreements and breakups happen over money and credit cards are often the root of the problem. Oh, I know the problem is really spending or more specifically, spending more than we earn. That is the root of the problem. A small article in the *National Post* gives the issue some dimensions. Here is the whole article:

National Post, Financial Post section, July 23, 2005 Headline: Lover's Quarrel Less Pillow Talk, More Money Talk, Would Reduce Spats About Cash

Arguments about money can still be a real spoiler between spouses, according to Decima Research, found that a quarter of adults (25%) describe their disagreements about finances as severe. And almost an equal portion (23%) say their disagreements affect other aspects of their relationships. At 31%, British Columbians were the most likely to say that money issues had affected their relationship. In fact, the survey results indicate the even mild and infrequent disagreements about money have an affect on the relationships between spouses. The most common source of marital spats about money was spending. Spending money, both in general and on specific purchases, was cited as the source of their most recent disagreement by 31% of Canadians. Borrowing and debt issues were the root cause of disagreements among 9% of respondents. *Financial Post*

One problem is that banks make the situation worse by using the money you pay on your card in the overnight interest market. If you pay on Monday, your account gets credited Tuesday or Wednesday. On top of charging nasty, greedy interest like 18% when the GIC rates are 2%, they use your money for their own growth and profit.

Another problem is that credit cards make spending all too easy. We all understand that problem. Here are some solutions:

How many cards do you have? The average Canadian has about 4 or 5 cards. Why? I don't know, I assume they are gathered over the years along with the mounting debt. If those cards are a problem, I suggest you have only one credit card, that's right only one. I only have one and I try to keep it manageable. Discipline is the key here. Have only one card from the bank you bank at and keep that card under control.

With the interest rates as high as banks charge, you must pay your card off every month. I suggest if you can't pay it off each month then don't buy the product. It sounds hard but that is the tough answer. So for proper care and feeding of credit cards just do two things:

1) Reduce your cards down to only one from the bank that you mainly deal with.
2) Pay that card off every month.

If you find that the total of the extra cards is too high to pay off at one time, you will have to take another action. Go to a bank and get a loan to pay off the rest of the cards. If you get the loan at 5% you are going to pay a lot less interest than cards at 18% or higher. Consolidate those debts into a low cost loan. Pay that loan off in a few years and as you are paying it off remind yourself that you got into this problem by overspending. Resolve never to get in debt like that again.

There are other good reasons to dump those extra credit cards. Your credit rating suffers if you have several cards. The rating agencies assume that you will spend to the limit on each of your cards even if you have only made one small purchase with that new card. If you spend $300 and have a $10,000 limit, the rating agencies think you will in time spend the whole thing. It is counted as though you already have spent to the limit. If you get rid of those extra cards you get rid of that problem.

There is only one reason to have two credit cards. If you are in a business that requires you to use a card, have a separate card for business and another for your personal expenses. East is east and west is west and never them mix them up. It makes keeping track of deductible expenses at tax time much easier.

Know the closing cycle of your credit card – what day do they send you the bill? Make a large purchase right after that date and you will have almost two months to pay without interest.

Here is a good trick if you are going on vacation. Pre-pay your trip. What I mean is say you expect to spend $6,000 on a vacation. If you want to avoid big charges on your card when you come home, try this. Deposit the $6,000 on your card before you leave. As you travel, use the card and spend down your deposit. When you come back, there may be a small balance or maybe a little debt from that big night in Paris. I believe you will enjoy your vacation more.

Above all, use your credit card or cards wisely.

Curve Balls from the Bond Curve

35

WHAT IS the bond curve? This stuff can get very academic and that is not the purpose of this book. I will simplify it here. The bond curve or yield curve is a shorthand for comparisons of interest rates on government bonds of different maturities. It compares the short term, medium term and long term interest rates on a graph. That makes a curve and that curve can tell us many useful things about investing.

For example, if investors think it is riskier to buy a twenty-year bond than a four-year bond they will demand a higher interest rate on the longer bond. In that case, the yield curve will slope upwards from left to right. That means that the curve is positive simply because investors demand compensation for the added risk of holding the longer-term bond. No one can predict what will happen in the next twenty years. That is the risk of a longer-term security. Now, if you buy a government bond, there is little risk that the government will default. But a corporate bond may be different. Can you tell me what will happen to Bell Canada or General Motors in the next twenty years? No, you can't, and that is the reason we have added risk and usually a higher rate of interest.

The bond curve can have many shapes and each one tells us something about the market.

If the **bond curve is inverted**. That is, the short-term rates are higher than the long-term rates. That is usually a sign of trouble. That could mean a recession is coming or at the least investors think that the Central Bank will cut short-term rates in the near future. In fact, the last five recessions in the United States have been preceded by an inverted yield curve. Remember what Trudeau said about U.S. recessions? He said, "When the

U.S. gets a cold, Canada gets pneumonia." Remember, if short-term rates are higher than long-term rates, prepare for a recession. How do you do that? You would sell certain securities and go to cash. When the market drops buy in again at a lower rate. The trouble is no one knows when to get back in and you may stay out of the market too long. It's a good idea to keep some of your cash available for a good opportunity when recessions come along.

A **flat curve** (yes, there is such a thing) is unusual and means that investors are indifferent to interest rates and maturity risk. As I said, that would be very unusual. However, you should not ignore a flat curve simply because it is not inverted. Flat yields from short to long-term rates can indicate a slowing of the economy and that will cause a lowering of interest rates in Ottawa and Washington.

When the yield curve as a whole **moves higher,** it means investors expect inflation and that will mean higher rates. If the entire curve **moves lower,** it means that investors expect a happier situation where inflation is under control and life is good.

If the direction up and down is **unchanged,** we can still get information about the difference in interest rate on different sorts of bonds with the same maturity. For example, you could compare government bonds versus corporate bonds or thinly traded bonds versus highly liquid bonds. (Liquid here refers to the ability to sell these bonds easily – that is, there is a large market for the bond in question.)

If the yield curve **is very steep**, it means that short-term interest rates have dropped more than longer-term rates. The gap, in this case, is wide between three-month Treasury Bills and 30-year Treasury bonds. Some economic force has caused the short-term interest rates to drop. A steep curve often forecasts a faster-growing economy because low short-term rates make it easier for companies to borrow to expand their staff and operations.

If the yield curve is **hump shaped,** it means that long-term rates and short-term rates are the same. People do not like a humped yield curve because it is an intermediate stage to an inverted yield curve. It signals slower growth. If the curve goes from hump shaped to inverted, then we may have trouble.

Here's the curve ball from the yield curve. Do you remember Cantor Fitzgerald? They are the Treasury bond brokers company, who had most of their staff killed during 9/11? Well, that company has regrouped and bounced back. Lately this company was in the news discussing the yield curve. Here is the whole story quoted from CNN Money as of July 8, 2005:

New York (CNN/Money) – One of the world's largest Treasury bond brokers has predicted that the so-called yield curve could invert by as early as next quarter, a move economists fear could precede a recession.

If the federal funds target rate hits 4.25% by the end of next year, the yield on the two-year note is likely to rise to 4.25%, as well, said a research note from John Herrmann, head of economic commentary at Cantor Viewpoint, a unit of Cantor Fitzgerald.

But the yield on the 10-year note was forecast to end the year at about 4.15%, not far from current levels.

The report said there was only a 20 percent chance that federal funds target rate would hit 4.25%, but the forecast made the top Treasury bond dealer one of the first voices to formally expect an inversion in the curve.

The yield curve refers to the upward sloping graph that's normally depicted by bond yields in the Treasury market: the yields on shorter maturity debt are lower than those on longer maturities.

Curves and conundrums

When short-term yields become higher than long-term yields, it is called an inverted yield curve. An inverted yield curve has preceded the nation's last two recessions. [sic]

The Federal Reserve has boosted short-term interest rates nine straight times since last June to 3.25%, and the central bank gave little indication that it would pause its monetary tightening campaign when it again raised last week.

Despite those increases, the long-term Treasury yields have not risen in kind and are in fact below where they were when the Fed started raising short-term rates last summer.

Fed Chairman Alan Greenspan has called that a conundrum and economists have struggled to predict whether the Treasury market is set to tumble, which would push yields higher. Bond prices and yields move in opposite directions.

Long-term yields have remained low despite a year of Fed fund rate hikes because they believe the hikes mean the Fed has inflation well in hand. Inflation hurts bonds by eroding the value of the fixed-income investment.

When the yield curve inverted in 2000, two-year yields exceeded 10-year yields by a little more than half a point. Cantor's recent forecast has pegged the two-year yield ending the year a quarter point higher than the 10-year yield.

But the firm said in its report that it believes the economy is "continuing to exhibit surprising economic resilience."

The report said there was a 20% chance of a recession. It may be higher today. If you watch the yield curve you will get a timely warning. If you have been reading the book in order then you should have understood that entire article. If not, go back and read the chapter on bonds especially the definition of yield. Here it is again:

Yield is the measure of the return on an investment and is calculated as a percentage. A stock yield is calculated by dividing the annual dividend by the current market price of the stock. For example, a stock selling at $25 with a dividend of $2.50 per share yields 10%.

A Bond yield is a more complicated calculation, involving annual interest payments plus amortizing the difference between its current price and the par value over the life of the bond. Always buy a bond based on the yield. That simply means exactly what interest rate you will ultimately receive.

Weeks before we go to press the yield curve has inverted (December 2005). That is a troubling sign.

Let's talk Risks

36

RISK IS a part of life. As soon as we leave the safety of our mother's arms we are at risk. I grew up in Niagara Falls and I didn't think about risk very often growing up. When I was 12 and 13, my friends and I would fish from a train bridge over the Chippewa Creek that had a sign, "Train Time Is Anytime." We noted the sign and got our fishing rods ready. We started fishing. Suddenly the bridge started vibrating just a little. We felt the track and it was shaking a little too. So we casually moved down on to the trestles of the bridge as the big freight train rumbled overhead. I think I got off a few successful casts from there. Trains just did not worry us.

Now that has changed. Risk for my clients is my chief concern. I have clients who are in their 70s and 80s. That is the time for no risk at all. At that time of life you probably cannot add to your portfolio since you are retired. The money you have is all you likely will ever have. The task of a good advisor is to make that money grow safely. That is easier said than done. People of that age often retreat to GICs – Guaranteed Investment Certificates. These seem safe and ideal, except for three kinds of risk.

The first risk is that GIC's are at 40-year lows. If you lock in you will make no money after inflation. Inflation is a bit less than 3%; at this time there are no GICs paying that much. Let's say that you bought a five-year GIC five years ago. You probably got 5.6% or even better. But now it is time to reinvest the money.

This second risk is called re-investment risk. If you stay in GICs, you have to re-invest the money at a very low rate. If you lock it in for another five years you will have less money due to inflation at the end of the contract. Consider something else.

The third risk is an opportunity lost risk. Where else could you have put that money safely? Did you miss an opportunity? And here is where the task of your advisor gets tough. Short-term government bonds are better, especially provincials, like Alberta or Ontario, but not by much. They are safe. Also, preferred shares from a secure company might pay better. Buy stock in a good firm that pays a safe dividend. A bank or insurance company's stock would fit the bill. An annuity is another option. The advisor has to search at bit and find an answer. It was certainly easier to simply buy GICs five years ago.

Many older investors told me about buying GICs at 18% back in the inflation driven 70s. I told them I remember I was paying 21% on my mortgage at the time. GICs and mortgages work hand in hand. The bank or insurance company lends out the GIC money on mortgages. That's why a bank advisor wants you to still buy GICs even when they are very low. He or she is not licensed to sell you provincial bonds or preferred shares or stocks. He or she has no other safe options.

If you are still at the bank when you are 70 or 80, do something you should have done years ago. Get a broker who can give you better paying safe options than super-low GIC's.

If you are in your 60s your risks are the same and they are different. If you invest in GICs the same advice applies. You cannot reinvest at super low rates and certainly do not lock in for five years. You may well be retired and looking for safety for your investments. However, if you are still working, it is a different situation. You still have time to add to your retirement savings. There will be no time later to add to your RRSP or non-registered account. Get busy! This is no time to take a flyer; however, I would settle on some good safe stocks that pay dividends and I would buy bonds whenever the rates go up.

If you are in your 50s, you know what to do. Invest all you can every month. Stocks and mutual funds are your answer. Top up your RRSP and put more money into a non-registered account. Now is the time that the sun is shining. Invest now for a much brighter retirement. Consider segregated funds for added safety.

Let's talk about mutual funds. Many clients tell me these days that they will never again invest in mutual funds. They were burned, they say, in the tech meltdown and want nothing to do with mutual funds. I can understand that, especially if you were invested in positively correlated mutual funds back then. Remember, if your investments are positively correlated they all go up and down together. That is not the way to invest.

I know it is time to reinvest in mutual funds. Many of them are well up and, frankly, the time to invest was two or three years ago when they were lower. If you are not back in, then get back in. This time get a broker who understands negative correlation. It is time in the market that counts. Do not try and time the market. Remember "time in the market" not "timing the market."

While we are talking about risk, it is time to discuss the opportunity in a crisis. This may be the way to get you back on top.

The Chinese character for crisis is composed of two other characters: one for danger and the other for opportunity. Most of us cannot remember the crash of 1929; but we can recall clearly the crash of October 19, 1987, a day known as "Black Monday." That morning the *Wall Street Journal* printed an eerie article that compared two periods from 1922 – 1929 and 1980 – 1987; the comparisons were remarkable. When that paper was dropped outside the city's front doors, the publishers had no idea that that day would witness the steepest drop in post-war history. The Dow Jones Industrial Average dropped 508 points or 22.6% that day. The volume soared to 600 million shares on Monday and Tuesday, a volume greater than the volume for the whole year of 1966.

In 1929, there was a famous crash, but the 1987 crash exceeded even that crash in volume. After the 1929 crash, there were runs on banks and bank closures. A dreary depression followed until the Second World War. What was different between the two huge crashes? In 1987 there were no runs on banks. There was no depression. The difference was the Central Bank in America. It did not hesitate to use its power as it had hesitated in 1929. This time the Central Bank had learned the painful lessons of its forefathers, and flooded the economy with money. The Central Bank pledged to stand by all financial institutions and bank deposits to make sure that the whole financial system worked properly. They saved the day. However, this bold move paved the way for many future unintended consequences (See Chapter Forty Four).

What followed was remarkably different. There was a depression in the 30s, but after Black Monday, starting in 1988, there was the greatest bull market in history. It lasted to the year 2000. It is too soon to tell if the current growth period is the beginning of a new bull market. However, North America is awash in baby boomers and they all have to invest to have a prosperous old age. When they all get back in the market, it could soar again. Get back in the market. Watch for an opportunity when stocks decline sharply. Pour more money in right after that crisis and take advantage of the lower prices.

If you are in your 40s, you likely still have many bills to pay with the kids in university. This can be a difficult time to invest. My advice is to still put away what you can every month even if it is only $200. It is the time to dollar cost average. Invest that money every month in a portfolio of mutual funds and let that money grow for years and years. Note that I said a portfolio of mutual funds. Brokers have those. They are made up of several funds negatively correlated that can be purchased as a group. Many good brokers have portfolio funds. Make sure they are negatively correlated. That was the advice of Harry Markowitz; invest in a portfolio not individual stocks. I add, especially if your total investments are less than $100,000.

If you are in your 30s, your job one is to pay off the house. I think you should dollar cost average with whatever money you can spare. Get the house paid off and invest something every month. Make saving for your old age a life long habit. Make it a habit to save $50 or as much as you can every month. The biggest risk you have is that you will not invest. Now is the time to get the foundation of your investments set.

If you are in your 20s no investment book in the world is going to make you invest. You have to see the need yourself and get busy. Job one is to buy a house, perhaps that is job two. Job one is to get married, then buy that first house. The house may well be the best investment you ever make. You may be doing very well and have no children yet. If you have the understanding, pour that extra cash into good negatively correlated mutual funds. Consider a mutual fund portfolio managed by professionals to guarantee the negative correlation. I can't tell you how important negative correlation is. This factor alone will help you sleep soundly.

Whenever you invest you will encounter risk. It is part of the market. If you have over $100,000 invested and are investing in stocks now, you know that risk and volatility are part of the same package. An investment that can go up sharply can also drop sharply - that is the essence of opportunity. When your stocks do drop, treat this as a time to re-invest. If you have the stomach for it, you can make risk and volatility your friend. Learn to invest in the dips, that is, when any of your stocks or stocks you would like to buy drop in value – invest swiftly. Use a broker you have primed for this task. He will set a watch on several stocks for you. When he or she calls, have the money handy. Right now trades are T plus 3. That means you have to have your cash in three days after you buy but that is changing. Soon it will be T plus 1 if the powers that be can work out the logistics. The best plan is to have cash with the broker with clear instructions to them to invest it when the time is right. You will have to check to see if your brokerage firm allows discretionary trades. They probably do not. In that case, your broker will have to call you before the money can be invested. Take his calls. They are likely important calls. Work with a good broker. He or she will reward you for your loyalty. Risk can be your friend if you handle it well, and your enemy if you don't.

It's Never Too Late

37

IF YOU read the last chapter with a kind of wistful manner, if you said to yourself, "I wish I had done all that when I was _____. You can fill in the blank. You are not alone. A great many people find themselves late in life with not much to show in their savings and investment accounts. It is a sad state of affairs to be sure, but I am here to tell you not all is lost. You need to start doing something today. Not tomorrow or the day after but TODAY. *Tempus fugit*. The Romans knew that time flies.

If you have worked in Canada you will have some Canada Pension Plan and Old Age Security Benefit. As I told you before, if you think you can live on that – think again.

There are three things you can do. One is buy some permanent life insurance so your heirs will not suffer for your lack of planning. Do not buy term life in this case. As you know, term life ends at 80 or in some cases 85. You may well be alive much longer than you think. Medical advances are incredible. In the past, people would usually die of heart attacks in their 60s. Today, you can survive with quick intervention. We all could live to 90 or longer. Then what? You will, it appears, definitely outlive your money.

The second thing you can do is buy a life annuity with whatever cash you can find. Right now the rates are not bad despite the low interest rates. Remember annuities are based on your age, mortality rates and interest rates. Check with your broker to see if the rates are high enough. Also consider a deferred life annuity if you are in your 50s. They are often a good way to force savings, and have the annuity start when you are older. That annuity will supplement your CPP for life. You won't get much return unless you can invest at least $100,000. But rates can change and you may be all right. Save for that annuity, starting today.

The third thing you can do is to start to aggressively pour money into your RRSP and your non-registered account. If time is short until you are 69 really put the coals to her. Invest all you possibly can.

It is too easy to hear this advice ringing in your ears and still do nothing. After all, the reasons you did not invest are still here. Right? The divorce, the kids, the long period of unemployment or under employment, as my father used to say, "I can feel for you, but I can't quite reach you." Get off the couch. Get a second job at night. See this as a big issue and just work harder. Get another job. Move to Alberta (bring a tent).

If you are good at your job and really add value to your employer's business – ask for a raise. If you have been working hard and haven't seen a raise in years, ask tomorrow. Aim for 10 percent. If you shoot for the stars, you will likely hit the treetops and 4.5% is good enough for this year.

But before you march out confidently, to corner the boss and ask for that raise, ask yourself honestly – are you worth it? If not, redouble your efforts so that next year you will be worth it.

If you are self-employed, increase what you charge for your goods or service by 10%. You will see an immediate jump in your ability to save. As I write this I am at the cottage on a lake in Muskoka. Yes, the same one in Chapter One. It looks like it will rain but there is a young water skier working at water skiing on one ski. He has fallen several times but each time he got up again and tried again. He reminds me of the truism, "Try, Try and Try again." Think about that if you think it is too late.

Also a person is not measured by how many times he falls, but by how many times he or she gets up off the mat and back into battle. Gird your loins! Get out there and do something to earn enough so you can retire in comfort. You cannot count on government you can only count on yourself – get going and do the three things I mentioned. 1) Buy some permanent insurance; 2) Save for a life annuity or deferred annuity and 3) add to your income with a raise, another job, a change in jobs or working two jobs. Get busy today. At work we don't get what we deserve… we get what we go for.

My Stock has Split and other Stock questions

38

ENOUGH OF the bad news. What if we get good news about our stocks? What does it mean if your stock splits? This topic was one that came up when I was out knocking on doors at Edward Jones. People knew something good had happened but what did it mean? Here is a definition from the Canadian Securities Institute *Investment Terms and Definitions:*

> *Division of a company's outstanding common shares into a larger number of common shares. A three-for-one split by a company with one million shares outstanding would result in three million shares outstanding. Each holder of 100 shares before the three-for-one split would have 300 shares after the split, but his or her proportionate equity in the company would remain the same – each share would just be smaller.*

Let's say you own 200 shares of Industrial White Lightning and the management declares that the stock will split 2 for 1 on a certain day. Let's pretend that IWL trades for $40 a share. You will have time if you want to buy more shares of IWL, but the market will immediately take the split price into account. When IWL splits you now have 400 shares and the price of the shares has dropped in half to $20 a share. Simple enough? You get twice the shares but at half the value so you are not really up any money. If your 200 shares at $40 were worth $8,000 now your 400 shares at $20 are still worth $8,000. The benefit is that when your share price is low again at $20, more people will be able to invest in IWL and the stock should go up.

Ok, then what is a reverse split?

A reverse split is not considered good news. A company wants to reduce the number of shares outstanding and force the share up in value. So they reduce the total number of shares in the market by splits like 1 for 3 or 1 for 2. If you owned shares of IWL and the market for illegal liquor had fallen, then your 200 shares at $40 might be reduced 1 for 2 and you would end up with half the number of shares but at twice the price. Your 200 shares at $40 become 100 shares at $80. Your value remains the same.

Why would a company do a reverse split? They could do it to make their share price look better, but the bottom line is that nothing really changes. This is also a strategy a firm could use to avoid stock market delisting.

I hear the term circuit breaker in relation to the stock market. What does that mean?

What are these circuit breakers? As a result of the crash of 1987, the New York Stock Exchange implemented rules that halt or restrict trading when certain price limits have been reached. When the Dow Jones Industrial Average drops by 2%, some trading curbs are quickly placed on index arbitrage between the futures market and the New York Stock Exchange. Remember *arbitrage* is the simultaneous purchase and selling of an asset in order to profit from a differential in price.

Other measures kick in when the Dow drops deep. At 5% decline, the NYSE stops trading for 10 minutes. If the Dow drops 10% by 2:00 in the afternoon, the Exchange declares a one-hour halt. If the decline by 2:00, is 20% a two-hour halt is called. And if the drop is 30%, the New York Stock Exchange closes for the day. Futures trading always halts along with the NYSE.

The rationale seems to be that a halt will give investors time to think again and develop a different strategy when the market re-opens. Also the time-out can bring buyers into the market to help stabilize the situation.

There may be a fatal flaw in these halts. On "Black Monday," the 350-point limit was reached and the market closed down for two hours, but when the market re-opened traders fell over themselves to sell their clients' positions and the 500-point limit was reached in minutes.

The legislated halts can also increase volatility by discouraging short-term traders from buying because they might be told they cannot sell because of a halt or because there are no market upticks. Remember short sellers can only sell short on a market uptick. There may be no upticks that day. Also keeping some buyers out will give the stock over to sellers who will only drive the price down sharply.

History has shown that investors, who are willing to step in and buy in a market when everyone else is in a panic to sell, get rewarded by the benefits of market volatility.

If you see this happening, it could be a great opportunity. Talk to your broker about being a buyer at discounted prices. Volatility and risk are the essence of the stock market. Learn to buy in the dips and not to sell emotionally. You can make volatility your friend or you can let it be your enemy.

My uncle is a Chartist. What does that mean? Is it contagious?

It almost sounds like a secret society. The Chartists! Protecting the Magna Carta from all evil. Something like that it is not. Being a Chartist is simply being a technical analyst. Most brokerage firms use Fundamental Analysis. They look at balance sheets, financial statements like the annual report, and they visit plants, talk to workers and management and speak to customers. They research exhaustively until they know that company very well.

A chartist, however, looks for information based on past price trends. They use terms such as "head and shoulders" formations, moving average convergence indicators and "saucers." They have their narrow base of support but academic economists dismiss Chartism as kin to astrology. However, some of what they say makes sense sometimes. What they try to do is to ride the bull market and avoid the bear markets. Wouldn't we all like to do that? The central problem, as I see it, is that stock prices do not follow a predictable path. It is more like a random walk in the woods than a charted path.

In the 50's, Professor Harry Roberts of the University of Chicago developed stock-type charts, which formed patterns that Chartists thought were significant. Roberts developed his data by the completely random flipping of a coin. Speaking of coins, there is another side to all of this.

Are stock movements completely random? Most economic activity is based on predictable events. Companies can estimate their gross sales every quarter; their earnings are fairly predictable, and they should know most of their costs each year. If it were not so, how could a company operate? Companies need predictability. Why shouldn't stock prices be predictable?

Are humans completely predictable? When otherwise normal people enter the market they do unpredictable things. I believe most people use emotion to sell or buy in the market and emotions en masse are completely unpredictable. In the chapter on hedge funds, I mentioned how investors over-react to market events and how they believe that a value stock will have some tough periods – so they do not buy it all. Or they believe that a growth stock will fly to the moon, that's over-believing - if there is such a word. They expect higher gains than are possible. It is all emotion. I'll say it again: Emotion has no place in a healthy portfolio. Be a Mr. Spock when you invest and it will serve you well. Live long and prosper.

Should I buy large companies or small ones?

This is a question I got often; Edward Jones is a large cap believing company. Large Cap refers to Large Financial Capitalization. These are the huge firms such as Bell Canada, Loblaws and Weston, Inco, Imperial Oil and other similar firms. Small cap firms are, as the term implies, are not huge, but they often are quite dominant in their niche market. They usually employ hundreds of people and have sales in the millions. They are not a mom and pop story; small cap companies are often stable employers with a unique product. The issue often comes down to liquidity. That is, is that small stock traded often and broadly? Or do the owners and management closely hold it? If you bought that stock, could you sell it quickly if you needed to?

Large brokerage firms cannot cover all small cap firms with quality fundamental research, there are just too many. If you ask your broker for an opinion, they will discuss the market with you, but cannot make any sound recommendation on most small cap companies.

I like a mixture of large cap and small cap in my portfolio. Large cap for stability and dividends and quality medium and small caps for growth; a small stock selling for $1.20 can double to $2.40 in a few years. That is easier than a $50 stock doubling to $100. I support small caps with about 15% of my portfolio. They are riskier than large cap simply because given enough bad news they can go under faster. That is the risk. Often small coal mines and oil companies fit the small cap definition. The upside is often hopeful; the downside always present. Keep in mind that my risk tolerance is different than yours. My portfolio may not be correct for you.

How do I find out about small cap firms? There are small cap mutual funds and that is the best bet for most people due to diversification. In addition, I read Canadian newsletters devoted to this. Either way I get professional money managers on my side. Then I investigate with phone calls, annual reports and the Internet. Then I buy or don't buy. Research is important, do not skip this step. My clients benefit as well.

When should I sell my stock or mutual fund?

I have broadly speaking two types of clients. There are the people who buy a stock or bond and hold it for years. In addition, I have many clients who trade in and out of stocks and enjoy the game. In general, I am a buy and hold believer but there is no denying the fun of a quick profit gained in a few weeks.

I know, however, that there are times when we must sell. If you need the money for some family emergency, then you must sell. However, if you are serious about saving for your old age, you will replace that cash as fast as you can. Remember, it is time in the market not timing the market that counts. Don't ever think you can decide the right time to get back in the market. Just get back in a soon as you can.

Every year there are only 12 to 15 days a year that really build your portfolio and you do not know when they will happen. If you are out of the market for just 1 or 2 of those days your annual growth will be lower. I would not sell if there were any way I could avoid it. It is like the advice I got at summer camp years ago: if you tip over in your canoe you hang on for three days and three nights. Hang on to those mutual funds and stocks and bonds. They are for your old age and not that fancy car or ski-chalet. It takes discipline and sometimes that is hard work, but in your retirement you will be happy you hoed to the end of the row.

What are the best investments?

This is a question only a novice investor would ask. The question implies that there is a best investment. There is no holy grail of investing. No mutual fund offers eternal growth. No stock comes without some headline concern. No bond is without worry at some point. Sometimes the best investment is the family home.

To answer this question properly I need to know how old you are and what your risk tolerance is. Every brokerage is concerned that the advisors know their clients. That means to know what risk they are comfortable with. You have to be able to sleep at night, if your investments are so risky they keep you up at night, get a new advisor. Your risk tolerance is important enough to be up-dated annually. In fact, a broker must keep a record that he has rewritten the Know Your Client Form every year. I usually do that when we have the annual review. It may seem like a waste of time to you, but believe me, your broker has to go through it annually with you - it's the law.

Back to the question, if you are 79, there is a simple answer. Something conservative that provides income. If you are 25, it is something quite different. At 25 you are trying to build your mutual fund portfolio; at 79 you want to hold on to your investments and get some income from them. Both are the best investments for the respective ages. At every other age, it is a variation on the same theme.

Is there ever a time not to be in stocks?

I am, as I said, a buy and hold advocate, but there are times I will call my clients and ask them to sell 50% of a winning stock. Take your profits. When I make that call I must have two ideas: 1) what to sell to take the profit, and 2) what is a better investment to put the money into. Sometimes I ask my clients to take a profit and then stay in cash until something good comes along.

I note with some interest that the Toronto newspapers are reporting in July of 2005 that many mutual funds managers are awash in cash. Some are up to 30% in cash. That is because right now everything seems expensive out there. Stocks are high; bonds are low. Actually anything with interest rates is down. Here again the broker must do his or her homework. How about preferred shares or some insurance product like a segregated fund or an annuity? The woods are full of good investment ideas if you know where to look and are using a full service broker.

If you want a broker to do his or her work, you must let them do it. We have to rebalance your portfolio to get back to your stated risk tolerance. We have to be able to reach you to sell 50% of a winning stock. Often all this seems self-serving on the broker's behalf because we get paid to do this. It may seem that way, but it is the right thing to do to keep your portfolio headed in the right direction and to limit your risk.

My broker has recommended I buy a bond rated C.
Is that a good idea?

Bonds are rated by the bond rating agencies based on the safety of the investment. A C- rated bond is a junk bond. I don't care what company it is – I would run from a C- rated bond. They may pay a higher yield but that is because you are taking more risk.

Let's do a quick review of Chapter 20. The rates go from AAA down. AAA bonds are federal bonds and they are the safest in Canada, investments such as Treasury bonds. AA bonds are top-drawer companies and some provinces. Single A ratings are good and still safe. They could be large companies or smaller provinces. The lowest investment grade is BBB; anything less than that is not investment grade and should be avoided. That is BB or B or CCC or CC or C. If they ask again, ask them what percent of firms rated C survive? It is not a pretty picture. Many do not make it. If you invest in a C rated firm you should just do it with money you can afford to lose - since you likely will lose it.

I used to keep a box of wooden matches in my desk drawer. I don't smoke but I had them there as a teaching aid whenever a client came in all hot and bothered and ready to emotionally buy some stock or junk bond. I would pull out the box and slowly take a match out and strike it. As the flame blossomed I asked, "Do you want to burn your money now or later? Here give me that cheque and we'll get it over with quickly."

I did that to get them to think a little. Remember Mr. Spock, "That's not logical," he used to say to Captain Kirk. Sometimes great ideas need a second opinion and a little theatre. It always worked.

One client came in wanting to buy *Krispy Kreme* Donuts. That company had just come into Canada and there were line-ups in Mississauga. I tried one and was appalled at the sweetness. Canadians are getting more and more health conscious, why would we flock to this and abandon Tim Horton's? I did not believe it would be a hit in Canada and told my client so. He disagreed and we settled on an investment in *Starbucks*. For the next year I ate crow. *Krispy Kreme* rocketed up and *Starbucks* slowly increased but not at the rate of the sweet donut company.

Then about a year later reason finally prevailed. *Krispy Kreme* announced a repackaging of their product and the closure of several formerly highflying outlets. The stock tanked. *Starbucks* just kept on growing. Sometimes it takes a while for good investment advice to be proven. Sometimes research is a simple as buying a donut.

There is nothing so certain

39

AS DEATH AND TAXES, is there any way to legally get around the truth of this maxim? Yes, but, of course not ultimately. Here is a tax idea known as the Mortality Swap. I had never heard of this idea until 1999. In November of that year, Moshe Arye Milevsky wrote an article in the *National Post Magazine*, which I have used to sell many insurance policies and annuities. Thank you, Moshe. I will use his article as the basis of this chapter. He called it the "Mortality Swap." Here is the strategy:

Generally in grade school math, one minus one is zero. But not always when it comes to insurance and annuities. Insurance companies give you protection for your loved ones for a large amount of money with small monthly payments. When you buy an annuity you give the insurance company a large amount of money and they guarantee to pay you small amounts of money every month as long as you live. Due to the way each investment is taxed, this can lead to an interesting opportunity when you are older.

At first glance, buying a $100,000 insurance policy and then buying a $100,000 annuity to make the monthly payments on the insurance would be like taking the above match to money. After expenses, commissions and fees it would seem pointless. However, the returns from this strategy can be better than a corporate bond. Doing this could be a sound investment.

Here is an example from Moshe's article:
Jo-Anne who is 65 buys a permanent insurance policy for $100,000 and then from a different insurance company (that is an important detail) she also buys an annuity for $100,000. Here is what would happen:

Jo-Anne would receive $8,112 per year from a life annuity. Of this amount $3,137 would be taxable given a 50% tax bracket. This would leave Jo-Anne with a cash flow of $6,543 per year ($8,112 –50% x $3,137). The insurance policy annual fee would be $2,566, which would leave Jo-Anne with a positive cash flow of $3,977 ($6,543 - $2,566). To generate an equivalent cash flow on her $100,000 she would have had to invest in an eight percent bond, which are unavailable today without large risks.

The older you are the better this works. Here is the chart taken from Moshe's article in 1999:

Age when Buying Mortality Swap	Annual Insurance Premium	Annual Life Annuity Benefit	Pre-Tax Return (50% tax bracket)
65	$2,566	$8,112	8.0%
70	$3,566	$9,357	8.4%
75	$4,919	$10,812	9.1%
80	$6,654	$13,162	10.9%

Since Moshe's article, the cost of insurance has gone down and the return from annuities has also gone down. See below. To repeat, it is important that you use separate insurance companies (the term is separate "underwriting"). If you don't, the taxman may not allow this benefit of the tax act.

Now I checked the idea at the office and right now it does not work. The annuity rates are just too low. I did the exercise for Mr. Sam Dominion, our fictitious investor, who is simultaneously aged 65, 70 and 75. Here are the costs based on whole life with some included life term to make it less expensive when compared with an annuity guaranteed to age 90. The costs just don't work now, even ignoring taxation, but when rates go back up, the Mortality Swap will make sense. Here are the numbers based on $100,000 of insurance and an annuity for the same amount for Sam Dominion in today's market:

AGE	Cost of Whole Life	Annuity payout
65	$592.92/ Month	$318.06 / Month
70	$640.00	$406.45
75	$793.27	$488.34

As you can see Sam is short every month. If you want to do this strategy when interest rates are higher call a good agent who understands this tax concept and see if it works at that time. With rates at 40-year lows, some good investment and tax ideas just don't fly right now.

What if you really DO win the lottery?

40

FOR MOST people this is just a pleasant daydream, winning the lottery or the man from Publishers Clearing House at your door. It won't happen. I had one client, who I'll call Phil, who won $2 million in the lottery. He is a good guy and has returned to home renovation work. The money did not affect him because he is a good man and the money only rested briefly with him before taking flight and leaving town. Here is Phil's true story.

Phil is a father of three children. Phil looks after the children himself since his wife left him. Legally they were separated. When Phil won the lottery, he just bought a ticket the day before the lottery on a whim. He was in the store and saw people eagerly buying the tickets. He bought what he had come in for and then asked for a Lottario ticket. It was a whim, just a simple idea and a way to spend some of his change - just a lark. He won.

Phil won two million dollars. Now years before, Phil was at a family reunion discussing the retirement plan of many Canadians called "win the lottery." I think in their hearts most people know that it is hogwash but some really believe that will save them instead of hard work and saving. The family, after a few ales, solemnly agreed that if any of them won the lottery, then one would share with all. Phil recalled the agreement and called his family together and gave them all equal portions of $1,000,000, or half of what he won. That had been the agreement. His family left happy to say the least.

Then his ex heard about Phil's good fortune. Dressed for the kill she came back to him. Do you remember a great line from *Frasier*, the television show? "Men can't do something for sex, since sex is what they want all the time." It is a failing of most men. Anyway Phil fell face first into the

243

trap. His ex stayed 91 days with him. If you know that number, you know that if a separated couple is reunited for more than 90 days the separation becomes null and void. She was his wife again. And she re-filed right away for divorce. Nice girl. She got $500,000 for her three months work.

Phil came to me with about $200,000. He had paid off his mortgage and fixed up the place a bit for $300,000. He asked me to not let this money disappear. We invested it and it went nowhere but up. Phil is sitting pretty now. The amazing thing is that all the money and its loss did not affect him. He is still a good family Dad and I count him as a friend.

This is opposed to another couple that won the lottery in Scarborough. One of the managers from Edward Jones came out door knocking with me and told me that the people in that house had won the lottery. I could see them inside through the front window so I knocked. They ignored me. The manager told me that the people had won and had closed up their house and left for about a year. Then they came back and would not talk to anyone. This is how winning the lottery often works out. People are worse off after they win than they were before.

What if you won the lottery? I have given this some thought. Perhaps it is my fascination too. Anyway, what if you won, would you like to know how to keep most of your winnings? Generally, windfalls tend to make you more of what you already are. If you are pleasant and generous you will be more pleasant and generous. If you are a cheap tightwad you will be more of that too.

If you can keep most of your winnings you will be better off needless to say. But how do you do that? Let's suppose you won $2 million. Here is what I would recommend you do:

Invest it wisely:
Put 10% to pay off the mortgage and fix up the place. That is $200,000.

Invest a further 15% in preferred corporate shares. Get safe solid preferred stocks from banks and insurance companies. You will need a good broker here. That is $300,000.

Then invest 45% or $900,000 in government bonds and solid safe corporate bonds. Then I would recommend you invest 25% in good worldwide stocks. With $500,000 you can buy a well-diversified portfolio. If you are adding up the percentages you know that we now have a total of 95% covered off.

With the remaining five percent, I want you to fulfill a heart's desire. Take that trip; with $100,000 you can have a fine time. Take a holiday on a cruise ship around the world. Buy that car you want or buy that boat you have seen. Spend it all if you want. Have a grand time. Then come home and let the rest of the money keep on growing and live off the interest and dividends.

The $900,000 invested at 5% will pay you $45,000 gross every year. The preferred shares and stocks total $800,000 and at 4% they will yield another $32,000. That is $77,000 a year plus any other pensions or work you may want to do. With the mortgage paid off, there is a fairly good life-style here. You will be tempted to live a little higher off the hog. I would caution you by telling you that it will be possible to live a bit better later when the stocks have grown in value. Give them time to grow. Then start taking money out of the stock market by withdrawing a certain amount every month from the growth in addition to the $77,000. Never let the total drop much. Your broker will show you how to do that. The idea is simple; sometimes the execution of the idea is different at each broker firm.

I asked the woman at work who buys the lottery tickets if we had won yet. She told me she would call a staff meeting in the boardroom, just like the television ad of a few years ago, and jump up and down. Good luck to all. I play, but I still think it is a form of voluntary taxation.

41

HOW DO you know if you have all the bases covered? You have a will and a good investment plan, some life insurance and so on but is it enough? If you have all five of these ideas covered then you are on the right track. These five ideas relate to your working life and all effect your retirement.

1) **Liquidity** – have you enough money to enjoy all that life has to offer? Can you save for your goals and live well at the same time? Even if you have a good job that may not be possible without some spending being curtailed. It is good to have at least three months expenses stashed away in a safe savings account.

2) **At Death is your family provided for?** – Is your insurance enough and is it up to date? Do you have enough? Even two million is not enough if you are going to live on the interest only. At 3% that is only $60,000. Most of us could live on that but it would be tight in most large cities unless your mortgage was paid off. Buy enough insurance. Many Canadians have small insurance accounts they purchased in 1966 or thereabouts. These people do not have enough insurance to pay for their burial, let alone help their family. Get enough insurance to pay off the debts, bury you, and help the family when you are gone. Don't be cheap in this area - it's your family's future.

3) **Disability** – There was a section on Disability insurance, if you are considering buy this worthwhile coverage, go back and read Chapter Seventeen. This insures you against the risk that you will be injured on the job or in a car accident or anything else that can

247

happen to us all every waking hour of the day. If you can't work, your family will suffer. Get some of the relatively inexpensive disability insurance. Do not count on the disability insurance you have at work. It is not large enough and if you lose your job or change positions you may be caught by an injury at just the wrong time. Get covered early and again it will not be expensive.

4) **Diversification** – This is important. Imagine years ago when railroads were all the rage you could have invested in nothing but railroads and for a while look like a genius to your family. Dividends would be pouring in and life would be sweet. Then came large trucks, other ways to ship grain, and millions of cars and suddenly your monopoly was gone. What happens then to your wise investment? Or perhaps more recently, you thought that tech was the key to investing happiness and you poured the money into Nortel, JDS Uniphase and AT&T? Where did your money go in the bear market of 2000- 2003? Down the rabbit hole into oblivion? Well some of in went to the Chairman's excessively fancy digs I'm sure. The rest went into vapour or so it seemed. Enough! We have to bounce back. How are we going to do that? We must diversify into mutual funds, and stocks and bonds. This is a must and make sure that your mutual funds are negatively correlated.

5) **Retirement** – We all want to retire well. Those who plan well will get what they want. Those who leave it to chance have little chance of making it. Retirement is what you make it. You can retire and live in your home and enjoy your grandchildren or you can sail the oceans of the world. It is up to you and whatever you and your spouse desire and have saved up enough to do. You can move out west to British Columbia or live in southern California. Whatever you wish for you must plan for it now.

There have been lots of strategies in this book on how to do that. Is this a good time to go back and read some chapters again?

If you have those five keys in your financial plan you will be well covered.

These can lead you to financial security when you are old and gray or in my case not quite old and bald.

Here is the true story of a good example of all five keys. I will change the name to protect my client but here is part of his story. Let's call him Hank. Hank worked as a lad on the CNR. He worked his way up the corporate ladder and when management asked him to move to a small town up north on the railroad line he picked up his wife and kids and made the move. Soon he was the boss of hundreds of men on the railroad. He was part of management and rose even higher.

He once told me that the best investments he ever made were three Canada Life Policies that he purchased when he was in his 20s. These policies were in the range of $25,000 to $40,000. Not huge and not expensive at his age, then. These whole life policies have matured and now pay him dividends every month. When he dies these alone will pay all the expenses. Now he has diversified, too. He owns stocks and bonds and some segregated funds. He is conservative, but once bought Red Hat and is still waiting for that to pay off. He has lost money, too. He helped his daughter and her husband out and lost $400,000. He still had enough since he has been investing all his life to pay off his house and have a grand portfolio. Did he do it all right? No; no one ever does. But here is what he did, and now he has the freedom to enjoy it. He follows the rules of **liquidity**: he keeps $60,000 at ING; he follows the rule **at death provide for your family**, he has a multi-million dollar life policy from Great West. He follows the rules of **disability** by having a disability policy that covered him all the years he spent with the railway. He follows the rules of **diversification** by having a broad portfolio with stocks, bonds, segregated funds and real estate. He **retired** to Orillia, a small town in Ontario, where he and his life-long wife enjoy life, their family and especially their grandchildren – just like they planned.

In short, Hank followed the rules of the five keys. I have had the privilege of getting to know Hank and I am a richer man for that relationship. He has been a friend when I needed someone to help and he has never let me down. Is there a better man than that? No, my pal Hank is one of the last really good men on the face of the earth. Thanks, "Hank."

Borrowing to Invest

42

THE IDEA here is a basic principle in investing and taxation. If you borrow for the purpose of investing the money for growth and it stands a realistic chance of growing, then it is tax-deductible. Now this can be applied to money you borrow from a bank, a friend or a loan against your permanent life insurance.

If you borrow a mortgage for your home and the house value goes up, that is not deductible. The law applies to real estate beyond the matrimonial home. However, if you borrow to invest in stocks and bonds, that money is tax-deductible.

There is a rogue agent at a company I have mentioned before who uses this strategy to line his pockets and along the way hurts his clients terribly. He asks people to re-mortgage their homes to build an investment fund. He then invests that money and is paid the commission. In the bear market some of his clients came close to losing or lost their homes. If you can't pay the mortgage because it has grown to an unmanageable size you are in trouble. I wonder how many husbands did this and didn't tell their wives? That made for some stormy family sessions, I would speculate. Of course he gets the usual risk letter signed by the client and so covers his backside but one day some badly burnt client should sue him. He is not alone. Some famous radio and television commentators were advising the same thing in 2000 and 2001. Funny, we have not heard from them for a while.

It's legal. To borrow to invest, even if that borrowing is re-mortgaging your family home. That money is tax-deductible. However, the last time I checked you couldn't live in a mutual fund. I would never advise a client of mine who did not have enough money to invest to enlarge his mortgage just to invest. It is way too risky for me and not suitable for my clients.

If you can handle the payments, borrow from the bank. Another way is to borrow against your own portfolio. That is called using margin and if done conservatively it is a sound strategy. Most brokerage houses employ strict guidelines on this practice, for example, you can only margin up to 40% or 50% of your portfolio. You are charged interest by the brokerage house. If you cash in your portfolio, the brokerage will pay off the loan first and give you what's left.

The best way to borrow is a loan that you do not have to pay back. That certainly will not be found at a bank. Your friend will insist he is repaid. Your re-mortgage must be paid off; but a whole life insurance policy loan is not required to be paid off. The hands down best way to do this is to borrow against the cash value of your whole life insurance policy. Keep in mind that if you do not pay the loan off the ultimate death benefit will be reduced.

To summarize this section, you can borrow from a bank, against your home if you dare, a friend, or your whole life insurance. Of all these options chose the last suggestion.

What can you invest in with this borrowed money? People have made fortunes investing in real estate. However, as this is written there are rumblings all over about a housing bubble bursting. That happens when the price of a basic house gets out of reach of first time buyers. If the real estate selling cycle is not being fed from the bottom who buys the houses of the ones who want to move up? There appears to be a bubble in California and some parts of the rest of the United States. In Toronto, the growth is fast and sustained as we are importing people from the third world by the hundreds of thousands. This is keeping the Toronto housing market buoyant but is changing the city in ways most people do not like. Twenty years ago homeless people and gunplay were unheard of in Toronto. Today, both are commonplace. But in normal times you can invest in real estate. You can also invest in stocks and bonds and mutual funds. Labour Sponsored funds are also OK, but I do not recommend them to my clients as you're locked in for eight years into very risky firms. In short, you can invest anywhere you want. As long as there is the opportunity to profit, that loan is tax-deductible.

You can use leverage if you have the stomach for it to really increase your retirement if you have 15 to 25 years to retirement. This is a long-term strategy. This is for sophisticated investors only. The sense of leverage is that the long-term growth of an investment should be higher than the cost of the loan if that amount of money was invested without leverage. For example, suppose you can afford to invest $10,000 a year. That would be OK and would build you a portfolio but at the end of 15 years you would have invested $150,000 and if your growth was 6% per year you have $166,142.30. Keep in mind that the 10,000 was invested every year and by year three you only had $30,000 invested.

Leveraging would look at this differently. Let's make the annual payment $10,000 on a loan for $200,000. Now you start off investing with a much higher number. After 15 years you would have paid out $150,000 and have a portfolio of $220,902 after paying off the loan. The difference of $54,760 is significant. Don't do this in your RRSP; you want to deduct the cost of borrowing, do it in a non-registered account, AKA a cash account. Also this example assumes a steady 6% rate of increase, and life is never like that. You could have lots more or lots less – there is risk to this strategy.

If you live in Quebec the laws are different. For example, the term of a loan is maximized at 20 years and the period of the amortization and the term of the loan must be the same. Also fixed rate loans are limited to five years and less and any loan over five years must be variable. Fast-rising interest rates could hurt you. Check with your local Quebec advisor.

This could be a strategy to use if you have not invested enough and time is getting on, but be very careful and know **that you know**, that you can afford it. In other words, be very sure you can pay the loan every year. There are no guarantees and you should make money over 15 years; but is it worth the risk? Only you can tell that.

Don't be in a big hurry for the Boomer's to retire.

43

PEOPLE BORN between 1945 and 1966 are baby boomers. That bulge in the population that has driven everything from Davy Crockett raccoon hats, hula-hoops and the Beatles to housing booms and stratospheric stock markets. But the boomers are retiring and dying off. I hear cheers from the so-called "oppressed X generations" who feel the boomers are hogging all the top jobs. We earned them and they will have their chance, too, with, I might add, a lot less competition for every job.

What will happen to your investments when all the boomers have retired? Retired people usually do not invest - they are taking their investments out. In short, the boomers will be selling. The last boomers were born in 1966. That was also the top year for immigration as well. That huge group of late boomers will be 65 in 2031. Most other boomers will be gone by then. Will the Third World pick up the slack in the stock markets? Can China and India's middle class step up to the plate? I do not know the answer, but I do know this, the stock market will not contain any of my money in 2018. That is when my RRSP wraps up. I will be almost entirely in long bonds. I'll tell you what I fear. I fear a deep depression caused by the fast fall of the stock market. If there are not enough buyers and yet masses and masses of sellers; the market will fall and fall fast. The only hope, I see is, what we call the Third World now, investing mightily. Right now that is not their tradition, so I will be in bonds and bond funds, and perhaps you should be there, too. I would start buying them as soon as the rates go up and keep adding them to your portfolio. Wean yourself slowly out of stocks and mutual funds. I aim to be clear about 2015. That's when boomers born in 1950 will retire. You can't buy bonds from banks.

You can only buy them at a good large brokerage house. So please take my advice and get clear of the bank and open that account with a real live stock broker or financial security advisor. Find someone you like and get going. Make sure he can sell bonds or bond funds.

What should you tell your children and grandchildren about investing after 2015? They need to stay in the market or the market could be in real trouble. Tell them what I have repeatedly told you: Invest, diversify and remember it's time in the market not timing the market. Their retirement will count on that advice too, even if it is in 2065.

The next chapter has another scary topic: the fall of the American dollar. Taken together the retirement of the boomers and the fall of the U.S. greenback will make investing in the future very challenging. You will need some savvy help to miss the potholes. Before you read the next chapter put the book down and pour yourself some drink you like. It may not be pleasant reading.

The Fall of the American Dollar

44

AT THE BEGINNING of this book I mentioned I would return to the question of whether you should be investing in American stocks, bonds and mutual funds. It is time to answer that question bluntly and directly. NO! Stop!

Here's why. The United States is awash in debt. As of July 6, 2005, U.S. government debt hit $7,836,653,815,732 - that is awesome debt. $7.8 Trillion and that number does not include the American government's Social Security and Medicare commitments, if they are included the number rises substantially. The nation is trying to spend its way to prosperity. Can you do that? Can you quit your job; refinance your home and live based on the debt you have created? Not for long. A nation is simply many families grown large and we all know that excessive debt is the well-trodden roadway to ruin. I fear for the United States; their dollar is on the brink of a massive devaluation. Other countries have pegged their currency to America's. When you see large countries like China dump the U.S. dollar and switch to another basis or just float their currency - that's when the big fall will come.

The United States has so many problems right now. The war in Iraq is sucking huge reserves from the American pocketbook. Truth is that the war, like all wars, is financed by debt. High-paying jobs in manufacturing are being shipped overseas to China and India. Hurricanes Katrina, Rita and Wilma were devastating to the South and recovery will be massively expensive and a gigantic drain on the country. There is a shortage of oil in in politically stable countries. Also millions of barrels of oil are flowing to China and India to help fuel their rapid growth. That is just another problem for Uncle Sam. Ben Bernanke, before he retires, will be asked to stop this fall. The usual levers of interest rates will not work this time.

I could write another book describing the demise of the dollar. But that has already been done. Please take some advice here: Read *The demise of the dollar* by Addison Wiggin. You can get it on Amazon.com; I paid $11.83 U.S. there. It is published by Wiley and the ISBN Number is 0-471-74601-0. For a discount, go to dailyreckoning.com and order there. Wiggin is a realistic gold bug, who wants a return to the gold standard, without government control. Don't let that throw you off reading his new book. It spells out the great problems of the American economy. Do not invest there right now.

What to do before it happens

Here is where I think you should invest. I have mentioned this before but I believe it bears repeating. Invest in whatever China needs but not directly in China. Invest in India. I would buy BHP Billiton PLC (symbol BHP), an Australian mining company. It's the largest mine company in the world, and ideally situated to satisfy the booming Chinese demand for iron ore and other minerals.

If you believe that the U.S. dollar is going down and I do - buy gold in some form. Gold and the U.S. dollar seem to work inversely to each other. When the greenback falls sharply, gold will head up sharply. You can buy bullion, but you always buy at retail and sell at wholesale. I owned gold bullion in the 1970s and it was hard to get down to the Scotia Bank dealer in Toronto to sell it. That is another story. Today I would not buy bullion but I would buy the ETFs for gold – GLD and IAU. I would add Newmont mining (NEM) as an unhedged stock holding. For a Canadian gold stock invest in Kinross Gold (K) on the TSE. Also there are good gold mutual funds at all major mutual fund companies. Invest in those if you have less than $100,000 invested. Remember, no stock or holding should represent more than 5% of your portfolio.

I recommend buying Canadian oil stocks like Suncor. The world demand for oil is insatiable and the easy oil supply will run out one day. The Alberta Tar Sands are ideally suited to an oil investment in that they are safe (not in the Middle East) and have huge reserves. With the high price of oil the expensive oil sand extraction method is quite affordable.

If you are a little aggressive in your portfolio, look for a stock that will really change the way the world does things. These stocks are rare. Microsoft did it. Microsoft software brought the power of computers to the common man. That really changed the world. Its stock soared, split, and soared again.

Two other stocks that may also do it are TKO and DCGN; both trade on the NYSE. TKO is Telkonet, which may change the way we access the net. It will enable us to inexpensively plug into any wall outlet for broadband lightning fast connections. It's called BPL – broadband through power lines. Look out, big phone companies with billions invested in broadband infrastructure.

DCGN is the stock symbol for deCODE Genetics, a new drug company based in Iceland. They tested the blood and analyzed the DNA of half the people of Iceland to make a scientific breakthrough. This will change how we build drugs; they will be tailor-made to our specific genetic code within a few years. They have a heart drug about to pass the third FDA test. Roche has partnered with them. This could be huge.

I own shares in these companies. I hope you are glad you read this far for those two ideas.

The United States has been with us at every turn. In the first and second world wars, they were there. I know they were there-late. When the world needed help the Yanks somehow were there. We aren't helping them in Iraq and that is the right thing for us, but wrong for them. I feel for them. I was shocked at the destruction of 2005's hurricanes. I believe that their wonderful land is in for another shock when the dollar falls fast. Living in denial does not postpone the end game. It just makes it more of a shock.

The American dollar is another bubble just like the tech bubble and the housing bubble. No one knows when it will burst, but it is inevitable that it will burst one day. The fallout will be awful. Inflation could return and all the ills that we recall from the 80s with it. As I said earlier, inflation can wipe out all the gains from bonds and stocks. That could be a real issue in the United States. Canada is American's largest trading partner. It will not be good for us either; that's for sure.

However, as Canada's dollar is not pegged to the U.S. greenback, our currency should soar and that will help importers and hurt exporters. In a time of a high Canadian dollar it could be the best time if you want to buy land in Florida or California.

Great thinkers on investing have come to the same conclusion. Warren Buffet has abandoned the U.S. Dollar. So has Sir John Templeton. These two wise men on investing agree. They have figured it out. Go against them at your peril.

Imagine the problem for the other countries all pegged to the U.S. dollar. That's most countries in Central and South America. They all depend on the strong greenback to support the value of their currencies. The fall will be heard around the world. The U.S. has been relying on the kindness of strangers for too long. When it becomes too expensive to base their currencies on the American dollar, large and small countries will move to the Euro; or in China's case, the Yuan will be allowed to float. China will be the largest producer and seller in the world in less than ten years. If I were younger, I'd learn Mandarin. China will be the whip hand and the rest of us the dogs, in terms of currency. If you go into any retail store and look at thousands of products on the shelves, you will see very few that are not made in China, only some Canadian and a few American products. That has long-term implications.

Wiggin, the author of the *demise of the dollar and Empire of Debt* with William Bonner, advocates a return to the gold standard. I don't see how that is possible in today's business climate. But if the world has hyperinflation as a result of the fall of the greenback, gold bugs and many others may demand a return to money backed by metal. We could live to see it. The odds are long but getting shorter as the years go by. Buy Addison Wiggin's book on the fall of the dollar. I found the information agreed with my opinions and went way further. He does make the case for the fall of the U.S. currency very well.

If we invest outside of the United States in oil, gold, BHP and all the other ideas I have mentioned in this book you should be able to avoid the problem. In fact, a fall in the greenback could accelerate your portfolio's growth dramatically.

When British Sterling fell in 1992, some investors like George Soros made a killing. He is rumored to have made two billion dollars in one day. He is called "The man who broke the Bank of England." Who knows if that kind of thing can't happen again?

Advanced Diversification

45

SOME CANADIAN investors are looking for a place that is less tax-happy than Canada. On the face of it I can see what they want to change. The past Liberal government fed its growth by imposing many endless taxes. In addition, they told us that the Federal surplus was only about one billion dollars. When the budget came down the surplus was over 9 billion dollars. They were touted as brilliant financial managers. I'm glad the people saw through this ruse and tossed the whole lot of them out.

Why are taxes so high? Because of the past government's policy of overtaxing us and using the surplus to buy our votes at election time.

It can make one want to leave Canada and her taxes and greedy Government's games of deception. The big money boys left years ago. Why should we be any different? How do you move offshore?

Years ago these schemes to move your assets offshore had a rough time in the media. It was as if people were taking their money and illegally stashing it with some bandit organization on some lonely island off Scotland or in the Caribbean. Some of that was true. There were, and likely still are, outlaw groups setting up phony tax havens. I would steer around those clowns so fast. Whatever you do, be sure it is legal or your money could go away like ice in spring.

The good news is that there are plenty of good, sound, tested and legal places to invest abroad. We have all heard of the Cayman Islands, Bermuda, Bahamas and the Isle of Man. More recently I have heard of Denmark, Liechtenstein and Malta. Of course, the granddaddy of all this is Switzerland but recently they have given some investors doubt. Whatever you do look, and look again before you leap.

Why do people use offshore investing as a part of their portfolio? I think there are at least four reasons:

1) **Tax Reduction** – Many investors use a foreign corporation to invest offshore. The corporation is based in, for example, Malta. There the corporation does no work and so pays little tax. That is the principle. No work, no wages equals no taxes. These small nations offer generous tax incentives to foreign investors. Many of these lands have little in the way of industry and relatively tiny populations. They cannot grow on the tax base they have, so they attract foreign investors and that provides economic activity and of course, some extra tax revenue for the nation. It seems like a win-win to me. If you set it up right, your foreign corporation can invest in the United States (later on) or Canada, and pay less taxes than you would buying the same investment from here.

2) **Diversification of Assets** – Let's suppose you have followed all the strategies in this book and you have stocks, bonds and mutual funds. You've added some real estate in a non-bubble area and now you are looking for a little more diversification. That's a good reason to put a little offshore now that the last budget did away with the foreign limit on registered assets. Now you can keep some, but not all of your RRSP assets in Canada and take some more of that money offshore if you want to. It extends your diversification. It also gives you more flexibility, and some day you will have to go and visit your money, so a tax- friendly business trip with your spouse is in order. Also, in some developing countries there are golden opportunities. I was down in Roatan (an island in the western Caribbean Sea) a couple of years ago and while driving around the island looking at properties – I saw an "ocean side golf course." What's unusual about that? The undeveloped land was for sale for less than a million U.S. and had demanding spectacular, world class golf course written all over it. It was not for sale as a golf course. It just looked like a natural championship course to me. It is still for sale now, though the price has risen sharply. Even if the island is too small to support a golf course, the land has jumped 30% in two years. Has that happened to your portfolio? See the concept?

3) **Confidentiality** – the laws in many of these tax havens are designed to protect the identity of the investors. This is important if you want to avoid (not evade) Canadian taxation. If you are a drug lord, crime kingpin or any other criminal there is no protection of your name and address. There must be a clear case for these crimes and the government cannot go witch hunting without a strong case against the individual. Most of these countries take this very seri-

ously and punish anyone who breaks this law. This precept is the cornerstone of offshore investing. Switzerland is giving investors trouble because they have seem to forgotten this basic rule.

4) **Protection** – if you are being sued or about to be sued, moving the money offshore can dodge domestic disruptions. This has to be done early. If you are expecting trouble, moving some assets offshore can protect those assets. Leave something here, so they won't go looking. See a lawyer on all this – that's important.

What are the disadvantages of investing offshore?

1) The tax loopholes are closing. The government is not blind to this and has let it go because not too many people are doing it (or so they think). Some day they may clamp right down.

2) The offshore corporations are a little pricey and the fees are annual, not one-time.

3) The legal fees will be high and some tax havens insist that you bring in at least $1,000,000 or more, but there are limits to this activity.

4) Safety – you must use a solid firm when you do this. A little fly splattered office is not the idea. Most world banks have branches in these areas so go with one of them. In Canada, Scotia Bank and CIBC maintain offices in most of these places.

What if you want to leave Canada entirely? You can do it, but there are strict government requirements. You really have to leave Canada *entirely*. That means no home here, no dependents that stay in Canada while you are gone, no personal property here, not even a car or stored furniture and no Canadian bank accounts or credit cards! Anything other than that and you must file taxes as though you never left, even if you haven't earned a dime in Canada all year. You will be termed a "factual resident" and must report all income from all sources, and pay federal and provincial or territorial tax where you have residential ties. You can claim all deductions, non-refundable tax credits and any refundable federal, provincial or territorial credits that may apply. You may also be able to claim a foreign tax credit on your Canadian income tax return if you paid income tax to another country on your foreign income. But filing takes little time and energy if you have nothing to declare.

This next part is a fun way to end this book. I read a method of moving money out of Canada in *Maclean's Magazine* a few years back. I can't tell if the magazine was having us all on or if they believed that this was a mainstream way to move money. Here with <u>tongue firmly in my cheek</u> is their advice.

Take the money out in cash and buy a money order or traveler's cheques for safekeeping. Now fly to Los Vegas and walk into a casino. Buy with all your money a large pile of chips. Handle them with care and do not lose them. Do not even think of playing them. Now go and have lunch. Later return to the casino and cash your chips. You have made your money disappear. If asked you can show the government your receipts for buying the chips but tell them all the money was lost in Texas Hold'em Poker. It can happen fast in that game. OK, you may have to lie to the tax people.

I hope you have enjoyed this book. I enjoyed writing it. For most of us there is plenty of time to build up a good portfolio of mutual funds, stocks and bonds. My advice is to get busy investing today. Don't forget the power of insurance.

The Best of British Racing and investing luck to you all and thank you for buying and reading this book. If you enjoyed it and learned something from it – I'm pleased you did.

Conclusion and Contact information

The power strategies in this book should be good for everyone, but I urge you to work with an investment broker who can advise you about your personal situation. One size does not fit all and one book cannot answer all questions. I hope I have shown you many strategies that you will find useful. They are sprinkled throughout the book. Use them in concert with a good broker who understands them.

If you are interested in working with me, this is how I work. I will never sit down with a person and tell him or her what to do until I have asked many questions to find out their specific situation and what they envision for the future. After this I go back to my office and analyze the answers. Sometimes I have to call back to explore a point that comes up in the analysis. Then I set up an appointment to make my recommendations for the business, individual or couple. You will never see me shoot from the hip. I take time with my recommendations, so I know they are in my client's best interests.

If you live in Ontario we can work together with no problem. If you live in northern Ontario or in Thunder Bay I can come, but it must be worthwhile. Call me and we can discuss it. If you live outside of Ontario, I am in the process of getting all my licenses for every province across Canada. I will come to meet you. Please call me and let's discuss it.

You can always reach me at: Cell: (416) 805 5158
Business Phone 416-777-7071
1(800) 547-6909 All Canada and continental USA. (Rings at home).
stocksandbonds@sympatico.ca

D. David Campbell

Appendix I

Alphabet Soup

ACSDP – Atlantic Canada Supplier Development Program
ACV – Actual Cash Value
CDIC – Canadian Deposit Insurance Corporation
CPI – Consumer Price Index
CPP – Canada Pension Plan
CSB – Canada Savings Bond
CSC – Canadian Securities Course
CTB – Child Tax Benefit
DIJA – Dow Jones Industrial Average
EI - Employment Insurance (formerly UI)
FCC – Farm Credit Corporation
FCS – Farm Consultation Service
FDMS – Farm Debt Mediation Service
FIRA – Foreign Investment Review Agency
FRM – Fixed Rate Mortgage
FRN – Fixed Rate Note
FSCO – Financial Services Commission of Ontario
FTAA – Free Trade Area of the Americas
FV - Future Value
GAAP – Generally Accepted Auditing Principles
GAAR – General Anti-Avoidance Rule
GARP - Growth At a Reasonable Price (an investing style combining both
    value and growth investing)
GDI – Gross Domestic Income
GIC – Guaranteed Investment Certificates
GIS – Guaranteed Income Supplement
GRIP – Gross Revenue Insurance Plan (farmer protection)
GST – Goods and Services Tax

HBP – Home Buyers' Plan
HST – Harmonized Sales Tax
IA – Investment Advisor
IDA – Investment Dealers Association
LIF – Life Income Fund
LRIF – A RIFF that has been converted to an annuity
LSVCCs – Labour-Sponsored Venture Capital Corporations
MER – Management Expense Ratio
MFDA – Mutual Funds Dealers Association
NAFTA – North American Free Trade Agreement
NASDAQ – National Association of Securities Dealers Automated Quotations
OAS – Old Age Security
OSFI – Office of the Superintendent of Financial Institutions
PFRA – Prairie Farm Rehabilitation Administration
PST – Provincial Sales Tax
PV – Present Value
REIT – Real Estate Invest Trust
RESP – Registered Education Savings Plan
RRIF – Registered Retirement Income Fund
RRSP - Registered Retirement Savings Plan
SBLA – Small Business Loans Act
WSIB – Workplace Safety and Insurance Board

Appendix II

Good Investment Books

I have read all of these books and I recommend you do too.

Bach, David, *Smart Couples Finish Rich*, Broadway Books, New York

Bach, David, *Smart Women Finish Rich*, Broadway Books, New York

Bonner, William and Wiggin, Addison, *Empire of Debt,* Wiley, New York

Cestnick, Tim, *Winning the Tax Game 2000*, Prentice Hall Toronto

Hagstrom, Robert G., *The Winning Warren Buffet Portfolio*, Wiley, New York

Hill, Napoleon, *Think and Grow Rich*, Fawcett, New York

KPMG, *Tax Planning 2005,* Thomson – Carswell, Toronto

Lowenstien, Roger, *Buffett, The Making of an American Capitalist*, Broadway Books, New York

McLean, Benjamin, *Your Child's Financial Future*, McGraw-Hill Ryerson, Toronto

Nazareth, Linda, *The Ever After Effect*, Stewart House Publishing, Toronto

Proctor, Bob, *You were Born Rich*, Life Success Productions, Phoenix, Arizona

Siegel, Jeremy J., *Stocks for the Long Run*, McGraw Hill, New York

Spenceley, Robert, *The Estate Planner's Handbook*, CCH Canadian Limited, Toronto

Wiggins, Addison, *The Demise of the Dollar*, Wiley, New York

Index

ISBN 141208205-6